An Altitude
SuperGuide

British Columbia

INTERIOR

An Altitude SuperGuide

British Columbia

INTERIOR

Meredith Bain Woodward
and Ron Woodward

Altitude Publishing
Banff & Vancouver

Photo, front cover:
The British Columbia interior is renowned for its lakes and its unique land forms, such as rock arch.

Photo, front cover inset:
Mattie Gunterman at Beaton in 1905. She is well known for her lively photographs of life in the Kootenays in the early 1900s.

Frontispiece:
A dramatic chain-saw sculpture greets visitors at Hell's Gate in the Fraser Canyon.

Photo, back cover:
The Clearwater River is among many in the Interior offering high adventure to whitewater rafters. Companies offering the excursions, such as Interior Whitewater of Celista, are licensed and regulated by the provincial government.

Extreme care has been taken to ensure that all information in this book is accurate and up to date, but neither the author nor the publisher can be held legally responsible for any errors that may appear.

Made in Western Canada
Printed and bound in Western Canada by Friesen Printers, Altona Manitoba, using Canadian-made paper and vegetable-based inks.

This book was published with the assistance of the Department of Communications, Book Industry Development Program.

Altitude GreenTree Program
Altitude will plant in Western Canada twice as many trees as were used in the manufacturing of this book.

Canadian Cataloguing in Publication Data
Woodward, Meredith Bain, 1944-
British Columbia Interior
(SuperGuide)
ISBN 0-919381-17-0
1. British Columbia – Guidebooks.
I Woodward, Ron, 1944- II. Title. III. Series
FC3807.W66 1993   917.1104'4
C93-091031-1   F1087.W66 1993

Editor: John F. Ricker

Maps: Paul Beck

Design: Robert MacDonald, MediaClones Inc.

Acknowledgments
Thanks to the following people for their help and advice: Garry Anderson, Alex Berland, Paul Dampier, Gerry Frederick, Joyce Johnson, Ken Mather, Margaret Panderin, Robert Pinsent, John Pinn, Donna Pletz, Al Smith, and Frances Surtees.

Altitude Publishing Ltd.

Post Office Box 490
Banff, Alberta T0L 0C0

402 West Pender Street, Suite 512
Vancouver, British Columbia V6B 1T6

Contents

How to Use the SuperGuide

BC's Interior covers a huge land area of approximately 900,000 square kilometres (350,000 square miles). The *SuperGuide* is a tool to help you create a unique travel experience among the Interior's many possibilities. In the *Superguide*, the "Interior" includes all of BC's mainland, excluding Vancouver, the Lower Mainland, and the coastal centres.

The introductory sections will provide you with background information about the nature of the landscape, flora and fauna, history, economy, and outdoor recreation.

The main section offers eight descriptive highway guides with maps and points of interest, emphasizing natural and historic attractions. Because most tourists to the Interior visit the southern quarter of the province, the emphasis is there. Guides for the **Trans-Canada Highway** (Highway 1) and the **Crowsnest Highway** (Highway 3), the two major east-west routes, begin this section. Then the north-south routes are listed: the **Coquihalla-Nicola**, the **Okanagan**, the **West Kootenay**, and the **East Kootenay**.

Two large circle tours complete the highway guide. The **Central Interior** circle tour begins at Cache Creek and includes highlights of the Cariboo-Chilcotin region north to Prince George, the Yellowhead Highway (Highway 16) east to Mt. Robson Provincial Park, and the Yellowhead South (Highway 5) to Kamloops.

The **Northern Interior** circle tour begins at Prince George and includes the John Hart Highway (Highway 97), the Alaska Highway (Highway 97), the Cassiar Highway (Highway 37), and the Yellowhead Highway (Highway 16) from Hazelton east to Prince George.

Throughout the text, boxes highlight selected subjects such as contemporary and historical figures, flora and fauna, historical events, and recreational activities.

A final **Reference** section contains useful information for vacationers, including addresses of river rafting companies, guest ranches, golf courses, and other resources.

British Columbia Interior SuperGuide does not include accommodations or restaurants except when they have historic or special significance. For accomodation and campgrounds, we refer you to *British Columbia Accommodations,* a comprehensive guide published annually by the provincial government. The booklet is available free at tourist outlets and Infocentres throughout the province. (Infocentres, identifiable by their red, white, and blue signs, are usually close to the highway and offer free maps and up-to-date local information. They are listed in the highway guide.)

Please note that all phone numbers in BC have the same area code: 604. Out of province numbers are given with their area codes.

We hope you enjoy your exploration of BC's Interior. From gold rush trails to Native pictographs, alpine views to sandy beaches, there is a lot to discover.

Introduction

Spectacular wild flower displays occur throughout the Interior in spring and summer. This field of yellow fawn lilies is in the West Kootenay's Slocan Valley. The species blooms from March through August, usually as the snow recedes.

BC's Interior is an ideal destination for vacationers who dream of losing themselves in the great outdoors. Part of Canada's westernmost and third largest province, the Interior covers about 900,000 of BC's 950,000 square kilometres and includes 18,000 square kilometres of inland water. Larger than any US state except Alaska and twice the land mass of Japan, the entire province has only three million people – a population density of only three people per square kilometre.

The Interior is famous for its variety; it includes deserts, glaciers, lava beds, and rain forests. Visitors can ride horses on the wide open spaces of Chilcotin cattle country, climb the spectacular and isolated peaks of the Rocky Mountains, boat on the warm waters of Shuswap Lake, water ski, snow ski, or pan for gold.

Visitors can also enjoy the cities. Kelowna, in the centre of the Okanagan, is the fastest growing city in the province and offers professional theatre, art galleries, fine dining, and winery tours. Nelson in the West Kootenay, with its picturesque heritage buildings, boasts more artists and writers per capita than any place else in the country. Kimberley, in the East Kootenay, is a Bavarian-style alpine town with internationally renowned skiing.

The history of human settlement is as varied as the landscape. A number of Native cultures thrived for centuries before the fur traders arrived in the 18th century. In 1858 thousands of gold miners hurried to the Fraser River looking for fortunes and sometimes finding them. The construction of the Canadian Pacific Railway in the 1880s and subsequent mining booms in the 1890s drew more settlers. Museums and archives throughout the Interior tell stories of early pioneers who include English orchardists, Chinese miners, Japanese fishermen, and Russian farmers – with an occasional marquis or mystic thrown in for good measure.

With its abundant recreational opportunities, variety of landscapes, and fascinating people, BC's Interior has a lot to offer.

Favourite Events and Attractions
(SuperGuide's recommendations.
Page numbers in parentheses.)

Top Ten Attractions
Cottonwood House and Barkerville (208-210)
Cranbrook Railway Museum (108)
Creston Valley Wildlife Centre (105)
Emerald Lake, Yoho National Park (73)
Hell's Gate on Fraser Canyon (50)
K'san Village, Hazelton (230)
LeRoi Underground Mine Tour, Rossland (99)
Old Grist Mill, Keremeos (89)
Painted Chasm Provincial Park, Clinton (196)
R.H. Atkinson Museum, Penticton (129)

Top Ten Events
100 Mile House Cross-country Ski Marathon (199)
Adams River Salmon Run, Fall (60)
Bulkley Valley Exhibition, Smithers, August (231)
Caravan Theatre, Armstrong, Summer (148)
Hedley Blast, July (87)
Iron Man Triathlon, Penticton, August (132)
Kamloops Cattle Drive and Trail Ride, July (59)
May Ball, Clinton (195)
Okanagan Wine Festival, Fall (123)
Williams Lake Stampede, July (202)

BC Facts

Provincial capital: Victoria
Provincial motto: *splendor sine occasu* – splendor without diminishment
Provincial flower: Pacific dogwood
Provincial bird: Steller's jay
Provincial tree: Western red cedar
Provincial stone: BC jade
Population: 3.2 million
Languages: English - 80% ; French - 1%; other languages - 15% (including Cantonese, Mandarin, German, Italian, Portuguese, Russian, Ukrainian); English + one other language - 4%.
Entered Confederation: July 20, 1871
Area: 948,596 km^2; 9.5% of Canada's land surface; 0.64% of the world's land surface
Highest point: Mt. Fairweather, 4663 m
Highest mountain (highway) pass: Kootenay Pass, 1774 m
Provincial sales tax: 6%
Legal drinking age: 19
Area code: 604
Total length of BC's highways: 44,300 km
Largest Interior cities: Prince George, Kamloops, Kelowna, Penticton

Lay of the Land

It has taken the milky waters of Tokumm Creek 8000 years to carve its path through the limestone walls of Marble Canyon in Kootenay National Park.

To many people, British Columbia is synonymous with mountains. Three-quarters of the land is over 1000 metres above sea level; less than 3 percent of the land is considered suitable for agriculture. But the landscape of the Interior has great variety.

Part of both the Cordillera and Great Plains regions of North America, the Interior has four major geographical components: the Western system dominated by the Coast and Cascade mountains; the Interior Plateau, which includes the relatively subdued contours of the Okanagan Valley and the Chilcotin;

the Rocky Mountain system; and the triangle of land in the northeast corner of the province that is part of the great Interior Plains.

When travelling through the Interior, it is interesting to notice evidence of its geological history. The earth was formed about 4.5 billion years ago. Over the next two billion years it cooled, forming land masses on the Earth's surface. For millions of years the land masses have been shifting in a process known as continental drift. It is caused by the very slow and complex movements of tectonic plates beneath the earth's surface. When these plates move they can collide, pushing material through the earth's crust, or they can pull apart, weakening the crust and creating opportunities for volcanic eruptions.

Throughout the Interior of BC it is possible to see evidence of both these processes. Volcanic rocks are abundant throughout the Cariboo and Chilcotin area. And a drive through any of the Interior's mountain ranges reveals layers of sedimentary and metamorphic rock jutting dramatically into the air.

The third major element, ice ages, probably had the most far-reaching effects in BC. The latest, the Wisconsin Glaciation, ended only about 10,000 years ago. Glacier National Park with its exciting views of the Illecillewaet and Asulkan glaciers offers accessible examples of the erosive power of ice. But evidence of the tremendous power of the ice-age glaciers, and resulting meltwater, can also be found in the terraced banks of rivers such as the Fraser and in the presence of huge boulders known as erratics in otherwise rock-free fields of the Columbia Valley.

The erosive force of weather since the last glaciation is a final element that shaped the landscape. The hoodoo formations that occur throughout the Interior provide immediate examples. Whether imperceptibly slow or cataclysmic, the transformation of the landscape is relentless. The Juan de Fuca Plate, for example, which lies off BC's coast, moves four to five centimetres a year in relation to the North American Plate. On the other hand, Mt. St. Helens in Washington state erupted violently as recently as 1980. BC experiences an

earthquake every day, according to the Ministry of Energy, Mines, and Petroleum Resources. Although most are not noticeable, experts predict a major event within the next 200 years.

Mountains

BC's many peaks are part of the Cordilleran mountain system of western North America.

The coastal mountain ranges contain both Mt. Fairweather (4663 metres) in the northwest corner (partly in Alaska), and the Chilcotin's Mt. Waddington (4019 metres), BC's highest peak entirely in the province. However, the Rocky Mountains are undeniably more famous. In the southern half of the province, the BC-Alberta border lies on the ridge of this range. But in the north, the Rockies are entirely in BC. The tallest peak at 3954 metres is Mount Robson, just west of Jasper, Alberta.

To the west of the Rockies and in the south lie the Columbia Mountains, separated by the wide Rocky Mountain Trench, a straight, flat-bottomed valley that runs the 1300-kilometre

Lichen is the first form of plant life to find a niche on inhospitable rock surfaces. It catches dust and other organic matter, providing a rooting place for simple plants that eventually build soil.

Glaciers often form in catchment basins known as cirques. As the glaciers melt, the basins enlarge, leaving behind formations such as this one on the Trans-Canada Highway east of Revelstoke.

length of the province and stretches from Montana into Alaska. The Columbia Mountains are made up of three parallel ranges: the Purcells, the Selkirks, and the Monashees, with the Cariboo Range to the north. In the far north the Cassiar-Omineca Mountains dominate the landscape.

Many of BC's mountain ranges contain ore bodies. The deposits of gold, lead, zinc, silver, molybdenum, copper, coal, and iron have led to human settlement of many areas, and mining will continue to be an important part of BC's economy.

Rivers

Cutting through the mountain ranges are the waterways that were a lifeline for early inhabitants as recently as 100 years ago. There are 843 rivers in the province and over 10,000 named creeks and brooks. The Fraser River, which begins in the Rocky Mountains,

travels 1370 kilometres through the province. The only major river in BC that begins and ends within the province's borders, the Fraser is a major spawning ground for Pacific salmon and steelhead trout.

The 2000-kilometre Columbia River, which also has its headwaters in the Rockies, is a major source of hydroelectric power for BC and the northwestern US.

The Thompson and Kootenay rivers are important tributaries of the Fraser and Columbia systems respectively. In the north the Skeena, Nass, Stikine, and Taku rivers drain into the Pacific. The Peace and Liard rivers are major waterways leading to the Mackenzie River system and the Arctic Ocean.

Weather

The mountains have a major effect on the weather in British Columbia.

Moisture-laden winds from the ocean make a roller-coaster journey east across the province until they reach the Rockies. Generally speaking, the western slopes of the higher mountains receive more precipitation, so the amount of snow and rain varies between areas. On the western slopes of the Columbia Mountain ranges, average rainfall is about 250 centimetres per year; in the arid areas of the Interior Plateau average annual moisture is 20 centimetres.

Weather-wise, come prepared for anything. In winter, snow and low temperatures are possible anywhere. In the summer months, most areas offer warm to hot days and cool nights. BC's warmest weather was recorded July 16, 1941, at both Lytton and Lillooet with a temperature of 44.4°C. The coldest temperature was –58.9°C at Smith River on January 31, 1947.

Weather at a Glance

Average Temperatures (°C)

	Jan	April	Jul	Nov
Castlegar	-4	8	20	2
Cranbrook	-9	6	18	-2
Creston	-4	8	20	1
Dawson Creek	-18	3	15	-6
Fort St. James	-14	3	15	-3
Kamloops	-5	9	21	2
Kelowna	-3	8	20	3
Osoyoos	-3	10	22	3
Prince George	-12	4	15	-3

Average Precipitation (mm)

	Jan	April	Jul	Nov
Castlegar	85	44	36	81
Cranbrook	49	26	22	33
Creston	73	35	25	66
Dawson Creek	33	16	58	28
Fort St. James	49	20	49	44
Kamloops	36	9	24	20
Kelowna	37	15	24	29
Osoyoos	41	20	19	30
Prince George	57	27	60	51

Bright Sunshine (Hours) 1951-1980

	Jul	Dec	Total
Blue River	245	30	1534
Burns Lake	258	42	1755
Castlegar	316	31	1876
Cranbrook	330	63	2244
Dease Lake	199	41	1634
Fort St. John	302	65	2192
Hope	258	4	1521
Kamloops	316	48	2048
Kelowna	311	41	1981
Kimberley	334	46	2152
Lytton	295	44	1987
Mackenzie	245	39	1651
McBride	245	39	1651
Oliver	310	41	2040
Peachland	328	45	1994
Penticton	311	39	2032
Prince George	293	47	1926
Puntzi Mountain	295	64	2084
Revelstoke	268	27	1628
Salmon Arm	289	11	1632
Smithers	243	39	1693
Trail	310	15	1717
Vernon	322	30	1903
Williams Lake	312	49	2124

What the Weather Warnings Mean in the Interior

Heavy snow Expect at least 10 centimetres of snow in the next 24 hours.
Heavy rain Expect 25 millimetres of rain in the next 24 hours.
High winds Expect speeds of over 65 km/h or gusts up to 90 km/h.

Weather information 1-660-1084

Ecology

The dappled colouring and instinct for stillness of this three-day old fawn provides a natural camouflage. Abandoned, it was rescued by hunters near Lillooet, but Fish and Wildlife Branch officials discourage human interference with the natural course of events.

A well-known Buddhist koan asks, if a tree falls in the forest, and nobody is around, will the tree make a sound? For centuries students have debated this riddle. But in the 1990s, the answer, ecologically speaking, seems to be yes.

Life on planet earth is a web of interdependent systems. Nothing happens anywhere without it having an effect somewhere else. Over the last two or three decades people have become increasingly and sometimes shockingly aware of this fact. Today, global warming, depletion of the ozone layer, and the effect of the destruction of rain forests are common topics of discussion.

Bugs introduced in a forest as pest control become pests themselves, destroying stands of trees and affecting logging jobs. A piece of plant material caught in the propeller of a boat floats loose in a lake, multiplies, and eventually chokes out other life forms. A fire burns hectares of forest land, destroying habitat for some wildlife species, creating space for other plants and animals.

Interior Habitats

Travellers have the opportunity to view a number of ecological systems in the Interior. The landscape ranges from sea level to Mt. Fairweather's 4663 metres, including everything from lush rain forests to deserts, and the land extends from the 49th to 60th parallels of latitude.

British Columbia has the greatest variety of wildlife habitat of any province in Canada. There are over 2000 species of flowering plants. Over a million birds per year migrate in the Pacific Flyway. The province has 75 percent of the world's stone sheep; 65 percent of the California bighorn sheep; 60 percent of the Barrow's goldeneye population; 50 percent of the trumpeter swans, blue grouse, and mountain goats; and 25 percent of the world's bald eagles and grizzly bears.

North America's largest wildlife viewing spectacle occurs in the autumn every four years at the Adams River salmon run near Kamloops.

Herb Hammond
Forester
Winlaw

My career is living, and I prefer most to live in a forest. Beyond that, you could call me a holistic forester.

One of the reasons I like BC is that it's a sea of lands and forests with islands of people in it. Our options are disappearing rapidly, but in BC, we still have a chance to show what it's like to be part of a forest in an ecologically and socially responsible way.

All organisms, whether they're human beings or bacteria or fungi or grizzly bears, are entitled to a fair and balanced part of the landscape.

Keeping all the parts in balanced use means zoning, making sure you have a plan that protects corridors, like 300 to 400 metres or so along the river systems in the watershed, where believe it or not, it's not even a good idea for people to live.

And you can zone a balance of human uses from timber to tourism to recreation to cultural and spiritual areas to wilderness areas.

When people look at the forest landscapes of BC, they need to recognize that the conventional way that we clearcut is a bankrupt system. It's not sustaining the forest, it's destroying the forest. Our forests have been living and dying for millennia. There's a biological legacy of dead tree bodies in the soil and above the soil that prop up the system.

The cutting and removal, with an underscore on removal, of even one tree is not a natural phenomenon. Mother Nature never cut down all the trees, loaded them on a truck and hauled them to the mill. When she burned up a forest or blew them all down, the bodies always stayed behind.

The fundamental principle is that the forest sustains us, we don't sustain the forest.

Herb Hammond is the author of *Seeing the Forest Among the Trees* (Vancouver: Polestar, 1991).

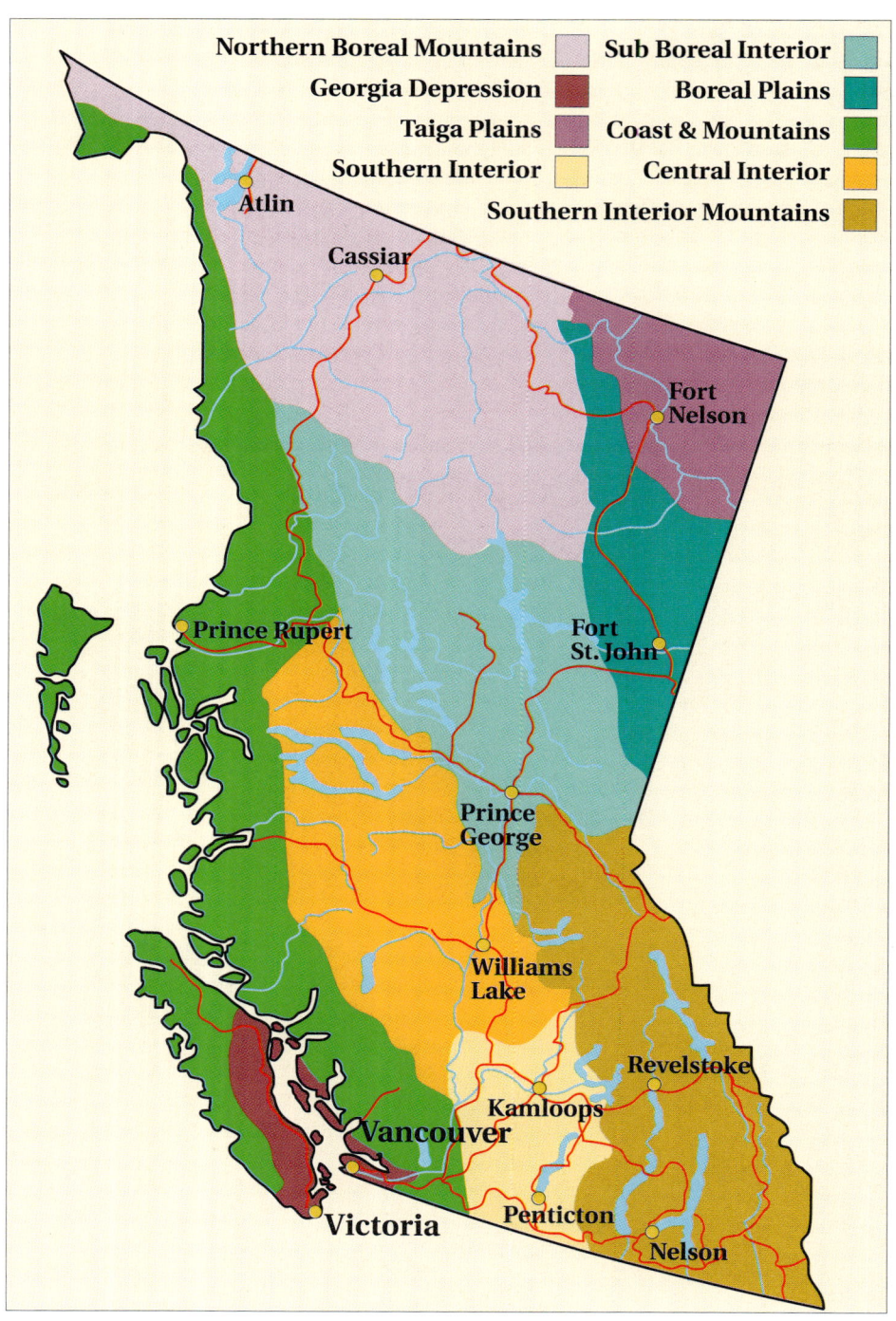

Northern Boreal Mountains
Georgia Depression
Taiga Plains
Southern Interior
Southern Interior Mountains

Sub Boreal Interior
Boreal Plains
Coast & Mountains
Central Interior

Atlin
Cassiar
Fort Nelson
Prince Rupert
Fort St. John
Prince George
Williams Lake
Revelstoke
Kamloops
Vancouver
Penticton
Victoria
Nelson

Ecoprovinces

Since the glaciers began retreating 12,000 to 15,000 years ago, the regrowth of plant and animal life that we see today has been controlled by a number of factors. Climate and topography are perhaps the most important, but animal migration patterns, soil conditions, and erosion rates also affect which species grow where and how well.

The provincial government has designated nine ecoprovinces which group plant and animal life into geographic areas. (See map.)

While most of the **Coast and Mountains** and the **Georgia Depression** ecoprovinces are not included in the *BC Interior SuperGuide*, the Coast and Mountains zone does include the lush rainforests and sparse alpine reaches of the eastern slopes of the Coast Mountains. The climate is determined by moist air masses from the Pacific Ocean. Western hemlock, western red cedar, and mountain hemlock are common tree species. Undergrowth is lush, typically containing mosses, ferns, devil's club, and thimbleberry. Animal species include deer, black and grizzly bear, and mountain goat.

The rolling plateau of the **Southern Interior Ecoprovince** is one of the warmest and driest areas of the province. Population centres include Lytton, Lillooet, Kamloops, Vernon, Osoyoos, and Princeton. Its vegetation is made up of dry grassland, ponderosa pine and Douglas fir forests, and many lakes, wetlands, and rivers – habitats which attract the greatest variety of bird species in the Interior. Other wildlife include reptiles, deer, grouse, bighorn sheep, and large runs of salmon.

The Chilcotin, Cariboo, and Nechacko plateaus make up the **Central Interior Ecoprovince**. The vegetation ranges from dry grasslands to forests of ponderosa pine and Douglas fir, and includes lakes, rivers, and wetlands. Smithers and Houston are in the north and 100 Mile House in the east. Highway 20 from Williams Lake to the Coast Mountains is included in this zone. Wildlife includes moose, cougar, black bear, coyote, wolf, California bighorn sheep, Barrow's goldeneye, and white pelican.

The **Southern Interior Mountain Ecoprovince** encompasses portions of the Columbia and Rocky mountains and the Rocky Mountain Trench. Population centres include Castlegar, Trail, Cranbrook, Fernie, Golden, Revelstoke, Clearwater, and Valemount. Dense conifer forests are common, although the Rocky Mountain Trench has dry grassland, and the high peaks of the mountains feature alpine tundra. The marshland of the Columbia and Kootenay rivers provide important habitat for wildlife. Species in this zone include tundra swan, Canada geese, mountain goat, grizzly and black bear, deer, elk, caribou, bighorn sheep, and the highest breeding concentration of osprey in the world.

The plateaus surrounded by the Omineca, Skeena, and central Rocky mountains in the north-central Interior make up the **Sub-boreal Interior Ecoprovince** including Quesnel, Prince George, Vanderhoof, Babine Lake, the headwaters of the Stikine River, and Williston Lake. Summers

Left: Larch is the only coniferous tree that drops its needles, providing a spectacular show of golden colour in the fall. All three varieties that grow in Canada occur in the Interior, with the western larch being the most important to the lumber industry.

Right: Mountain asters are a common roadside wildflower throughout the Interior. There are 4000 species of flowering plants in Canada; 2000 of them are found in British Columbia.

are warm but winter temperatures are affected by cold Arctic fronts. Forests are spruce, fir, pine, and deciduous trees with some wetlands at the lower levels and alpine tundra at the higher elevations. Grizzly bear, moose, black bear, wolf, beaver, muskrat, boreal owl, trout, and salmon are included in the wildlife population.

Rolling alpine tundra and lodgepole pine and spruce forests make up much of the vegetation in the **Northern Boreal Mountains Ecoprovince.** The region includes the plateaus and mountains of the far north-central Interior. Summers are mild and winters are long and cold. This is a relatively unpopulated area containing some of the largest expanses of wilderness in BC. Included are Atlin, Telegraph Creek, Muncho Lake, and the headwaters of the

Stikine and Finlay rivers. Caribou, moose, grizzly and black bear, wolf, and mountain goat are common. Birds include Bohemian waxwing, ptarmigan, loon, gyrfalcon, and snow bunting.

The **Boreal Plains** and **Taiga Plains** ecoprovinces are the extensive lowlands and plateaus in the northeastern corner of the province. Generally, summers are warm and dry and winters are cold. Both areas have many wetlands and small lakes.

Fort St. John, Hudson's Hope, Dawson Creek, and the area stretching to just south of Fort Nelson are included in the **Boreal Plains**. Aspen, spruce, and subalpine fir forests and grasslands are the dominant vegetation. Common wildlife species are moose, deer, black bear, caribou, lynx, wolverine, sharp-tailed grouse and broad-winged hawk.

Fort Nelson and the area north are in the **Taiga Plains**, typified by muskeg and tamarack and spruce forests. Wildlife include black bear, moose, lynx, caribou, snowshoe hare, spruce grouse, and sandpipers.

Ecological Reserves

The provincial government has established 131 ecological reserves, about half of which are in the Interior. Although most are open to the public for wildlife viewing, bird-watching, and photography, access to some particularly sensitive areas is restricted. The reserves were established for scientific study and education, not recreation. Motorized vehicles are not allowed and hunting, tree-cutting, and camping are prohibited.

The Kootenay River, part of the Southern Interior Mountain Ecoprovince, joins the Columbia River at Castlegar.

Protect Ecosystems

The Interior is an increasingly popular tourist destination. Although its vast area makes it seem there is room enough for all, carelessness or ignorance can be destructive to the fragile ecosystems. Consider the following:

1. Don't disturb fragile habitats, protected areas, or native animals.

2. Don't introduce new species of plants or animals into an area. In the Okanagan be aware of milfoil. In the Cariboo, the spread of knapweed is a major concern. Loosestrife is another problem weed in many areas.

3. Remove your garbage. Don't dump plastic or non-biodegradable items overboard or leave them in the woods.

4. Don't collect or buy specimens or products that threaten wildlife or fragile plant species.

Highlights of History

Entrepreneurs imported camels into the Interior in 1862, reasoning that the animals' ability to travel great distances without food or water would be useful. However, other packers objected to the foul-smelling, ill-tempered beasts. They were released into the desert near Cache Creek. The last one died in 1905.

ca. 10,500 BC Native people live at Charlie Lake near Hudson's Hope.

ca. 7000–9000 BC Natives live at sites such as Milliken near Yale in the Fraser Canyon.

ca. 1750 Volcanic eruption at Tseax, near Terrace. Native villages are destroyed.

1793 Fur-trader Alexander Mackenzie of the North West Company travels through the Rocky Mountains to the Bella Coola area on the Pacific Ocean. He is the first known European to cross the continent north of Mexico.

1805 The North West Company's Simon Fraser establishes the first fur-trading post west of the Rockies on McLeod Lake. He calls the area New Caledonia.

1807 David Thompson, also of the North West Company, explores the Columbia River, establishing Kootenae House near present-day Invermere.

1807–08 Simon Fraser establishes Fort George, the site of present-day Prince George, and follows the hazardous Fraser River to the Pacific Ocean.

1811 John Jacob Astor's Pacific Fur Company establishes Fort Astoria at the mouth of the Columbia River just a few weeks before David Thompson arrives.

1812 David Stuart of the Pacific Fur Company establishes a fort at Kamloops. Later that year, the North West Company buys Fort Astoria for about $80,000, gaining control of the fur trade north of the Columbia.

1821 The Hudson's Bay Company absorbs the North West Company, settling a long and bitter animosity.

1827 Fort Langley is settled on the lower Fraser River.

1832 Fort Simpson is established on the coast near present-day Prince Rupert.

1833 Scottish botanist David Douglas travels in the Okanagan, identifying the species known as Douglas fir.

1841 James Sinclair and a contingent of Red River settlers from Manitoba travel through the Rocky Mountains near Radium Hot Springs on their way to Oregon Territory, hoping to maintain a British presence in the land north of the Columbia River.

1846 The Oregon Treaty defines the US-Canada border as the 49th parallel of latitude. The Hudson's Bay Company establishes Interior fur-trade routes entirely within British jurisdiction. A new Brigade Trail heads south from Kamloops to newly established forts at Yale and Hope.

1858 Prospectors discover placer gold along the lower Fraser River. In just a few months, between 20,000 and 30,000 people swarm into the area. New Caledonia becomes the colony of British Columbia as the British government takes over its administration from the Hudson's Bay Company.

1859 Miners follow the Fraser River north, and on the tributaries of the Quesnel and Horsefly rivers, they discover more gold.

1860 Roman Catholic priests, under the leadership of Father Charles Pandosy, establish the first mission in the Okanagan and plant fruit trees.

Walter Moberly and Edgar Dewdney begin work on the Dewdney Trail from Hope to Rock Creek.

1861 Prospectors discover gold in the Cariboo at Williams and Lightning creeks. Barkerville becomes the biggest city north of San Francisco.

1862 The Overlanders, lured by advertisements of easy travel to the goldfields from the Prairies, make their perilous journeys from the east to Jasper and down the Fraser and North Thompson rivers.

A severe smallpox epidemic decimates BC's Native population, (some estimates indicate 20,000 Native people died).

1864 The Cariboo Wagon Road is completed between Yale, Cache Creek, and Clinton. The B.X. Line begins its service and a number of businesses spring up, including way stations, truck gardens, hotels, and grist mills.

Gold is discovered at Wild Horse Creek near present-day Fort Steele and on the Big Bend of the Columbia River.

Road builders and Natives clash in the Chilcotin War when Alfred Waddington attempts to build a road from Bute Inlet north of present-day Vancouver to the Cariboo. It is one of the few violent clashes

Interior Natives can be divided into four broad cultural groups: the Kutenai, the Interior Salish, the Tsimshian and the Athapaskan. These Kutenai women, photographed near Windermere in 1922, are pulling a travois. The sled-like device was used extensively by nomadic tribes.

between Native people and Europeans.

Sir James Douglas retires as governor of the colonies of Vancouver Island and British Columbia.

1865 The Cariboo Wagon Road is completed.

The Big Bend Gold Rush brings settlers to the area east of Cache Creek.

1866 Vancouver Island and the mainland unite as the crown colony of British Columbia.

Edgar Dewdney completes the Hope-Rock Creek Trail to Wild Horse Creek in the East Kootenay.

In the Bulkley Valley area, the Collins Overland Telegraph Company abandons its ambitious project to connect North America with Europe by telegraph through Siberia.

1869 The first transcontinental railway in the US is completed.

1870 A wagon road is completed from Savona to Kamloops.

1871 After several false starts, British Columbia enters Confederation. The federal government promises to build a national railway which will link BC with the rest of the country. Surveying begins.

Prospectors discover gold on the Omineca River tributaries east of Takla Lake. Hazelton becomes an important supply centre as the head of navigation the Skeena River.

1872 Chinese and Native people are disenfranchised.

A public school system is established in the province.

The first homesteader arrives at the site of present-day Douglas Lake Cattle Ranch, today one of the largest in the world.

1874 Another gold rush occurs, this time in the Cassiar region of northwestern BC.

1876 A wagon road from Kamloops is completed to Okanagan Mission where Father Pandosy and the Oblate Fathers have settled on Okanagan Lake.

1880 Crews begin construction of the CPR in BC. Revelstoke and Golden on the Columbia River become supply centres. All along the line, towns are created. Contractors import 9000 to 17,000 Chinese workers.

1881 Major A.B. Rogers finds a pass through the Selkirk Range.

1882 Silver, lead, and zinc are discovered on Kootenay Lake at what is to become Blue Bell Mine, the earliest lode claim in the Kootenays.

1885 The CPR is finally completed through the Rockies via the Kicking Horse, Rogers, and Eagle passes. Kamloops becomes a divisional point.

1886 Regular steamer service is inaugurated on Okanagan Lake.

1887 Copper, high-grade silver, and iron pyrite are discovered near Nelson. The Hall and Silver King mines are established.

1888 Grateful to Sam Steele for peacefully settling a conflict with the Kutenai, grateful citizens of Galbraith's Ferry rename their settlement Fort Steele.

1889 The Great Northern Railway (GNR) and CPR lay tracks through Creston area.

1890–92 Mining booms begin in the West Kootenay at Rossland (gold), Slocan and Kaslo (silver and lead), and Greenwood and Phoenix (cop-

per). Deposits of silver, lead, and zinc result in the establishment of the Sullivan Mine at Kimberley. (The Sullivan Mine will become BC's largest over the next century.)

1892 The Shuswap and Okanagan Railway is completed from Sicamous to Okanagan Landing near Vernon. Lord and Lady Aberdeen grow apples as a commercial crop and a land boom begins.

1894 A great flood on the Fraser River washes away much of what was left of the Cariboo Road through the Fraser Canyon. The CPR becomes the main means of transportation.

1895 F. Augustus Heinze from Montana builds a small smelter at Trail. (It

University of BC archeology students excavated the Milliken site near Yale between 1959 and 1961. Charred cherry pits and other evidence suggest Native tribes used the site 7000 to 9000 years ago.

Guards watch over a gold shipment at the Bullion Mine in the Cariboo, probably in the early 1900s. Some say the mine produced 30 to 40 million dollars in gold during its lifetime.

will become the largest lead-zinc smelter in the world.)

1897 The discovery of gold in the Klondike attracts the first European settlers to the Peace River country.

The CPR agrees to build a rail line through the Crowsnest Pass and to lower freight rates.

1898 Mines are established at Moyie (gold) and Fernie (coal) in the East Kootenay. Intensive mining development begins at Copper Mountain, Hedley, and Tulameen in the Princeton area.

1900 The CPR's Crowsnest route goes through Cranbrook, not Fort Steele, effectively destroying Fort Steele's position as the major settlement in the East Kootenay.

1900–20 British setters, attracted by land developers' advertisements, and encouraged by the CPR and the federal government's National Policy, settle in the Kootenays and the Okanagan and Thompson valleys.

1901 The federal government establishes the Dominion Telegraph line over the old Overland route between the Yukon and Port Simpson near present-day Prince Rupert.

1903 Richard McBride becomes premier of BC at 33, the youngest in BC's history. Political parties are established. McBride's 12-year tenure oversees an economic boom that includes railway construction, reform of labor laws, and the establishment of BC's first university.

1906 With the discovery of coal near Merritt, a spur line of the CPR is completed from Spences Bridge to Merritt.

One of America's most wanted outlaws, Bill Miner, is arrested for robbing a train near Kamloops.

Simon Gun-an-Noot is wrongly

The Construction of the CPR

One of the most important events in the development of BC's Interior was the construction of the CPR. Not only did it provide much needed jobs, but it linked BC with the rest of the country.

Sir John A. Macdonald's Conservative government in Ottawa agreed to the construction of a transcontinental railway within 10 years as part of Confederation with BC in 1871. Realization of the agreement faced many difficulties.

The route in BC had to cross four mountain ranges before reaching the Pacific Coast. Surveying was difficult. Planners such as Walter Moberly and Sanford Fleming couldn't agree where the line should cross the mountains. Rocked by "the Pacific Scandal," Macdonald's government was forced to resign in 1873 when it was revealed some cabinet members had taken bribes in return for construction contracts.

The contract was eventually awarded to Donald A. Smith, J.J. Hill, and George Stephen of the Canadian Pacific Railway Company. In BC, construction began at Yale in 1880.

Thirty-year-old New York engineer Andrew Onderdonk obtained the contracts to build most of the railway through British Columbia. Unable to find enough workers, he subcontracted for laborers from southern China. It is estimated that between 9000 to 17,000 Chinese were employed during construction of the railway. Onderdonk later noted that likely three Chinese died for every kilometre of track laid.

As the railway pushed west from the Rockies and east from the coast, towns like Revelstoke and Golden were born, others like Kamloops and Yale were rejuvenated as railway divisional points and supply centres. The coal-mining community of Merritt flourished. Lumber mills were set up supplying railway ties and building materials.

The "Last Spike" of the CPR was driven by Donald Smith at Craigellachie on November 7, 1885, pictured above. The first passenger train reached Port Moody the following July.

William Van Horne was appointed president of the CPR in 1888. Under his guidance the company encouraged land settlement, developed a telegraph service, launched an international steamship line, and built tourist hotels. The introduction of elegant CPR paddlewheelers on Kootenay, Arrow, and Okanagan lakes in the 1890s encouraged settlement and tourism. Van Horne negotiated the Crowsnest Agreement in 1897, which initiated the CPR's entry into the mining industry.

accused of a murder near Hazelton. He and his family elude capture for 13 years in the wilderness.

1907 Work begins on the Grand Trunk Pacific Railway, opening the Nechako and Bulkley valleys to European settlement.

1908 Peter the Lordly leads his Doukhobor followers to the West Kootenay from Saskatchewan in search of "toil and peaceful life."

1909 Charles Walcott discovers the fossils of the Burgess Shale near Field, which many claim are the most important paleontological find in human history.

1910 Construction begins on the Kettle Valley Railway, which eventually will stretch from Midway to Hope.

1911 The federal government establishes Yoho National Park in the Rockies.

1912 Pacific Great Eastern Railway (PGE) is incorporated to build a line from North Vancouver to Prince George.

1913 Mt. Robson becomes the first provincial park in the Interior.

1914 The Grand Trunk Railway is completed from Edmonton to Prince Rupert. Prince George also thrives.

Mt. Revelstoke National Park is created.

Canadian Northern Railway (CNR) construction seriously damages the fishery in the Fraser Canyon.

1914–18 World War I. Many British settlers return to their motherland to fight. BC's pre-war population is 450,000.

1915 The CNR is completed connecting Vancouver to Edmonton via the Yellowhead Pass.

1916 The Kettle Valley Railway is completed from Midway to Hope.

1918 The Panama Canal opens, giving BC easier access to world markets.

1920 The mining industry in Greenwood and Grand Forks collapses due to a strike in the East Kootenay the previous year.

1923 The federal Chinese Immigration Act effectively stops Chinese immigration into Canada.

1930 On August 13, "Black Wednesday," 45 miners die in an underground explosion at Coalmont in the Tulameen region near Princeton, one of the worst mining disasters in the province's history.

1931 The Edmonton, Dunvegan, and British Columbia Railway line is completed to Dawson Creek.

1937 Doukhobor lands go into receivership, effectively ending their communal experiment.

1938 Tweedsmuir Provincial Park, BC's largest, is created.

1939–45 World War II.

1942 The Alaska Highway, a US military project connecting Dawson Creek to Fairbanks, is completed, stimulating the economy and attracting settlers.

1944 Japanese Canadians are interned in "relocation camps" in several Interior communities.

1944–46 The International Joint Canada and US Fisheries Commission builds fish ladders in the Fraser Canyon to restore the salmon fishery.

1946 The Alaska Highway is opened to the public.

1947–49 Chinese, Hindu, and Japanese citizens are re-enfranchised.

1948 The Great Flood on the Fraser River leaves 9000 homeless.

1949 The Hope-Princeton Highway opens.

1952 Hardware merchant WAC Bennett becomes premier of the province and will remain so for the next 20 years, the longest tenure of any premier in the province's history.

The John Hart Highway is completed from Prince George to Dawson Creek.

1953 When the provincial government refuses to participate, Chilcotin residents build the "Freedom Road," connecting Bella Coola with the Interior.

1956 The Pacific Great Eastern Railway is completed from Quesnel to Prince George and North Vancouver to Squamish.

1957 Copper Mountain Mines, once one of the largest mines in the British Empire, closes.

1961 The Kettle Valley Railway is abandoned.

1962 Rogers Pass is opened on the Trans-Canada Highway.

1964 The Columbia River Treaty, renegotiable in 30 years, becomes effective between the US and Canada. Under the terms of the controversial treaty, Canada builds three dams on the Columbia: the Duncan (1967), the Keenlyside (1968), and the Mica (1973). The Arrow Lakes are flooded, submerging farmland and entire towns.

1965 The Hope Slide dislodges half a mountain and kills four people on the Hope-Princeton Highway.

1968 The largest freshwater body in BC, Williston Lake, is created when the WAC Bennett hydroelectric dam is constructed on the Peace River.

1970s As a reaction to the Vietnam War, thousands of Americans, some of them avoiding military conscription, settle in BC. The West Kootenay, Okanagan, Bulkley Valley, and Lillooet areas are among popular destinations for "back-to-the-land" advocates.

1971 BC Rail (formerly the PGE) extends its line from Prince George to Fort Nelson, serving the resource industries of the north with 2300 km of track.

1972 Libby Dam is built on the Kootenay River in Montana, creating 128-kilometre Lake Koocanusa in the East Kootenay.

1984 Construction of Revelstoke Dam is completed on Columbia River, one of North America's largest hydroelectric developments.

1986 The province hosts Expo 86, a world exhibition. The first phase of the Coquihalla Highway is opened, providing fast access to the Interior.

1988 The federal government makes a formal apology to Japanese-Canadians interned during World War I; each survivor is awarded $21,000.

1992 Federal and provincial governments make an historic agreement to address Native land claims in BC.

Cassiar in northwestern BC becomes BC's latest ghost town when the asbestos mine goes bankrupt.

Economy

BC's Interior waterways provide an ideal system of transportation and storage of logs. This boom is on Slocan Lake in the West Kootenay region.

Resource extraction has always been a strong component of BC's economy. Prehistoric Native cultures used natural resources such as trees, animals, fish, and minerals for trade and sustenance. In the 18th and 19th centuries European furtraders explored BC's Interior (New Caledonia) looking for better trade routes and new territory. Logging began with the gold rush in 1858 as towns were constructed, and it continued with the building of the CPR. Today, most of the people who live in the Interior rely on its natural resources for their livelihood.

Mining

Although logging is the number-one resource industry in the province, mining has played a more dramatic role in the development of the Interior. A gold rush on the lower Fraser River in 1858 began a stampede of men and women began into the Cariboo, the Big Bend of the Columbia River, and the Kootenays, opening up the province for development. Logging, ranching, and road and railway building quickly followed.

In 1990, the total value of mineral production in the province (including oil and natural gas) was $3.96 billion. Copper accounts for 40 percent of mineral and petroleum production, with coal following at 27 percent, gold at 24 percent, and petroleum and natural gas at 23 percent. However, the mining industry employs only about two percent of the total workforce in the province.

Always a "boom or bust" industry, mining shutdowns are a major occupational hazard, and BC's Interior is full of ghost towns that were once thriving communities. Some, like Barkerville, have become major tourist attractions. Cassiar, an asbestos-mining town until 1992, is a more recent casualty. Other communities that have always depended on mining are facing closures during the next decade. Places like Kimberley and Princeton are turning to tourism for an alternate economic base.

Forest Products

Sixty percent of BC is forested, about 52 million hectares. The province produces 63 percent of Canada's sawn lumber, most of its plywood, and 24 percent of its chemical pulp. In 1992, forestry made up 49.6 percent of BC's economy, directly and indirectly employing 272,100 people (18 percent of the province's workers).

Although the coastal logging industry has been dominant for much of the last 150 years, logging began in the Interior in the 1860s as mining developed and towns sprung up. With the construction of the CPR, enterprising mill operators supplied lumber for railway ties, tres-

Treeplanting

In BC, all logged public land must be reforested. Approximately $200 million is spent by the private sector and over $80 million by the provincial ministry of forests annually on forest renewal. By 1990, nearly 2.5 billion trees had been planted since the provincial government began its program in 1930. Although the first concentrated effort at treeplanting in BC occurred in 1936 on Vancouver Island, extensive planting in the Interior didn't begin until the early 1970s.

In 1990–91 nearly 250,000 trees were planted on over 200,000 hectares of private and crown land.

The provincial government contracts with private companies for its replanting programs. At present, 150 companies actively compete for contracts. In 1992 about 11,000 workers, one-quarter of them women, were employed as tree planters. Province-wide the season can stretch from January to November, but the most concentrated planting occurs in May and June, making it ideal employment for students. Planters usually earn $100 to $200 per day.

In the Interior, most planting begins in the spring at the lower elevations when the land is moist, and it moves to the higher elevations as the snow melts. Equipped with digging tools called "dibbles" and bags of seedlings, planters work across a site, planting a tree every two to four metres. Planters may carry three or four species in their bags, making a planting decision based on soil, location, amount of light, and other factors. Depending on the terrain, a worker could plant as many as 1000 or more trees a day.

tles, and avalanche sheds. Once the rail lines were completed, mill owners exported lumber to the developing towns of the Prairies. But it wasn't until the mid-1970s that Interior operations began providing half the province's forest products.

Although pulp mills were established in the coastal area in the early 1900s, they did not appear in the Interior until the mid-1960. Today there are nine pulp and paper operations in the Interior.

In the 1960s most of the Interior's small independent mills disappeared, bought out by larger, often multinational, interests. The practice concerns many residents who fear the longevity of the forests is not a priority of out-of-province corporations. A fiery debate currently rages between the forest industry and environmentalists about how to best manage this valuable resource.

Fishing

Most of BC's commercial fishing takes place on the coast, although the major spawning grounds are located in the Interior. Five Pacific salmon and two salmonid trout species breed in the Fraser and Skeena river systems. The Interior also plays an important role in the province's sportfishing industry. Anglers spent about $1.3 billion in BC in 1989.

Agriculture

Not surprisingly, since most of its land is mountainous and unsuitable for agriculture, BC only supplies five percent of Canada's total agricultural products. However, agriculture is still vital to the economy in the Interior. The Okanagan area, well known for its orchards and vineyards, is one of Canada's three main fruit-growing areas and one of the country's two wine-producing areas. The Creston Valley is also valued for its orchards and farm produce, and the cattle ranches of the Cariboo and Nicola Valley have been an important part of the economy since the gold rush. But most of BC's cultivated land is found in Peace River country, tucked away in the northeast corner of the province, accounting for 90 percent of the province's grain production.

BC's net farm income in 1990 was $220 million, with livestock and related products comprising 64 percent of the industry.

Energy

The geography and climate of the Interior create abundant opportunities for hydroelectric development. The Kootenay River was dammed early in the twentieth century to provide power for mining projects. Since the 1960s the Columbia River has been flooded and dammed to increase hydroelectric potential both for export and domestic use. Further north, the Peace River project is currently the third largest producer of hydroelectric power in the country.

Like other forms of resource development, hydroelectric power takes an environmental toll, disturbing delicate aquatic habitats. A public increasingly concerned with environmental protection is constantly challenging BC Hydro proposals to further develop the province's waterways for power exports.

Although BC imports most of its oil, it is a net exporter of energy due to its hydroelectric, coal, and natural gas developments.

Tourism

With resource based industries facing an uncertain future, tourism is becoming more and more important to the economy of the Interior. The beautiful scenery, clean air and water, and wide variety of outdoor recreation activities attract visitors from around the world. In 1990, over five billion dollars was spent by over 23 million overnight visitors travelling in BC.

Ginseng

In the arid areas of the southern Interior, travellers may see evidence of one of BC's newest cash crops: ginseng. Farmers have been cultivating the plant in Asia for 7000 years and in the United States since the 18th century, but commercial cultivation in BC

didn't begin until 1982, near Lytton. Identifiable by the large sheets of black plastic which protect the delicate plant from excessive moisture, ginseng fields bring about $20 million to BC's economy annually. By 1998, that total is expected to rise to $100 million.

There are between 55 and 60 large- and small-scale farms in the Interior ranging anywhere from one-tenth of a hectare to 60 hectares. About 400 hectares of land are under cultivation in the province.

According to Al Smith, President of the BC Association of Ginseng Growers, machinery, shading structures and other start-up costs are high. Seed alone can cost up to $20,000 per acre. The root takes three to four years before it can be harvested, but returns can be up to $200,000 per acre. On average in BC, farmers can harvest 500 to 600 pounds of seed per acre yielding $100 to $200 per pound. Anywhere from 2800 to 3400 pounds of root can be harvested per acre at $50 to $60 per pound.

Ideal growing conditions exist around Kamloops, Merritt, Lytton, and Lillooet, and in the Okanagan Valley, with some farms in the Grand Forks and Creston areas.

Native to northern Manchuria, the northeastern United States, southern Ontario, and Quebec, ginseng is regarded as a "cure-all" by many. Although in BC, farmers sell either dried root or seed, processed ginseng is sold as tea, capsules, soups, gum, and health drinks.

Outdoor Recreation

BC has 843 rivers and over 10,000 named creeks and brooks. Thousands of Interior lakes offer recreational opportunities. Above, children swim and fish on Slocan Lake near Silverton.

From the warm-water lakes of the Okanagan to the icy glaciers of the Selkirks, opportunities for outdoor recreation are plentiful in BC's Interior. Whether horseback riding on a Cariboo guest ranch, powder skiing in the Kootenays, or rafting on the Thompson River, many activities are near major highway routes. Travellers with a desire to get off the beaten track can hike, drive, or fly to more remote destinations and enjoy activities such as alpine hiking, heli-skiing, and fly-in fishing.

SuperGuide focuses on noncommercial outdoor recreation activities.

The Outdoor Recreation Council of British Columbia, an umbrella organization that provides information on outdoor recreation opportunities and safe use of the outdoors, is a useful resource. (See Reference.)

When planning your vacation, be aware that areas like the Okanagan and Shuswap lakes tend to be quite popular in the summer months, whereas areas like the Kootenays and the Cariboo provide a little more breathing room.

If you really want to get away from it all, try one of the wilderness parks in the northern half of the province. Liard Hot Springs Provincial Park close to the Yukon border has a unique ecosystem with subtropical plant life. Guides offer trail rides into remote Spatsizi Plateau Wilderness and Mount Edziza provincial parks near Highway 37.

For reader convenience, some commercial listings are given in the Reference section, such as river-rafting companies and guest ranches, but these are not recommendations.

However you use BC's natural areas, remember they are for everyone. "Take only photographs, leave only footprints," and "Pack it in, pack it out," are good pieces of advice.

Summer Activities

The summertime is when BC's diverse landforms can be most appreciated. Landscapes ranging from ancient glaciers and dormant volcanoes to arid grasslands and sandy beaches translate into a wide variety of recreational choices. Here are a few possibilities.

Camping, Hiking, and Mountaineering

From the rolling grassland of the Thompson region to the rugged alpine peaks of the Bugaboos, BC's Interior offers an incredible variety of terrains for hikers, climbers, and campers. There are hundreds of parks and recreation areas spread over thousands of hectares of land to meet the needs of everyone from RV users and day trippers to experienced mountaineers.

Campgrounds in the Interior range from commercial ventures with swimming pools and laundromats to spartan sites in the mountain ranges.

The provincial government oversees approximately 500 provincial parks, ecological reserves, and recreation areas and there are more privately owned facilities. The 389 provincial parks include day-use only picnic areas, wilderness parks, and marine parks, containing over 11,500 campsites covering 5.4 million hectares. BC Parks publishes a variety of free maps and brochures about provincial parks and their facilities (available at Infocentres and parks offices).

BC Forest Service Recreation areas, containing over 1200 campsites and 5000 kilometers of trails, offer more rustic camping and an alterna-

BC has almost 400 provincial parks providing a variety of facilities. At Champion Lakes Provincial Park near Trail visitors can view flora and fauna from a boardwalk around the lakes.

An airborne skier enjoys the challenge of Old Granite Mountain in Nancy Green Recreation Area, near Rossland. Red Mountain is in the background.

tive to the sometimes crowded provincial campgrounds. Each forest district has detailed maps and information. Local regional districts also maintain parks for public use. Contact local tourist associations and Infocentres. Some ecological reserves are also open on a limited basis to visitors, but they are not recreation sites.

Mt. Revelstoke, Glacier, Yoho, and Kootenay are the four national parks in the Interior. All but Mt. Revelstoke National Park have campgrounds. Maps and interpretive literature are available by mail or at the park gates. (See Reference section.) Inexperienced hikers and climbers may want to contact the Association of Mountain Guides, Box 1537, Banff, Alberta T0L 0C0, 403-762-3761.

There are a number of books on the market which offer descriptions of hiking trails, climbing, and wilderness camping in specific areas, including Altitude's *Walks and Easy Hikes in the Canadian Rockies.* Information is also available from the provincial tourism department, local tourism associations, and Infocentres.

Among the popular hiking routes in the Interior are the Mackenzie Grease Trail in the Chilcotin, the Pacific Crest Trail in Manning Park, and the Earl Grey Trail in the Purcell Wil-

Forest Fires

Firefighters deal with about 3000 fires in BC's forests every year. Please make sure you are familiar with regulations and restrictions regarding the building of campfires. Infocentres and forestry offices have brochures. If you see a forest fire, Dial "0" and ask for ZEnith 5555.

derness Conservancy. Abandoned rail lines such as the old Kettle Valley Railway between Hope and Midway, historic trails, and old fur brigade routes are currently being reclaimed by outdoor groups. Many communities have short nature walks on their list of local attractions.

The Centennial Trails Trust in Vancouver is working on a national heritage trail. BC's 1400-kilometre section will travel across the southern province, with some sections between Victoria and Banff already in use. (See Reference section.)

Serious climbers will find many challenges on alpine peaks throughout the Interior in such areas as the Rocky Mountains, Glacier National Park, the Purcell Wilderness Conservancy, and the Bugaboo Alpine Recreation Area. Contact the BC Federation of Mountain Clubs. (See Reference section.)

Fishing

BC is famous around the world for its sportsfishing, with thousands of Interior lakes to choose from. Almost every area claims superior fishing opportunities, among them the Lakes District and Bulkley Valley east of Prince George, the Interlakes region in the Cariboo, and the many lakes in the Nicola Valley and Kamloops region.

The provincial government takes pride in its freshwater stocking program. In 1989, 12 million fish, the majority from wild stock, were released into 1220 lakes and streams. Nine to ten million fry are produced annually in the inland fish culture program at five major provincial

hatcheries. Three are located in the Interior at Summerland (Okanagan), Cache Creek (Cariboo), and Wardner (East Kootenay). They grow about 50 strains of 10 salmonid species including Dolly Varden, kokanee salmon, rainbow trout, and steelhead. All three hatcheries are open to the public and have interpretive services.

A number of angling options are available from flying in to remote

A fisherman tries his luck at Dutch Creek in the East Kootenay. Twenty species of game fish are commonly caught in the Interior.

Game Fish in the Interior

Trout
rainbow (includes
    steelhead and Kamloops)
cutthroat
brown
char (includes Dolly
    Varden/bull trout, lake
    trout, and brook trout)

Bass
smallmouth
largemouth

Whitefish
mountain whitefish
lake whitefish

Other
Kokanee
Arctic grayling
burbot (ling)
white sturgeon
black crappie
yellow perch
walleye
northern pike

Angling Guidelines

• Familiarize yourself with fishing regulations. Most areas have some restrictions.
• Respect catch limits.
• Help protect the integrity of our fishery. Do not introduce aquarium or foreign species.
• Leave the fishing site in the same, or better, condition than you found it. Fines of up to $1 million are in effect for destruction of fish habitat.
• A private landholder has the right to grant or refuse access. Make sure you get the necessary permission.
• Voluntary "Catch and Release" is being adopted by more and more anglers and in some places is mandatory. (See below.)

Catch and Release

Many anglers enjoy the sport of fishing, but elect to help sustain BC's fishery by releasing some or all of the fish they catch so the fish may spawn or be caught again. However, fish that you plan to release must be handled properly, or despite good intentions, they may not survive.

• Use barbless hooks.
• Play and release a fish as quickly as possible. An exhausted fish may not live.
• Keep the fish in the water as much as possible. A fish out of water is more likely to injure itself or damage its scales.
• When handling the fish be as gentle as possible. Make sure your hands are wet; keep your fingers out of the gills; don't squeeze the fish or damage the scales.
• Use longnose pliers to remove the hook as rapidly, but gently, as possible. If the hook is deeply embedded, cut the line and leave it in.
• When reviving the fish, hold it gently in the water, moving it back and forth to pump water in its gills. Point it upstream. and when it begins to struggle and swim normally, let it go.

resorts and guided wilderness trips, to solitary fly-fishing or leisurely family outings. Local tourism associations can provide current information about guides and excursions as well as where the fish are currently biting.

Many anglers prefer the voluntary "catch and release" approach to fishing, which fisheries management staff endorse. The practice, enabling fish to spawn or be caught again, is mandatory in some waters because of stock depletion.

In order to protect and maintain the fishery, a number of freshwater fishing regulations and licensing fees are in effect, which include ice-fishing. These vary from area to area. All non-Native anglers 16 years of age and older must buy a licence. Provincial licences are not valid in national parks. Copies of the provincial government's *Freshwater Fishing Regulations Synopsis* and licences are available from government agents, sporting goods stores, Infocentres, or the provincial Ministry of Environment (see Reference section.).

Water Sports

Marinas at most resort areas rent power boats, canoes, and other water sport equipment. At remote locations, rental facilities vary. Enquiries should be made in advance.

Arrow, Shuswap, Christina, and Kootenay lakes are among those that have marine parks. Part of the provincial park system, these areas are accessible only by water.

Kootenay, Windermere, Skaha, and Nicola lakes are good windsurfing locales.

PADDLING

Canoeing and kayaking are popular activities on the Interior's thousands of lakes and rivers. Possibilities include a slow meander down the Columbia River between Golden and Radium, an exciting whitewater journey on the Chilcotin River, and a seven- to ten-day paddle on the Bowron Lake circuit. Popular paddling trips are listed below.

Moving water is rated on a scale of one to six, with six being the most treacherous. Make sure you match your ability with the challenge of the river. Paddlers should always check locally as conditions vary seasonally.

RIVER RAFTING

River rafting is popular on a number of Interior rivers including the Fraser, Thompson, Chilcotin, Adams, Stikine, Tatshenshini, Kicking Horse, and Kootenay. Several private rafting companies offer excursions lasting a few hours to several days. (See Reference.) Rafting has been under intense provincial scrutiny because of a number of fatal accidents several years ago. As a result, strict licensing and operating regulations are now in effect for rafting companies, with safety the number-one priority.

BOATING

Water lovers who prefer a slow boat to nowhere may want to rent a houseboat. Shuswap, Okanagan, Mara, and Kootenay lakes are favourites. Sailing is more popular on the coast, but most large Interior lakes are favourable.

SCUBA DIVING

Scuba diving is more commonly practised on the coast, but tales of buried treasure under several Interior Lakes keep the sport alive. Regulars at coffee shops in downtown Nelson may provide the latest rumors on Kootenay Lake's sunken treasure. Ellison Provincial Park on Okanagan Lake is the Interior's only underwater marine park.

Golf

A great many Interior communities have golf courses, with new ones constantly being developed, and many older ones being upgraded. In areas

Popular Canoe Routes

1. **Bowron Lake Circuit** in the Cariboo near Barkerville. Seven to ten day circuit covers 10 lakes, some portaging, through wilderness area.
2. **The Similkameen River** from Princeton to Cawston. Described as "a classic whitewater experience," this two-day trip covers 100 kilometres.
3. **Wells Gray Provincial Park** in the Cariboo Mountains. Clearwater, Mahood, and Murtle lakes offer 170 kilometres of wilderness paddling.
4. **Fraser River.** Several portions have canyons and rapids of advanced difficulty.
5. **Columbia River.** Novice to intermediate paddling from Canal Flats to Golden, and from Revelstoke to Arrow Lakes.
6. **Slocan Lake and River** in the West Kootenay. Forty kilometre-long lake and 60 kilometre river. For beginners and experienced paddlers.
7. **Thompson River,** from Clearwater to Kamloops. Ideal for novice or intermediate. Savona to Goldpan Campground near Spences Bridge is more challenging. Dangerous waters south to Lytton.

Among the may choices for golfers in the Interior are the championship links at Fairmont Hot Springs in the East Kootenay.

with milder climates such as the Okanagan, the season can stretch from March to November, sometimes year round. (See Reference section.) Even the experts haven't played all the 170 regulation-sized courses in the province, but from Lillooet's unique Sheep Pastures to Castlegar's championship greens, the possibilities are varied.

Wildlife Viewing

BC's wide variety of terrains and ecosystems means an equally wide variety of wildlife habitats. As a result BC has the largest number of species in the country. The 700 species of

Popular Wildlife-viewing Sites

Trans-Canada Highway
• The Adams River near Kamloops: salmon spawning
Crowsnest Highway
• Between Hedley and Keremeos on the Similkameen River: mountain goats
• Creston Valley: birdwatching
• Elk Valley: elk, deer, bear, and bighorn sheep
Coquihalla-Nicola
• Highway 5A south of Kamloops: birdwatching
Okanagan
• Kalamalka Lake Provincial Park: rattlesnakes
• Vaseux Lake: California bighorn sheep and birdwatching
West Kootenay
• Kokanee Creek Provincial Park: spawning kokanee
• Kootenay Lake and River: osprey
East Kootenay
• Columbia wetlands: birdwatching
• Kootenay National Park: elk, wolves, and Rocky Mountain bighorn sheep

Central Interior
• Alkali Lake: birdwatching
• Bowron Lake Provincial Park and Mt. Robson Provincial Park: moose
• Chilanko Marsh and Cranberry Marsh: bird watching
Northern Interior
• Pink Mountain: mountain caribou, wild buffalo, and butterflies
• Stone Mountain Provincial Park, Dunlevy Creek, and Muncho Lake Provincial Park: stone sheep

Tips for Wildlife Viewing
1. Check the season.
2. Check the time Best wildlife viewing times are early morning and early evening.
3. Hide behind natural or artificial screens.
4. Keep silent.
5. Be patient.
6. Read wildlife clues such as nests, tracks, and droppings.
7. Use aids such as field guides and binoculars.

vertebrates found here include 448 species of birds, 143 species of mammals, 19 species of reptiles, 20 species of amphibians, and 73 species of fish. A number of "viewing corridors" have been identified by the BC Wildlife Branch where the opportunities are better than average to catch sight of certain species. These are listed in the highway guides.

Guest Ranches and Horsebackriding

Guest ranches provide an authentic western experience, with the Cariboo-Chilcotin and Nicola Valley considered by many to be the heart of cowboy country. (An annual rodeo circuit travels around the province, but if you want to see how they do it back home on the ranch, look for the "real" rodeos in places like Anahim Lake and Riske Creek in the

Chilcotin). There are a number of guest ranches in the East Kootenay as well. (See Reference.)

Horses are for hire at stables throughout the Interior, with guided trail rides lasting from a few hours to several days. Some communities such as Kamloops sponsor an annual trail ride.

Above: Rancher Lloyd Jones' Top of the World Guest Ranch is one of many in the Interior. This working ranch attracts guests from as far away as Germany and Italy.

Below: The smallest members of the squirrel family, chipmunks are commonly seen at campgrounds throughout the Interior. Seeds are their most important source of food, but a chipmunk's diet may also include fruits, mushrooms, insects, and flowers.

Spelunking

Spelunking, the underground cave exploration sport for non-claustrophobics, is gaining popularity in the Interior. One of the more popular sites is the Cody Caves near Kaslo in the West Kootenay where the limestone formations date back 600 million years.

Hang Gliding

Hang gliding is probably the closest you can come to flying without actually flapping your wings. If leaping off the edge of a mountain into thin air is how you want to spend your vacation, BC's Interior will provide you with an opportunity. Twice a year hang gliders from all over Western Canada converge on the Cariboo community of Clinton to pursue this passion. The West Kootenay, the East Kootenay, and the Okanagan are among other popular areas.

Rockhounding and Goldpanning

With BC's varied terrain and history of volcanoes and glaciers, rockhounds can spend many rewarding hours poking around canyons and mountainsides. On the Cassiar Highway, Jade City and Dease Lake are popular stops. The Fraser Canyon, the Similkameen region, the Okanagan, and the East Kootenay are among other good places to look.

Gold panners work creek beds in former gold strike locales such as the Fraser Canyon, the East Kootenay, and the Barkerville area. But many of these areas still have active claims. Check with local government agents or Infocentes for regulations.

Bicycling

In response to the growing popularity of cycling, several communities have developed bike trails. At Vernon's Silver Star Provincial Park aficionados can take the chairlift up and rent a bike at the top for the trip down. Rossland declares itself the "Mountain Biking Capital of BC." And cyclers are a common sight along BC highways. Golden promotes a "Golden Triangle" bike route that takes in Radium Hot Springs and Lake Louise.

Winter Activities

Skiing is probably the province's number one outdoor winter sport, from heli-skiing in deep powder to cross-country skiing on well-groomed trails.

Downhill (Alpine) Skiing

In the Interior, popular downhill ski areas include Red Mountain and Whitewater in the West Kootenay; Apex Alpine, Big White, and Silver Star in the Okanagan; Tod Mountain near Kamloops; Mt. Mackenzie near Revelstoke; North Star, Fernie Snow Valley, Radium, and Fairmont in the East Kootenay; Ski Smithers in the Bulkley Valley; and Gibson Pass in Manning Provincial Park. Many communities have family slopes.

Cross-country (Nordic) Skiing

Some provincial parks and forestry recreation areas have marked cross-country or nordic trails, but many skiers prefer to search out logging and access roads in rural areas. In recent years, telemarking has become popular. It is not uncommon to see nordic skiers on alpine (downhill) slopes. Many downhill ski resorts have groomed cross country trails.

For those who like skiing in a crowd, the Cariboo community of 100 Mile House sponsors an annual cross-country ski marathon that attracts hundreds of participants from around the world. Many private companies have ski-touring packages that offer everything from half-day outings on local trails to longer expeditions in remote backcountry. Revelstoke, Golden, Nelson, McBride, Smithers, and Invermere are headquarters for some of these outfits. Contact local Infocentres.

Heli-skiing

For the more adventurous, heli-skiing offers the double thrill of virgin powder and an absence of lift lineups. A number of private companies will fly you into otherwise inaccessible areas. The Bugaboos in the Purcell Mountains and the Premier Range in the Cariboo are well-known for this particular type of euphoria. Smithers, Revelstoke, Nelson, Invermere, Golden, McBride, and Valemount are among the communities where heli-ski operators are located.

Snowmobiling

Logging roads are popular in the wintertime for snowmobiling. Because of its relatively flat terrain, the Nicola Valley and the Cariboo are particularly popular. Some communities have specially designated areas for snowmobiling. In multi-use areas, snowmobilers should be on the lookout for cross-country skiers and others using the same trails.

Other winter activities include snowshoeing, ice-fishing, ice climbing, and winter moutaineering. For details, contact local tourism associations.

Hot Springs

No matter what your activity or what your season, a good soak in a hot mineral pool is often a good way to end the day. The East and West Kootenay have a number of natural and developed spas. Check the Reference section.

Be Prepared

No matter where or how you enjoy the snow, make sure you are aware of the danger of frostbite, hypothermia, and avalanche potential in the area you plan to visit. Regretfully, every year there are fatalities due to avalanches. Do not minimize the risks involved; respect avalanche warning signs and learn avalanche safety techniques.

In winter carry tire chains, and keep essentials for several days survival stored in your vehicle.

For more information see the Reference section.

Trans-Canada Highway

Sagebrush and ponderosa pine are typical vegetation of the arid Thompson River area in the southern Interior.

The scenic Trans-Canada Highway (Highway 1) is the longest paved highway in the world. Although a disarmingly easy journey through spectacular terrain today, the route through the Interior was agonizing for early travellers.

The first portion of the Trans-Canada Highway passes through the historic Fraser Canyon. Here, in places, early Native residents used a system of rope ladders to travel along the steep rock walls above the turbulent Fraser River. In the 1860s, an eastbound traveller would board a stagecoach at Yale and then trans-fer to a paddlewheeler at Savona, for a journey to the north end of Shuswap Lake. From there, a narrow mountain trail continued to the goldfields on the Big Bend of the Columbia River.

The Big Bend Highway from Revelstoke to Golden was the only road through to the central Rockies until 1963.

Today's modern two- to four-lane paved highway makes the journey pleasant and manageable. Highway 1 is the most well-travelled route in the province.

The semi-nomadic Interior Salish are indigenous to the region. Many

Interior towns and attractions on the Trans-Canada lie close to ancient villages and fishing and hunting grounds. Cities such as Lytton and Kamloops were Native encampments for thousands of years before Europeans and Asians settled here.

The first non-Native settlements were established by fur traders who built forts and brigade trails in the early 1800s. Beginning in 1858, several gold rushes – notably on the lower Fraser River, in the Cariboo, and in the East Kootenay – brought an influx of people to the southern Interior. The construction and expansion of trails and wagon roads soon followed, with the Canadian Pacific Railway track laid in the 1880s. Farming, logging, and service communities quickly sprung up along the railway route. The Trans-Canada Highway parallels the rail line in many places.

Hope

150 km (93 mi) east of Vancouver. Population: 3280. Infocentre: 919 Water Avenue, Box 370, V0X 1L0. 869-2021; Fax: 869-2160

Hope is the gateway to the Interior and the intersection of Highways 1 (the Trans-Canada), 3 (the Crowsnest), 5 (the Coquihalla), and 7 (the Lougheed). (The signs can be confusing: watch carefully.) At Hope the Fraser River leaves the Coast and Cascade mountains to begin the final portion of its journey west to the Pacific.

Simon Fraser passed this way on his 1808 expedition in search of the Columbia River. In 1846, a Hudson's Bay Company fur-trading fort was established here at the end of

the Brigade Trail from Fort Kamloops. Hope was an important centre during the 1858 gold rush on the lower Fraser River and again with the development of the railways. The Canadian Pacific Railway (1885), the Canadian National Railway (1915), and the Kettle Valley Railway (1916) all converged here.

The **Hope Museum** (869-2021), located at the Infocentre on Highway 1

Hope's Christ Church was consecrated in 1861 and is one of BC's oldest churches. Reverend Alexander St. David Francis Pringle arrived in 1859 from London and raised the money for its construction from the gold miners.

Trans-Canada Highway Facts

- It is the longest paved highway in the world.
- It was constructed during the 1950s and 1960s to connect Victoria, BC, with St. John's, Newfoundland.
- The Roger's Pass, in the Selkirk Range, opened in 1963. The visitor centre draws 160,000 visitors per year.
- Total length: 6888 kilometres
- Cost: $1 billion
- Cost of BC portion: $280 million
- Distance from Hope to the Alberta border: 623 kilometres
- Highest passes: 1327-metre Rogers Pass in the Columbia Mountains and 1643-metre Kicking Horse Pass in the Rockies
- Campgrounds: on average, one every 160 kilometres

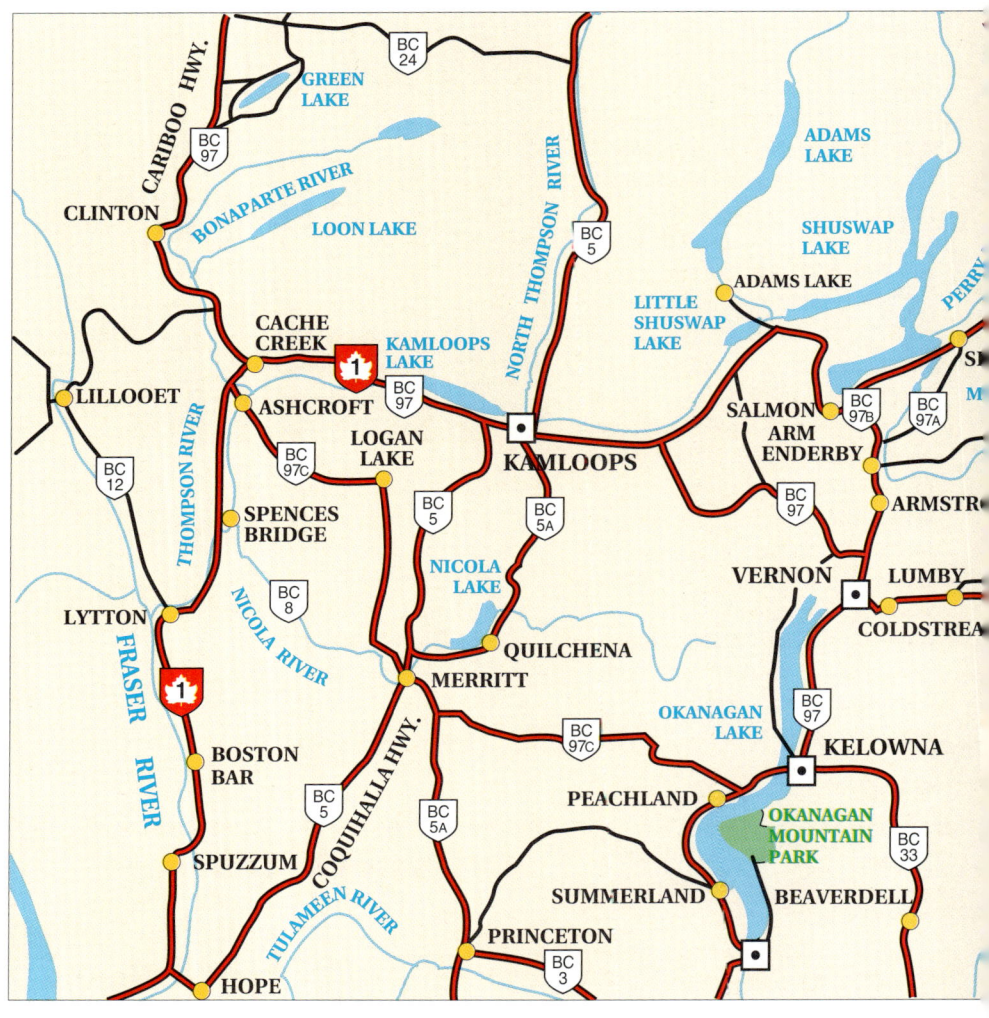

in the city centre, has an interesting collection of local history; outside is a restored gold-ore concentrator. Other points of interest include **Christ Church** (869-7320), consecrated in 1861, and the H-tree in Memorial Park, a legacy of Hudson's Bay Company days. A signpost at Centennial Park along the Fraser River points out several mountain peaks with their elevations.

The annual **Brigade Days**, held the second weekend after Labour Day, is a three-day event that includes fireworks, logging sports, a parade, a demolition derby, and dancing.

Recreational activities include fishing, canoeing, gold panning, river rafting, glider flying, and rockhounding.

Access to the scenic **Skagit Valley Recreation Area** is just three kilometres southwest of town via Silver

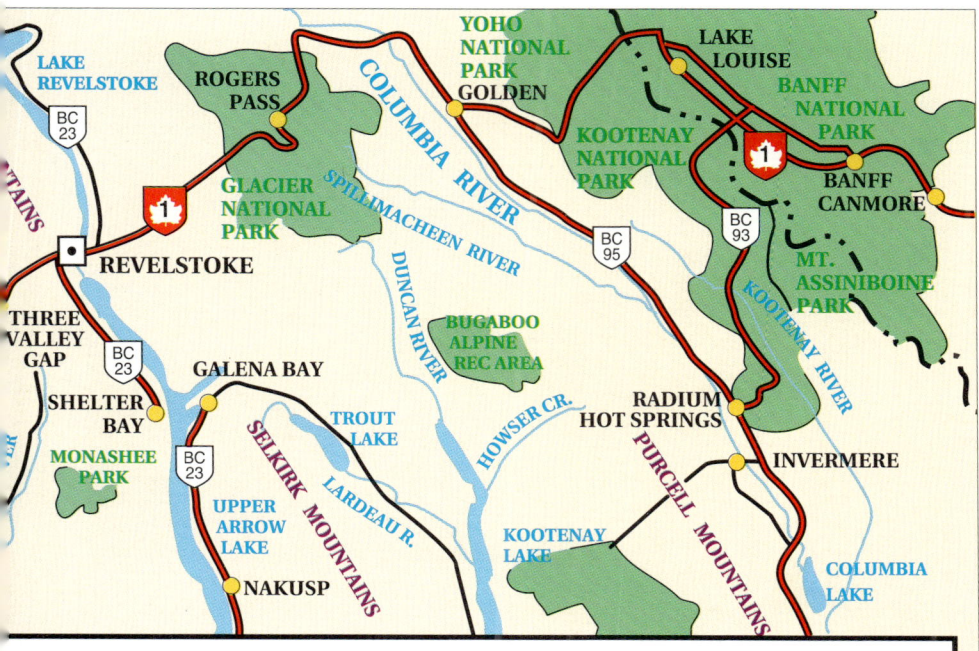

Distances

ncouver to Hope — 150 Km	Salmon arm to Sicamous — 31 Km
pe to Lytton — 108 Km	Sicamous to Revelstoke — 70 Km
tton to Cache Creek — 95 Km	Revelstoke to Golden — 148 Km
che Creek to Kamloops — 84 Km	Golden to Lake Louise — 71 Km
mloops to Salmon Arm — 108 Km	

Creek on Silver Skagit Road. The 32,508-hectare park is home to bear, deer, coyote, cougar, mountain goat, and over 200 species of birds. The Skagit River is a noted fly-fishing stream and a favourite with canoers.

Several Hollywood film companies have used Hope as a location in recent years, among them *First Blood* which gave birth to the infamous Rambo. Pick up a map of the Rambo walking tour at the Infocentre.

One favourite movie location is the historic **Othello and Quintette tunnels,** carved out of solid mountain rock for the **Kettle Valley Railway.** The line ran from Hope to Midway in the Kootenays from 1916 to 1961, and now with rails removed, some portions are used as hiking and biking trails. Accessible downtown from the parking lot of the **Coquihalla Canyon Recreation Area** (or from the Kawkawa Lake

The Fraser River

- Length: 1360 kilometres
- Headwaters: Near Mt. Robson in the Rocky Mountains at an elevation of 1109 metres
- Drainage area: 238,000 square kilometres, about one-quarter of the province. Sixty-three percent of BC's population lives in the Fraser River Basin, about 1.8 million people, most of them between Hope and Vancouver. It's the fifth-largest drainage area in Canada.
- Major tributaries: Nechako, Chilcotin, Quesnel, and Thompson rivers
- Annual average discharge: 3475 cubic metres per second. Over 80 percent of the flow occurs between May and mid-July. The greatest flow is 15,000 cubic metres per second in the spring. The smallest flow, 400 cubic metres per second, is in winter.
- Biggest fish in the river: white sturgeon, which can range from 13 kilograms to 180 kilograms and can live to be 100 years old. Large sturgeon are increasingly rare.
- What it moves besides water: about 20 million tonnes of clay, silt, sand, and gravel per year
- Memorable description: "Too thick to drink, and too thin to plough." Ray Mueller, riverboat man from Sinclair Mills, east of Prince George (*Vancouver Province,* Sept. 15, 1991)
- First European to travel the river: Simon Fraser in 1808. The trip took him 35 days from Fort George (present-day Prince George) to the Pacific. He thought he was on the Columbia River.
- Industry on the river: the six pulp mills contribute up to 75 percent of the waste waters discharged above Hope. To date, there are no dams.

The world's most productive salmon waterway:
- The river supports five species of salmon. At any one time, at least one species is travelling through the estuary.
- The river accounts for one-half of BC's annual commercial salmon catch, worth about $270 million.
- Over 800 million juvenile salmon migrate to the sea via the Fraser River system annually.

turnoff on the Coquihalla Highway), there are four tunnels and two railway bridges offering a view of the Coquihalla River raging below. In the fall, spawning salmon make their way up Kawkawa Creek and steelhead spawn in the Coquihalla River.

Lake of the Woods Rest Area, five kilometres north of Hope on Highway l, has a small public beach popular for swimming, fishing, and canoeing.

The Gold Bars

Between Hope and Yale there are many gravel bars on the Fraser River that yielded great riches during the 1858 gold rush. **Emory Creek Provincial Park,** 15 kilometres north of Hope, marks one such site. Once the initial rush was over most of the miners followed more promising rumors north. But many Chinese miners stayed behind here and at similar claims to dig a little deeper. Their patience and vigilance was often rewarded by less dramatic, but respectable finds. Today gold panners still hunch at the river's edge, looking for glittering nuggets in the gravel.

Hoping to become the terminus of the CPR in the 1880s, Emory boasted 13 streets, 9 saloons, a newspaper, and a sawmill, but it became a ghost town when the railway bypassed it.

Hill's Bar, four kilometres south of Yale, was one of the first and most lucrative finds in the lower Fraser gold rush. Less than one square kilometre, it has been estimated that $20 million worth of placer gold was discovered here between 1856 and 1875.

Experts claim there are many varieties of rock on Fraser River banks, including nephrite, jasper, rhodonite, and garnet. The Coquihalla River, and Emory and Ruby creeks are also good places for rockhounding.

Yale

32 km (20 mi) north of Hope. Population: 200. Infocentre: Highway 1, Box 74, V0K 2S0. 863-2324. Seasonal

Yale is rich in history. Archeologists, excavating the Milliken Site near Yale in the 1950s and 1960s, found evidence of human settlement dating from 7000 to 9000 BC. When Simon Fraser made his historic journey through here in 1808, he recorded that he obtained canoes from the resident Natives.

Yale was established as a fort in 1848 by the Hudson's Bay Company, and a decade later it was a riotous gold town – 30,000 prospectors passed through its saloons and hotels. Rivaling Fort Hope as the dominant settlement on the lower Fraser River, Yale gained the upper hand when it became a terminus for steamships on the Interior route to Fort

Alexandra Bridge was built in 1863 by Joseph Trutch as part of the Cariboo Wagon Road at a cost of $45,000.

Kamloops, and the starting point for the Cariboo Road in the 1860s. The treacherous waters of the Fraser Canyon were deemed unnavigable north of here, despite the S.S.*Skuzzy* (see box). When the CPR was completed in the 1880s, the Cariboo Road was eradicated and Yale's importance diminished.

Yale's rich history has been preserved at the **Yale Historical Museum** (31179 Douglas Street, 863-2324). On Highway 1 at the traffic light, **St. John the Divine Church,** built in 1859–60 by the Royal Engi-

neers, is one of the oldest on the mainland. Reverend William Crickmer petitioned his bishop for this new parish once it became clear that his current posting, the much touted community of Derby near Fort Langley (in the Fraser Valley), did not have the future early administrators had envisoned. The Reverend's new church was built just one block from the saloons and hotels that formed the centre of Yale, which provided a source of serious competition to Reverend Crickmer's ministrations. The nearby **Pioneer Cemetery** has its

S.S. *Skuzzy*

In order that CPR construction proceed as quickly as possible, contracts were let for sections of the line. Andrew Onderdunk, a thirty-year-old engineer from New York won the contract for two of the sections in the difficult Fraser Canyon. Obviously he thrived on challenge, because he then bought out two other contractors, taking responsibility for the entire 200 treacherous kilometres between Emory's Bar and Savona.

Onderdonk was not one to let anything get in his way. Unable to find sufficient numbers

of qualified workers, he imported thousands of laborers from China. One source claims he had 7000 men working for him and contracts worth $18 million at the height of his projects in BC.

Because the tolls on the Cariboo Road were costing Onderdonk dearly in freight costs, in 1881-2 he had a boat built that would meet the mighty Fraser head on. The *Skuzzy* was 37 metres long and 7.5 metres wide with a hull divided into 24 watertight bulkheads, a paddlewheel aft and a steam winch in the bow.

The reputation of the Fraser Canyon was well known and no one wanted the dubious honor of captaining the vessel. After two unsuccessful attempts, two daring brothers, Captains S.R. and D.S. Smith, who had successfully challenged dangerous portions of the Columbia, Snake, and Willamette rivers, were hired for the job at a fee of $2250. In the spring of 1882, with a crew of 17, they began a two-week trip up the canyon to Lytton from Spuzzum, battling the fury of Hell's Gate, and a drop in the river of nine metres in five kilometres on one stretch of river. Eventually 150 Chinese winched her through Hell's Gate by using a separate line from the shore.

The valiant *Skuzzy* made it through the Canyon, but it was a one-time only trip.

own stories to tell of the gold rush and railway construction days.

Lady Franklin Rock, just north of town, was named as a tribute to the tenacious spirit of the wife of the noted Arctic explorer. Sir John Franklin disappeared in 1845 while looking for the Northwest Passage. Thirty-nine expeditions searched for his party, among them Lady Franklin herself in 1861. According to one source, her determination to sail up the Fraser River on her quest was blocked by the rock that bears her name. While Lady Franklin remained in Yale, she was the centre of a social whirl and organized the building of pews and choir stalls at the new church. The remains of Sir John's expedition was finally discovered in 1880 on King William Island in the Arctic.

Spirit Cave Trail one kilometre south of town offers a one-hour hike to spectacular views of the Cascade mountains.

Special events in Yale include the **Strawberry Social** in July and the **Fraser River Barrel Race** in August.

Lower Fraser Canyon

Carved by centuries of glacial torrents, the Fraser Canyon was, and remains, a daunting sight. Originally, Natives used a series of ladders and paths along narrow ledges to travel this route. The Europeans first tried to bypass it by establishing the Harrison-Lillooet and Coquihalla trails. But at the urging of Governor James Douglas, in the 1860s a precarious trail was widened into the celebrated Cariboo Wagon Road. It was supported by log cribbing and

stone retaining walls. The CPR destroyed much of the road when building its line through the Fraser Canyon in the 1880s, but some portions are still visible, such as the old original bridge at **Alexandra Bridge Provincial Park** one kilometre north of Spuzzum. A 15-minute walk from the

Simon Fraser's Journal
June 26, 1808

[Hells' Gate and the Black Canyon] *This morning all hands were employed the same as yesterday . . . the navigation was absolutely impracticable . . . as for the road by land we scarcely could make our way in some parts even with our guns. I have been for a long period among the Rocky Mountains, but never have seen anything to equal this country, for I cannot find words to describe our situation at times. We had to pass where no human being should venture. Yet in those places there is a regular footpath impressed, or rather indented, by frequent travelling upon the very rocks. And besides this, steps which are formed like a ladder, or the shrouds of a ship, by poles hanging to one another and crossed at certain distances with twigs, suspended from the top to the foot of immense precipices and fastened at both extremities to stones and trees, furnished a safe and convenient passage to the Natives — and we, who had not the advantage of their experience, were often in imminent danger, when obliged to follow their example.*

The tram at Hell's Gate carries visitors 500 metres, from the highway to the Fraser River below. The 34-metre-wide gorge is the narrowest point on the Fraser River.

had travelled up the Columbia River and through the Okanagan Valley.

Hell's Gate
31 km (19 mi) north of Yale

One of the most spectacular portions of the Fraser Canyon is Hell's Gate, named – with indisputable logic and firsthand knowledge – by Simon Fraser. At peak flow (35 kilometres per hour), 908 million litres of water per minute pass through the 34-metre-wide gorge – twice the volume of Niagara Falls. A 500-metre-high air tram gives visitors an only slightly terrifying ride over the chaos below. (Hell's Gate Air Tram, 867-9277, is open May to October.)

Those who want to walk down to Hell's Gate can do so via a path that begins in the parking lot 500 metres south of the tramway concession on the highway. A suspension footbridge crosses the river at the lower level.

In 1914, when the CNR was blasting bedrock for its track, a slide blocked the river, destroying the salmon run. Recorded catches of 31 million fish in 1913 were reduced to 1.8 million in 1921, and some say they have never recovered. Between 1944 and 1946, a Joint Canadian and US International Fisheries Commission built concrete fish ladders that have since restored the run, although the gorge is narrower than before the blasting. An interpretive display at river level explains how the fish ladders work. The concrete structures slow the water to about five kilometres per hour, giving the fish a fighting chance to swim upstream.

parking area goes down the old road to the bridge for a walk across the Fraser River. The original Alexandra Lodge, a roadhouse on the Cariboo Wagon Road, is nearby. With the advent of the automobile, a highway was re-established in the 1920s.

Access to the 13-kilometre round-trip **Old Brigade Trail** is 300 metres north of Alexandra Lodge. Built in 1848 by the Hudson's Bay Company, the Brigade Trail was the main transportation route into the Interior after the Oregon Treaty was signed and the border with the US established in 1846. Prior to that, the fur brigades

Local rafting companies offer expeditions through Hell's Gate from Boston Bar to Yale. The **Nahatlatch River**, accessible via a secondary road across the Fraser at Boston Bar, is another popular whitewater-rafting trip close by. The Nahatlatch Lakes chain is also a favourite with canoers.

In a route filled with challenges to early travellers, **Jackass Mountain**, 25 kilometres north of Boston Bar, must have been rated high on the list. Some say the name was a comment on the foolishness of the men and women who travelled the route in search of the elusive mother lode; others claim the namesake was a fully loaded mule who fell off the narrow roadway in the 1860s to its death in the canyon below.

Lytton

108 km (67 mi) north of Hope.
Population: 335. Infocentre: 400 Fraser Street (city centre), Box 460, V0K 1Z0. 455-2523; Fax: 455-6669

Lytton, at the confluence of the Thompson and Fraser rivers, was called *camchin*, "the place that crosses over," by the Native people.

An early fur-trading post and stop on the Cariboo Road, the town now bills itself as the "Whitewater Rafting Capital of Canada." There are 18 major rapids in the 37 kilometres of the Thompson River between Lytton and Spences Bridge, with such encouraging names as the Frog, Devil's Kitchen, and Jaws of Death. Other local attractions include gold panning and rockhounding. The Infocentre also houses local history displays and the archives. One story tells of Jessie Ann Smith, a young widow who allegedly

Tne muddy Fraser and the clear green Thompson rivers dramatically join together at Lytton. They are part of the largest watershed in British Columbia.

developed the famous Granny Smith apple here in the early 1900s.

Just down the street, the waters of the muddy Fraser and the clearer green Thompson rivers provide a stark contrast before blending together and continuing to the Pacific Ocean. A reaction ferry – a small vessel attached to a cable that uses the river's current for locomotion – crosses the Fraser here. The free ferry carries only two or three cars a trip.

The ferry provides access to the **Stein Valley**, an old-growth forest that the Lytton Band is trying to protect. Regarded as a sacred site by the Lytton people, the 109,000-hectare watershed is the last completely unlogged watershed in BC that is close to a heavily populated area. Containing three glaciers, four lakes, and 250 square kilometres of alpine meadows, the valley has become a focus for environmentalists around the province. For several years the band hosted a three-day event every August in the Stein Valley to draw attention to their cause, but recently the **Earth Voice Festival** has been moved to the Lower Mainland in order to protect the ecosystem from the thousands of visitors who attend. With its giant trees, petroglyphs, and pictographs hundreds of years old, it remains a popular destination for hikers. The Lytton Infocentre has maps and information.

The **Multicultural Heritage Park,** eight kilometres north of Lytton on Highway 12, is expected to be open in 1993, offering nature trails, a reconstructed Native pit house and archeological dig, and gold panning.

Besides outdoor recreation, logging is a mainstay of the local economy and woods tours and self-guided forestry highway tours are available through the Infocentre. Residents are proud to point out that the sawmill is locally owned, an unusual claim in this day of multinational ownership.

Across the street from the Infocentre is a relief display of a "jelly roll," a geological record of the swirling sediment created by melting glaciers. Although a common occurrence, this sample is unusual because it measures in metres what normally occurs on a much smaller scale.

Be prepared for hot summer temperatures. The second highest temperature recorded in Canada was at Lytton and Lillooet on July 16, 1941 when the thermometer soared to 44.4°C. Annual events include the **Lytton Rodeo** in May.

Sidetrip: Highway 12 to Lillooet

Just north of Lytton on Highway 12, Botanie Road offers the opportunity of viewing Rocky Mountain bighorn sheep and alpine meadows. There are also ginseng farms along this route, a relatively new agricultural pursuit in the province. (See page 31.) Highway 12 follows the Fraser River northwest of Lytton to Lillooet, head of the old Harrison Lake route to the Interior. (See page 192.)

Thompson Canyon

The Fraser Canyon is impressive for its imperviousnes, but the Thompson Canyon is breathtaking for its geological spectacle. Pinnacles, out-

croppings, sheer cliffs, slides, shadowy canyons, and waterfalls in colours ranging from deep reds and oranges to cool greens and greys line the route, with the waters of the Thompson travelling swiftly below. The high river terraces and white silt bluffs visible along the highway are evidence of the mile-thick ice sheets that once covered the province, receding as recently as 10,000 years ago. As the glaciers melted, huge volumes of meltwater containing sand, gravel, and boulders carved new paths, shifting the river's course, creating the terraces.

The Trans-Canada Highway veers away from the Fraser River at Lytton to follow the Thompson River, passing through several old communities. The Thompson River was named by Simon Fraser in honor of his contemporary David Thompson, who explored the eastern part of the Interior, but never saw this waterway.

In the Thompson Canyon, the transformation from wet coastal rainforest to arid desert vegetation is complete, as sagebrush and pine replace cedar and thimbleberry. Known today as "the Arizona of Canada" because of its desert ecology, this hot and dusty section must have tested the stamina of even the most intrepid stagecoach travellers in the 1860s. Hikers should be aware of small prickly pear cactus and rattlesnakes that hide in the sagebrush and rocks. (See page 132).

South of Spences Bridge, a marker tells of the Great Landslide, a 1905 event that dammed the Thompson River for several hours and killed 18 people.

The Canadian National Railway, completed in 1915, parallels the CPR line from Kamloops to Vancouver. From Kamloops it runs north through the Yellowhead Pass to Edmonton. VIA presently operates a passenger service on the CNR.

Built in 1862, Ashcroft Manor was a favourite roadhouse on the Cariboo Wagon Road. The manor burned down in 1943, but original artifacts and outbuildings remain.

Spences Bridge

40 km (25mi) north of Lytton.
Population: 138

Just off the highway, the beautifully restored **Spences Bridge Hotel,** surviving today as the Steelhead Inn, claims to be the oldest existing hotel in BC. While sipping a beer in the pub, it could do no harm to nonchalantly inquire about the treasure supposedly buried here. The story goes that a prospector, returning from the northern fields with a smile on his face and a bag of gold, was robbed and killed nearby. The thieves were caught and hanged, but not before they stashed the loot – which no one has ever found.

On a hot day, there is no point in looking to the Thompson River for relief because the current moves too fast for swimming. But at Spences Bridge the slower moving Nicola River is fine for a dip. The area is also noted for steelhead fishing. Watch for bighorn sheep that live on the rocky bluffs above the highway between Spences Bridge and Ashcroft. The sheep often come down to drink from the river.

Highway 8 offers a side trip to Merritt and the historic Nicola Valley. Besides great fishing, the area boasts Canada's largest cattle ranch at Douglas Lake.

Look for volcanic rock at **Red Hill Rest Area**, 28 kilometres north of Spences Bridge, evidence of activity that occured before the last glaciation.

Ashcroft

43 km (27 mi) north of Spences Bridge. Population: 1600. Infocentre: junction of Highway 97C and 1, Box 183, V0K 1A0. 453-9533. Seasonal

In this sparse landscape the oasis of **Ashcroft Manor** (March to November, 453-9983) on the Trans-Canada Highway is a welcome relief on a hot summer day. Built in 1862 as a roadhouse by the Cornwall brothers, it was considered one of the most reputable and hospitable hotels on the road. Englishmen to a "T," Clement and Henry Cornwall imported fox hounds and instituted the coyote hunt, a Cariboo version of the traditional British event. Clement Francis Cornwall later became one of BC's first senators after Confederation and the province's lieutentant-governor in 1881.

The original manor was destroyed by fire in 1943, but travellers can still get refreshments in the tearoom, and the several restored buildings on the site offer interesting displays. The original roadhouse served as the first courthouse in the area with the legendary Judge Begbie in attendance.

In town, the Infocentre houses the museum and local history displays. There is also a replica of small coal mine (453-9232), and on the main street the tiny red building that was the first firehall is still standing. Ashcroft is the gateway to the Highland Valley via Highway 97C. Tours can be arranged for **Highland Valley Copper Mine** (575-2443), one of the largest open pit copper mines in the world. The tours are two-and-a-half hours long and operate twice a day during the summer.

Annual events include the **Ashcroft Rodeo** in May.

Cache Creek

50 km (31 mi) north of Spences Bridge. Population: 1020. Infocentre: 1340 Highway 97, Box 460, V0K 1H0. Phone and Fax: 457-5306. Seasonal Cache Creek was a trading site for Native people long before the arrival of the Europeans. Fur traders used to stash their furs here, thus "Cache" Creek. Later a fur-trading post was built, and then the settlement became an oasis on the hot and dusty Cariboo Wagon Road.

The town is on the edge of a long-dormant line of ancient volcanoes stretching into the Cariboo. Rock formations million of years old make interesting exploration for rock-

Wild Grasses

Many of the grasses seen along the highways we regard as useless weeds, at best providing interesting shades and textures to the landscape. But most were put to a variety of uses by the Native people.

A number of species that are not true grasses, including sedges, tule, cattail, and bear grass, shared common uses with rye, sweet, pine, and reed grasses.

The Kutenai used the leaves of the bear grass plant for making their distinctive hats, whereas the Okanagan wove the highly prized material into their birch-bark baskets. Only the Kutenai had direct access to bear grass, so Okanagan, Thompson, and Chilcotin people had to trade for it.

Rye grass, a robust species commonly found in a wide variety of habitats in the Interior, was used in a number of ways. The Thompson people used the hollow stems to decorate cedar root baskets. Some Okanagan tribes made arrows from the stems and used the leaves as a lining material for floors or steaming pits in food preparation. The Prairie Blackfoot used the leaves for bedding.

Rye grass is found in such diverse conditions as moist river banks or dry gulleys, on slopes or plains from the Thompson to the Rocky Mountain Trench. Among its uses, Flathead Native boys put hawthorn points on the stems and used them to inflict pain when preparing for battle.

hounds. The Cariboo Jade Shoppe downtown (1093 Todd Road) has jade-cutting demonstrations.

Kamloops
80 km (50 mi) east of Cache Creek. Population: 63,110. Infocentre: 10 -10th Avenue, Box 488, V2C 5L2. 374-3377; Fax: 828-9500

People of the Secwepemc (Shuswap) nation have lived in this area for at least 7000 years, naming the site *Cumloops*, "meeting of the waters," due to its location at the merging of the South and North Thompson rivers.

Fort Kamloops was established in 1812 by David Stuart of the American-based Pacific Fur Company. Both the Hudson's Bay Company and the North West Company also vied for supremacy, and fur traders fought at least one bloody battle for control of the area.

In the 1820s Fort Kamloops was a way-station on the early Fur Brigade Trail to the Columbia River, and over 600 horses pastured on the lush sur-

---

Walhachin

Between Cache Creek and Kamloops, look for fragments of a wooden flume along the north side of the highway, the vestige of a dream that flowered and faded in the early 1900s.

An American developer, C.E. Barnes, decided to transform the sagebrush and desert into lush orchards and genteel living. He bought land and called the site Walhachin, attracting upper class English families with his claims of "heaven on earth."

In 1907 Barnes oversaw the building of a dam on Deadman Lake near Cache Creek and the construction of a two-metre-wide wooden flume to carry water over the dry ravines and hillsides for 30 kilometres to the settlement.

The flume as it was in 1907 and as it s today.

A hotel was built, the wealthy Marquis of Anglesey created a luxurious estate and invested money, and the town and orchards thrived.

When World War I broke out in 1914, many of the men rallied to the call of the motherland. Of 107 men in the community, 97 eventually enlisted, the largest number per capita in the British Empire. The lack of manpower and financing, combined with a devastating flood and an untenable original goal, led to the demise of the experiment. By the end of the war, Walhachin was finished.

Today, a small community remains on the site of the original townsite on the south side of the Thompson River.

Kamloops

To TOD MOUNTAIN SKI AREA
BARRIERE, JASPER and EDMONTON

BC 5

INDIAN

WESTSIDE RD.

YELLOWHEAD

NORTH THOMPSON RIVER

ROAD

LAKE

PAUL

NORTH KAMLOOPS

BROCKHURST
PARKCREST AVE
HALSTON AVE.
KINGSTON AVE.
12TH ST.
8TH ST.
SINGH ST.

BROCKHURST RECREATION CENTRE & PARK

TRANQUILLE RD.

To AIRPORT & GOLF COURSE

THOMPSON RIVER

MacARTHUR ISLAND PARK

MacKENZIE AVE.

FORTUNE DR.
TRANQUILLE RD.

RESERVE #1

To WILDLIFE PARK & GOLF COURSES

3

2

RIVERSIDE PARK

VICTORIA ST. W.

LORNE ST.

MT. PAUL WAY

HIGHWAY

1

S. THOMPSON RIVER

BC 97

VALLEYVIEW DR.

HIGHLAND RD.

4

1ST
2ND
3RD
4TH
SEYMOUR ST.
COLUMBIA ST.
5TH
10TH

1

VALLEYVIEW

To LAC LE JEUNE

SUMMIT DR.

CARIBOO COLLEGE

NOTRE DAME DR.

JUNIPER RIDGE

1
BC 97

DUFFERIN

COPPERHEAD DR.

PACIFIC WAY

HILLSIDE WAY

SOUTH SHORE

BC 5

COQUIHALLA HIGHWAY

LAURIER DR.

ALBERT McGOWAN PARK

SAHALI HEIGHTS

1 Secwepeme Indian Band Office & Museum
2 Overlander Bridge
3 St. Joseph's Church
4 Kamloops Museum Archives & Art Gallery

● Information Centre
■ Park
Indian Reservation Boundary
Golf

N

ABERDEEN HILLS

ABERDEEN DR.

BC 5A

To MERRITT

rounding grasslands. In the 1850s and 1860s, as the fur trade waned, Kamloops became a stopover on the route to goldfields in the Cariboo and the Big Bend of the Columbia. The **Overlander Bridge** commemorates a particularly courageous group of gold seekers who made a perilous journey down the North Thompson River in 1862. (See page 216.)

In the 1880s vast numbers of Chinese laborers were imported for the construction of the CPR, and they settled at Kamloops. A separate **Chinese Cemetery** (on Fernie Road) was established for the workers. The cemetery, unique in Canada because it fulfills all of the ancient burial requirements, is a designated heritage site. Every April, Ch'ing Ming, the Spring Festival for Departed Souls is held here. Contact the Chinese Heritage Cemetery Society, Box 1421, Main Station, V2C 6L7, 573-4593.

Access to markets was enhanced by the completion of the CPR in 1885, and ranching and farming became the economic mainstay of Kamloops. Since the 1960s logging and mining have become economically dominant. Industrial tours include **Highland Valley Copper Mine** (575-2443) in Logan Lake and the **Weyerhauser Pulp Mill** (828-7363).

Swimmers enjoy a late afternoon dip in the Thompson River at Riverside Park in Kamloops. The North Thompson starts in the Rocky Mountains near Tête Jaune Cache and the South Thompson empties the Shuswap Lake system at Chase. They join together at Kamloops.

The Kamloops Band was one of 20 groups that made up the powerful Secwepemc (Shuswap) nation. The **Secwepemc Museum** (345 Yellowhead Highway, 828-8777) is housed in the reserve's former residential school and features Secwepemc cultural traditions and a gift shop. A celebration of the living culture, the **Kamloops Indian Pow Wow**, is held annually in August (828-9700). **Four Corners Native Art Gallery** offers a variety of work by Native artisans (119 Palm Street, North Shore, 376-0550).

St. Joseph's Church (200 Chilcotin Road, 828-9700), also on band land, has been restored to its 1900 condition, although parts of it are older. Father Le Jeune, an early Oblate misionary, was instrumental in building this and several other Interior churches. Le Jeune has been honored for developing a written form of several Native dialects.

The **Kamloops Museum, Archives and Art Gallery** (207 Seymour, 828-3576) emphasizes Native culture, the fur trade, and the railway. The museum and the Infocentre have maps of the heritage walking tour, which includes buildings dating back to 1887. The **Rocky Mountain Rangers Military Museum** (1221 McGill Road, 372-7424), preserves the history of a cavalry group that was first formed to fight in the "Riel Rebellion."

A two-hour trip on the locally built paddlewheeler *Wanda Sue* is another way to enjoy the Thompson River area. The vessel departs from the old Kamloops Yacht Club (1140 River Street, 374-7447) on varying schedules between May and October.

One of Interior's few professional theatre groups, the **Western Canada Theatre Company** (372-3216) presents a full season during the winter months in the **Sagebrush Theatre**. Kamloops also has a symphony orchestra (374-9200) which offers classical programming during its season.

Other special events include the **Kamloops Pro Rodeo** in April; the **BC High School Rodeo** in June; the **Folkfest**, the **Bluegrass Festival**, the **Cattle Drive (372-7075)**, and **Rangeland Days** in July; the **Kamloops Rivers Meet** and the **International Airshow** in August; and the **Provincial Winter Fair** in September.

Bird-watchers can visit Tranquille Marsh, 10 kilometres west of North Kamloops on Tranquille Road. During spring migration, over 2000 Canada geese rest here as well as snow geese, blue heron, pelicans, trumpeter and whistling swans. Mule deer, coyotes, and bighorn sheep are also residents. On Highway 1 east of Kamloops watch for swans, Canada geese, and osprey. Take Highway 5A, the old route to Merritt, to see sandhill cranes in September and April, as well as birds of prey such as hawks, kestrels, and owls.

Nearby provincial parks include **Paul Lake** and **Lac Le Jeune**. Both are within a half hour's drive from town and offer trout fishing, hiking, swimming, and wildlife viewing.

Tod Mountain (578-7222), north of Kamloops on Highway 5, has 47 alpine runs and several nordic trails. In summer, it is popular for hiking and fishing. Also north of town, **Harper Mountain** (372-2119/573-5115) is a family ski slope.

Twelve kilometres east of Kamloops on the Trans-Canada Highway, the **Kamloops Wildlife Park** (573-3242) is the largest non-profit zoo in

the province. Over 70 species of indigenous and exotic animals from coyotes to camels range over 20 hectares of land. Besides educational programs, the wildlife park has a captive breeding program for two endangered species, the burrowing owl and the Asian wild horse, and has won several awards for its educational programs .

The park is also the site of Bill Miner's big mistake. One of America's most wanted outlaws in the 1900s, he robbed the wrong CPR train here for a gross return of $15. He was captured and sent to the BC Penitentiary in 1906, but escaped a year later. (See page 120.)

Thompson River

The Thompson River and its north and south arms are very popular with canoers, kayakers, and rafting enthusiasts. Degree of difficulty varies from place to place, so ask locally. A one- to two-day trip between Chase and Kamloops is very popular, with either direction possible in the gentle current. Watch for hoodoos, unusual pillared rock formations, along the

In the 1800s, the government was happy to pass responsibility for Native populations to the church. Different denominations claimed control over different geographic areas. St. Joseph's Church was built on the Kamloops Band's land in the 1870s by Roman Catholic missionary Father Le Jeune.

Many original log buildings from pioneer days remain throughout the Interior. This barn is near Shuswap Lake Provincial Park.

South Thompson. These geological statues can be found throughout the province and are formed by erosion, in this case on clay benches that once formed the bottom of a glacial lake.

Chase

56 km (35 mi) east of Kamloops.
Population: 1980. Infocentre:
124 Chase Street, V0E 1M0.
679-8432; Fax: 679-3120

Chase is located on **Little Shuswap Lake** and the South Thompson River and is surrounded by a profusion of wildflowers in spring and summer. To the west lie dry rangelands and sagebrush hills, and to the east lie the lusher forests of the Shuswap Lake area. Wildlife viewers can look for bighorn sheep on the surrounding hills, or take the short hike to **Chase Creek Falls** at the rest area just east of town. The 57-kilometre gentle paddle down the South Thompson to Kamloops reveals hoodoos, *kekulis* (Native pit houses), and a variety of birds.

Special events include the **Squilax Pow Wow,** an annual intertribal gathering with traditional singing, dancing, and drumming in July. Members of the public are invited to attend the celebration. (Contact: Box 1100 Chase, V0E 1M0, 679-3203.)

Roderick Haig-Brown Provincial Park

66 km (41 mi) east of Kamloops,
5 km (3 mi) north of Squilax. 955-2217

The annual **Adams River salmon run** in October is a major wildlife-viewing attraction. When the run peaks every four years (1994, 1998, 2002), an estimated two million sockeye find their way home – one of the largest spawning phenomena in the world. Thousands of people come to witness this mysterious event as the river changes colour with the thrashing red bodies of the dying salmon. In off-years, lesser numbers of sockeye, spring, coho, and pink salmon, and steelhead trout repeat the marathon upriver battle – 485 kilometres from the Pacific Ocean via the Fraser and Thompson rivers.

The 988-hectare park, named after conservationist and writer Roderick Haig-Brown, runs along both sides of the 11-kilometre Adams River between Shuswap and Adams lakes. Whitetail and mule deer, black bear, beaver, river otter, mink, osprey, bald eagles, harlequin ducks, and mergansers are among the other species.

In the fall, the entire river is utilized for spawning although most people watch from platforms on the eastern bank on the lower part of the river. The area also is of archeological interest. Evidence of *kekuli* and pictographs can still be seen.

Hiking, boating, and fishing are all permitted in the park. Visitors are asked to remember that this is a conservation site: any interference with artifacts or spawning fish is illegal. Beware of poison ivy along the dry exposed slopes. Remember the rule of thumb: "Leaves in three, let them be."

Shuswap Lake

With over 1000 kilometres of warm navigable waterways and 20 provincial and marine parks, Shuswap Lake attracts large numbers of summer vacationers. Visitors can rent a variety of aquatic devices for enjoying the lake, including the ever-popular houseboat. The fishing is excellent for rainbow and lake trout, Dolly Varden and whitefish. Other good fishing lakes close by are Adams, Little Shuswap, White, and Mara.

At Scotch Creek and Herald provincial parks watch for the shallow depressions that are remains of Native pit houses used for winter dwellings. On the cliffs of the lake itself are fading ochre pictographs, over a hundred years old

The odd H-shape of Shuswap Lake converges in Cinnemousun Narrows, evidence of the glaciation that rounded mountain peaks and steepened valley walls in the last Ice Age. The rock is mostly metamorphic, altered extensively by heat and pressure. Rockhounds should look for blue-grey and banded agate, crystalline geodes, and amethyst, particularly on Squilax Mountain near Chase, the Enderby Cliffs, and Mount Ida near Salmon Arm.

Shuswap Lake is one of the Interior's most popular destinations, with over 20 marine and provincial parks.

Salmon Arm, the largest town in the Shuswap area, is a service centre for agriculture and forestry. Settlement occurred with the construction of the CPR in 1885.

Salmon Arm

52 km (32 mi) east of Chase.
Population: 11,610. Infocentre:
70 Hudson Ave NE, Box 9999, V1E 4P2.
832-6247; Fax: 832-8382

Salmon Arm's name dates back to the days when salmon were so abundant settlers scooped them out of the lake and onto their fields for fertilizer. Today, Salmon Arm calls itself the "Gem of the Shuswap."

The **Waterfront Nature Enhancement Preserve** (follow the signs on Lakeshore Drive) is home to over 150 species of birds and waterfowl and one of four places in the province to view nesting western grebes. In May, these elegant birds skitter across the water in a remarkable courtship dance. Other wildlife include red-winged and yellow-headed blackbirds, osprey, and painted turtles.

Haney Heritage Village (June to September, 832-5243), just south of town on 97A, is a 16-hectare park featuring turn-of-the-century heritage buildings, a two-kilometre nature trail, and a forest that features most species of local flora.

The area abounds in lakes and trails. One easy-access walk is to **Margaret Falls** in **Herald Provincial Park** just east of Tappen. Nearby **Larch Hills** is a popular cross-country ski area with 150 kilometres of trails. The **Reino Keski-Salmi Loppet** is a cross-country ski marathon held here every winter. (Contact: Box 218, Salmon Arm, V1E 4N3.)

Other special events include the **Strawberry Social** and the **Salmon Arm Rodeo** in June and – believe it or not – a world-famous **Sonnet Festival** in April.

Sicamous

25 km (16 mi) east of Salmon Arm. Population: 2345. Infocentre: Main Street and Riverside Avenue, Box 346, V0E 2V0. 836-3313; Fax: 836-4368

Idyllically situated between Shuswap and Mara lakes, Sicamous calls itself the "houseboat capital of Canada," advertising over 350 vessels for rent. For those who don't have a week or two to lollygag about the lake, the modified sternwheeler *Phoebe Anne* (836-2200) takes visitors on a historic trip up Seymour Arm and back on daily sailings during July and August. In 1865, miners in search of gold on the Big Bend of the Columbia River made the same journey, disembarking at Ogdenville to make their way overland through the Monashee Mountains to the goldfields. Ogdenville was once a bustling town with six saloons, thirteen stores, five bakeries, and one bathhouse. It became a ghost town in two short years as the promise of gold dwindled.

The **Blue Manor Art Gallery** (12 Bruhn Road, 836-2854) on CPR Hill is set in a 1922 vintage home and features the work of Okanagan artists. The **Dutchman Dairy** (836-4304), one kilometre east on the Trans-Canada, offers free admission and self-guided tours of a barnyard which includes a camel, llamas, and exotic birds. The dairy sells 56 flavours of homemade ice cream, among other delights, and has a picnic area.

Other outdoor recreation includes hang gliding in summer and nordic skiing in winter.

Once a CPR construction site, Sicamous is now the "houseboat capital of Canada." Its name is a Salish word meaning "narrow" or "squeezed in the middle."

Craigellachie

One of the most important moments in BC history occurred at Craigellachie, 30 kilometres east of Sicamous in the Monashee Mountains. It was here on November 7, 1885, that Donald Smith drove the CPR's famous "last spike" into the rails to complete the transcontinental railway. In return for completing the project, the CPR was awarded generous land grants and began a huge financial empire that grew to include hotels, airlines, shipping, and mining. There are picnic tables and an Infocentre (836-2244) on the site. (See page 25.)

Eagle Valley

About 20 kilometres farther east on the Trans-Canada Highway is Eagle Valley and 1790-metre Eagle Pass. One of the great natural clefts in the mountains, the pass was revealed to surveyor Walter Moberly when he watched eagles fly through in the summer of 1865. The CPR took advantage of the route to construct the railway in the 1880s.

Three Valley Gap

The original town of Three Valley had its heyday in the 1880s. The present ghost town has been reconstructed from 20 buildings collected around the province. Along with a resort hotel (837-2109), there are displays of Native artifacts, live performances in the Walter Moberly Theatre, and a flower garden beside Three Valley Lake. (The attractions are open May to October.)

Although many people think they're entering the Rockies as the mountains emerge on this portion of Highway 1, in fact the peaks are the Columbia Mountains. The Rockies

Steller's Jay
Cyanocitta stelleri

Jays belong to the same family as crows and magpies. Of the 37 species of jay that exist, the three that occur in Canada also occur in the Interior: the blue jay, the gray jay, and the Steller's jay.

The bright blue Steller's jay, BC's unofficial bird, is the only crested jay found west of the Rockies. In Canada, it is only found in BC and southwestern Alberta. Common in coniferous forests, it is known for its gregarious and sometimes cheeky scolding. Fearless as well as curious, the Steller's jay will frequently demand handouts in campsites and picnic areas.

First noted in the mid-1700s in Alaska by Georg Wilhelm Steller, a naturalist on the Bering expedition, the Steller's jay is found from Alaska to Central America, and throughout BC's Interior.

Their natural food supply includes carrion, insects, eggs, nestlings, fruit, nuts, and berries. They have the capacity to carry nuts and other food in pouches to storage caches. Research indicates they can remember the location of hundreds of food caches.

Not a true migrator, the Steller's jay tends to disappear deeper into the woods when nesting, becoming more acquiescent and secretive.

are on the other side of the Columbia River and the Rocky Mountain Trench beyond Golden.

Revelstoke

70 km (43 mi) east of Sicamous.
Population: 7620. Infocentre:
300 First Street West, Box 490, V0E 2S0.
837-3522; Fax: 837-4223

Once a sleepy railway town, with its heritage buildings and outdoor recreation, Revelstoke has become one of the Interior's hidden treasures. First settled in the mid-1800s, it was originally called Big Eddy and later Second Crossing, in reference to its location on the Columbia River. In 1880 a townsite was laid out called Farwell. But in 1886, when an English banker named Lord Revelstoke put some money into the CPR, the town got a new name and it soon became an important centre on the rail line.

For many years Revelstoke was the western entrance to the infamous Big Bend Highway, a long, dusty route around the Selkirk Range that followed the Columbia River, in the days before the Rogers Pass route opened in 1962. Mining and the railway had a big role in the town's development, and more recently logging and then hydroelectric projects have kept the economy alive.

The Infocentre has a walking tour brochure of many of the town's heritage buildings. The beautifully restored **Revelstoke courthouse** (1100 Second Street West, 837-7636) has original stained glass windows, marble panelling, fixtures, and furnishings. The **Revelstoke Museum** (315 First Street, 837-3067) features displays of railway, riverboating, and other early area history. A very

Three Valley Gap is a resort complex located in the Eagle Valley. Surveyor Walter Moberly discovered this route through the Monashee Mountains in 1865.

Top: The Revelstoke Dam, completed in 1984 under the terms of the 1964 Columbia River Treaty, hosts 68,000 visitors a year.

Bottom: Revelstoke's courthouse, built in 1912, is the centrepiece of a $2.3 million heritage revitalization project completed in 1987.

pleasant feature of the revitalized downtown area is the pedestrians-only **Grizzly Plaza** and its powerful bronze sculptures by West Kootenay artist Tom Lynn.

One of North America's largest hydroelectric developments is the **Revelstoke Dam** (837-6211), four kilo-metres north of the city on the old Big Bend Highway. Over 68,000 people visit the site each year. Self-guided "talking wand" tours include an elevator trip to the top of the 175-metre-high concrete structure and information on the Columbia River system. (Open March to October.) An-

---

Vern Enyedy, Revelstoke
Curator
Piano Museum

Everybody keeps telling me it's pretty bizarre to have a piano museum in Revelstoke. But Revelstoke has a very nice quality of life. You're not in a rat race here. The old heritage houses are being fixed. It's a nice atmosphere, nice people. The cultural scene is slowly improving.

My pianos are all in the old heritage house that I have here. I think I have roughly 33 pianos in my museum collection and it's still growing. They range from 1783 to 1937. Seventy-five percent of them are playable.

It started as a hobby. I've been in the piano tuning and restoring business for years and I noticed all these old pianos around BC, not cared for.

We brainwash people to think certain ways. We condemn the old and think new ways are superior. But there never were bad pianos in the past. They were very adequate and very beautiful. It's just that they were different sounding.

There's no market for these old pianos, so if I take one it has to be because it has historical significance. Most of my pianos have been collected from this area.

One of my best finds was an oak-case Broadwood in Vernon. It's one of the most illustrious names in the piano business. Beethoven had a Broadwood. When I was told it was oak, I said that was impossible. But sure enough I got in the house and it was oak with brass corners and everything. It was beautiful.

Another unusual find was an 1830 Robert Wornum; Wornum was one of the inventors of the upright piano. And that was in Lumby. I have no idea how it got there.

Last January I got a call from a guy in Kamloops. He said he had an old Broadwood grand. So I said OK. And the next Sunday he parked it right in front of the house. It's an eight-foot grand, 1835.

Our house is a bed and breakfast called the Piano Keep. We have about 4500 square feet, lots of room, but I'm running it right out, of course, with the pianos. Sometimes I think I should go back to stamps.

The Enyedy's are looking for a building to house their piano collection. Until the museum is open, you can call for an appointment at 837-2120.

Locals cut a trail to the top of Mt. Revelstoke in 1908. Today a 26-kilometre drive over a paved road takes visitors to spectacular alpine wildflower displays and picturesque Balsam Lake.

other 145 kilometres north, **Mica Dam**, the highest earthfill dam in North America, has a generating capacity of 1.731 million kilowatts. The tourist centre (834-7382) is open from the end of June to Labour Day

Most people come to Revelstoke for the mountain scenery and four-seasons outdoor recreation. Privately run chalets offer hiking and skiing tours in the alpine areas. Man-made Lake Revelstoke offers good fishing (a world-record-size Dolly Varden was caught here in 1991) and camp-

ing. Watch for bears. (See page 77.)

Goldstream Provincial Park is a good place for rockhounding (garnet, soapstone, and serpentine) and recreational gold panning. (Contact the government agent on First Street.)

The two- to three-day paddle down the Columbia River to Shelter Bay is a popular trip. Revelstoke is also headquarters for both Glacier and Mount Revelstoke national parks (313 Third Street West, Box 350, V0E 2S0, 837-8155).

In 1990, *Powder* magazine called **Mount Mackenzie** (837-5268), six kilometres south of town, "the best skiing in North America." Locals say Frisbee Ridge has the best snowmobiling in the country.

Highway 23 south of Revelstoke connects with Highway 6 at Nakusp and the West Kootenays. The schedule of the free ferry across the Arrow Lakes from Shelter Bay to Galena Bay is posted on the highway in Revelstoke. It does *not* run 24 hours and there are no concessions at the ferry docks.

National Parks

• Motorists planning to stop in national parks, must have valid permits on their vehicles. The single-entry, four-day, and annual permits are good for any national park while they are valid, but do not cover camping or other service fees. The permits can be obtained at highway booths at the entrance to the parks.

• It is illegal to feed, touch, disturb, or hunt wildlife in a national park. Poachers can be fined up to $150,000 or imprisoned for six months.

• Pets must be leashed at all times in national parks. Dogs are not permitted overnight in the backcountry.

• Provincial fishing licences are not valid in national parks. Park information centres sell national park fishing licences and have information on regulations.

• For overnight stays in the backcountry, free park-use permits must be obtained from information centres or warden offices.

• It is illegal to remove or destroy plants and other natural or historic objects in national parks.

Mt. Revelstoke National Park

Bordering the town of Revelstoke is 260-square-kilometre Mt. Revelstoke National Park, created in 1914. Summit Drive, one kilometre northeast of Revelstoke on the Trans-Canada Highway, is a 26-kilometre drive up a paved road providing easy access to the 1938-metre summit of Mt. Revelstoke. Pull-outs allow spectacular views of the Columbia River, Eagle Pass, and surrounding mountains. In the summer, the alpine meadows are filled with brilliantly coloured wildflowers. Trails at the top lead to nearby lakes. Camping is not permitted in the park, but there are private campsites in Revelstoke and several provincial parks nearby.

The Trans-Canada Highway follows the southern border of the park and the Illecillewaet River. There are many trails off the highway that lead to alpine meadows, passing near waterfalls and through forest land. Near the western entrance to the park, **Skunk Cabbage** and **Giant Cedars trails** offer easy self-guided nature walks.

Albert Canyon

37 km (23 mi) east of Revelstoke, 837-2420

At the end of a long hard day of sightseeing, Albert Canyon Hot Springs provides happy relief. Besides 26°C and 40°C pools, there is a commercial campsite with all the amenities plus trail rides, whitewater rafting, fishing, and hiking.

Glacier National Park

Not to be confused with the American park of the same name just south of the BC-Alberta border, the Canadian Glacier Park covers 1349 square kilometres. Over 400 glaciers sit on the lofty peaks of the Purcell and Selkirk ranges.

Glacier National Park lies in particularly rugged country, inhospitable to all but the most tenacious wildlife – mountain goat or hibernators like marmot or black and grizzly bear. Evidence of frequent avalanches is found in the treeless slides that line the highway, an occurrence which constantly challenges those charged with keeping the road and rail line clear.

One of the most photographed points along the Trans-Canada is the 1327-metre **Rogers Pass.** Staff at the Infocentre (837-6274) greet 160,000

Rogers Pass, discovered by Major A.B. Rogers in 1882, eluded CPR surveyors looking for a route through the Selkirk Mountains in the 1870s. Highway construction through the rugged area began in 1956 and took six years to complete.

Illecillewaet, "the Great Glacier," is one of 400 in Glacier National Park. The CPR built Glacier House near the base of the glacier in 1886, attracting tourists from around the world. It was here that mountaineering began as a sport in North America.

visitors a year. The facility has a number of displays and in the summer months, the staff offer interpretive programs.

Major A.B. Rogers, chief engineer of the CPR, first found this pass through the Selkirk Range in 1881. Strong-backed men armed with picks and shovels created a track for the CPR which linked BC with the rest of Canada in 1885. But it wasn't until 1962 that the Trans-Canada Highway was built.

The Illecillewaet, Asulkan, and Swiss glaciers can all be seen from the Infocentre. The Illecillewaet Campground affords a closer view of the glaciers and has trails to the alpine areas.

Hikers can pick up information on the park's 140 kilometres of trails at the Infocentre. (Overnighters must register with the park staff.) Of the 21 routes in the park, one of the easiest, the 30-minute **Abandoned Rails Trail**, starts just behind the Infocentre. Two other gentle 30-minute walks are the **Meeting of the Waters Trail,** starting at the Illecillewaet Campground, and the **Loop Trail** at the Loop Brook Campground.

Much of the park is alpine tundra that includes many flowering plants. Incomparable photography opportunities are available from May through August. The eastern boundary of the park marks the beginning of the Mountain Time Zone: eastbound travellers should put clocks ahead one hour.

Golden

150 km (93 mi) east of Revelstoke. Population 3700. Infocentre: 10th Avenue North, V0A 1H0. 344-7125; Fax: 344-6688

Golden was visited by David Thompson as early as 1807. But the first building was not erected till 1882, when the settlement was known as "The Cache." Major Rogers used it as his headquarters while surveying his route through the mountains to the west. From the time the CPR was completed until the spur line south was finished, Golden also enjoyed a memorable era as the northern terminus for sternwheelers on the Columbia steaming north from Lake Windermere. The town has the distinction of having the oldest curling club in Western Canada. Curlers first hurled their stones on the frozen Columbia River in 1892.

As soon as the railway was completed, the CPR began working at ways to keep the railway viable, and a strong interest in tourism was born. The company hired Swiss guides in the 1890s to ensure the safety of trekkers and mountaineers. Memorabilia can be found in the **Golden and District Museum** (1302-11th Avenue and 13th Street, 344-5169).

Outdoor enthusiasts will find Golden a centre for a variety of activities including river rafting on the Kicking Horse and Blaeberry rivers, hut-to-hut high-country hiking, skiing,

---

Jean Feuz Vaughan
Edelweiss Village Golden

Jean Feuz Vaughan was born and raised in Golden and hopes to stay there until she dies. "I've never left the area," she says. "I never saw the need. It's warm in the summer, not too cold in the winter."

Possibly another reason she stays is the Edelweiss Village, which she looks after with her husband Allen. Jean's grandfather, Edward Feuz, was one of the first Swiss guides employed by the CPR to guide tourists in the Rockies in the 1890s. His three sons, Walter, Ed Jr., and Ernest, followed as teenagers. In 1912 the CPR built houses for the guides so they wouldn't need to return to Switzerland each year, and the Feuz brothers moved to Canada permanently.

Jean, the youngest of Walter's eight children, says the brothers never had an accident. Walter eventually developed goiter, gave up guiding, and managed the boats at Lake Louise for several years. But Ed Jr. climbed until he was 84, leading first ascents of 78 area mountains. The last of the original Swiss guides, he died at Golden in 1981, at the age of 96.

Jean and Allen Vaughan now own the six restored gingerbread-trimmed chalets and rent out all but one. That's the one Jean was raised in. Visitors are welcome to view the site. Go up the hill at 14th Street, beside the Esso station, just off Highway 1.

Emerald Lake was discovered in 1882 by CPR surveyor Tom Wilson. Today it is one of the most popular stops on the Trans-Canada Highway.

fishing, and mountain biking. **Burges and James Gadsden Provincial Park** is a wildlife sanctuary and nature study area on the north side of the Columbia River west of Golden. The Columbia wetlands south to Radium Hot Springs is also popular with paddlers and wildlife viewers. "The Golden Triangle," a 316-kilometre biking route, travels through magnificent scenery, connecting Golden, Lake Louise, and Radium Hot Springs. A number of private resorts and outdoor adventure companies offer package hiking, rafting, and biking tours.

Special events include the **Golden Rodeo** on Labour Day weekend and the February **Sno Fest**. **Whitetooth Ski Area** (344-6114), with 560 vertical metres, six runs, and a 480-metre double chair lift is the local alpine ski slope northwest of town.

Yoho National Park

East of Golden, the highway finally enters the Rockies and Yoho National Park.

With its lofty peaks, glaciers, spectacular waterfalls and lakes, Canada's second oldest national park is often compared to the Himalayas and the Swiss Alps. Thirty of its peaks are over 3000 metres. Yoho is one of several parks in the area (Banff, Jasper, and Kootenay are the others) which, along with the Burgess Shale, have been designated by UNESCO as world heritage sites, in recognition of their continuing natural, historic, and recreational value.

We have the CPR to thank for this national treasure. Once workers had pushed the track over the majestic Kicking Horse Pass, the company built their first hotel at Field to avoid hauling a dining car up The Big Hill to the east. At the encouragement of the CPR, tourists, climbers, and artists migrated to the town, and in 1886 Mt. Stephen Reserve was set aside. Yoho National Park was established in 1911.

The highway follows the Kicking Horse River through the 131,300-hectare park, within close range of several popular attractions. (The information centre at Field has maps and descriptions.)

The river was given its name when James Hector, a 23-year-old geologist with the Palliser Expedition of 1857-60, was searching for a route through the Rockies to the Columbia River. Stopping near Wapta Falls, young Hector was kicked in the chest by a pack horse and rendered unconscious. His colleagues presumed he was dead, and it was a momentous occasion when he revived – so momentous that they renamed the Wapta River to mark it.

Thirty-metre-high **Wapta Falls** is visible by taking the two-kilometre Wapta Falls Road south just past the west entrance to the park and then embarking on an easy one-hour hike. Other falls in the park are higher, but the width of these carry a spectacular peak flow of 255 cubic metres per second. The marsh along the side of the road is home to beaver, muskrat, blue heron, and moose.

Back on the highway and across the bridge, the Hoodoo Creek Campground road leads to a more vigorous, but short hike to hoodoo formations. These sculpted pillars of glacial sediment have boulders balancing on their peaks – evidence of their relative youth. Some geologists feel these are the best example

of hoodoos in the world.

Lakes, waterfalls, and magnificent scenery line the drive to the **Natural Bridge** turnoff, where the ceaseless action of the river over thousands of years has worn a hole in solid bedrock. Six kilometres along the same road is **Emerald Lake,** (particularly breathtaking on a bright day). Visitors can hike around the lake, go for a horseback ride, rent a canoe, or wander through the world-famous chalet, built in 1902. This is the one of the most photographed lakes in the Rockies – if there are too many people, trails from the parking area lead to more pristine experiences.

Formerly a waterfall, the Natural Bridge has been created as the waters of the Kicking Horse River have encountered a resistant limestone layer in the bedrock.

Fossils of the Burgess Shale

In the summer of 1909, Dr. Charles Doolitte Walcott, head of the Smithsonian Institution and an eminent paleontologist, was conducting field research at the higher elevations of Mt. Stephen, near Field. On the last trip down the mountain, as the first snow was falling, Mrs. Walcott's horse stopped at an obstruction. As Dr. Walcott stooped to lift the rock from the path, he discovered the fossilized remains of a 500-million-year-old creature embedded in the shale. It was one of the most important paleontological discoveries in human history.

The Walcotts had literally stumbled upon the vestige of a vast prehistoric sea that once lapped the shores of the Rocky Mountains. The Cambrian creatures had become embedded in the silt on the ocean floor, immune to predators and rapid decay. As time passed, more and more layers of material pressed down, hardening into rock, and the earth continued to shift and change. Miraculously the fossils remained perfectly preserved, in some cases right down to the contents of their stomachs. An incredibly wide variety of species were represented.

Prevailing scientific biases resulted in a rather conservative original evaluation of the find. It wasn't until 1966, after chipping out 10,000 more specimens, that Cambridge paleontologist Harry Whittington and his colleagues discovered that there were at least 15, perhaps 20 creatures in the Burgess Shale fossils that defied classification in currently existing categories.

These fossils are not only objects of great beauty, says Harvard paleontologist Stephen Jay Gould, but they challenge the foundations of our ideas about life itself. For more information, read Gould's book, *Wonderful Life: The Burgess Shale and the Nature of History* (New York: Norton, 1989).

Field

55 km (34 mi) east of Golden.
Population: 280. Infocentre: Trans-Canada Highway, Box 157, V0A 1G0.
344-7574; Fax: 343-6721

The tiny town of Field exists because of the CPR. A railway camp was constructed here in 1884, and in 1886 Field House was built, drawing visitors from around the word.

Field is the closest settlement to the Burgess Shale, a major paleontological discovery. In 1909, Charles Walcott first came across the perfectly preserved fossils near a massive limestone reef dating back over 500 million years. The sites are very delicate and access is extremely limited. Parks officials report that viewing is disappointing to ordinary mortals who will find the displays at the information centre and the Takakkaw Falls turnoff much more informative. Parks staff are emphatic in discouraging all but the most serious visitors. However, there are hiking tours available for those with a unabiding, passionate interest, through park headquarters (343-6324) or a private company (343-6470).

Field is also a base for the slightly exotic sport of ice climbing, best attempted between December and March. Features not normally regarded as attractive, such as subfreezing temperatures, blue ice, and spindrift avalanches have made the area's many frozen waterfalls excellent training ground for some of Canada's top climbers.

Yoho National Park East of Field

East of Field, a road at Kicking Horse Campground leads through the Yoho Valley to **Takakkaw Falls.** In Cree Takakkaw means magnificent, and it certainly is – at 380 metres, one of the highest waterfalls in Canada. Although the falls are visible from the parking lot, a 10-minute walk will bring visitors close enough to need a raincoat. (There are several sharp hairpin turns on this road. Unhitch trailers in the parking lot near the turnoff.) Mountain goats who like to hang out on precipitous ledges to avoid predators can be seen in this

One of the highest waterfalls in Canada, Takakkaw Falls has a combined drop of 380 metres. In 1974, four locals climbed its frozen waters, an action that marked the beginning of ice climbing as a significant winter sport in the Rockies.

The Upper Spiral Tunnels Viewpoint, right beside the Trans-Canada Highway, offers visitors a fascinating look at a unique solution to a railway engineering nightmare. Built in 1909, the track loops in a figure eight under Mount Ogden and Cathedral Mountain. It is possible to watch one end of a train leaving the tunnel while the other end is entering.

area. Good viewing places are at the turnoff and the Lower Spiral Tunnels Viewpoint farther up the valley.

The next stop on the highway is the **Upper Spiral Tunnels Viewpoint.** This engineering masterpiece was built in 1909 to prevent trains from derailing on the steep downhill grade from Kicking Horse Pass known as the Big Hill.

"The fairest of mountain lakelet tarns" is how mountaineer James Outram described **Lake O'Hara** in 1900. Motor vehicle access to this glacial lake and the many other beauty spots in the area is limited – a bus service takes hikers and day trippers to a campground and lodge (343-6418), the starting point for over 30 trails. Because of the number of visitors attracted to this fragile alpine

zone, reservations must be made in advance to stay overnight or ride the bus.

Kicking Horse Pass (1625 metres) sits on the Continental Divide: on the west, streams and rivers flow into the Pacific Ocean via the Columbia River system, and on the east, they flow to Hudson Bay and the Atlantic Ocean via the Saskatchewan River system. A three-kilometre drive along the Great Divide Parkway allows visitors to actually stand with one foot on either side of the divide.

For a more detailed description of this and other parks and attractions in the Rockies, refer to the *Canadian Rockies SuperGuide* and *Walks and Easy Hikes in the Canadian Rockies* published by Altitude.

Bears

Bears are the largest hunting carnivores on land. They are not generally aggressive, but under certain circumstances they can be. Because of this unpredictability, all bears should be regarded as dangerous.

In the Interior there are two species: black bears and grizzlies. Grizzlies average 3 metres, weigh 150 to 400 kilograms, have a large hump on their shoulders, and range in colour from pale yellowish to dark brown with white tips on the hairs. Black bears average 2 metres and weigh 125 to 300 kilograms, and range in colour from white to dark brown and black.

Since bears require many kilometres of foraging territory, they rarely congregate, unless at rich feeding grounds such as spawning runs and garbage dumps. Except for people, bears have few natural predators.

Bears hibernate during the winter, so an encounter is unlikely between November and April. During the rest of the year, they range throughout the Interior. Disastrous encounters beween bears and people are rare, but they do occur. In 1992, there were four reported cases of severe maulings in BC.

Consider the following:
• Always check locally for bear warnings and advice. Let someone know your backcountry route and schedule.
• Don't store food or garbage in tents or leave it unattended. In the backcountry, elevate food and garbage at least five metres between two trees.
• Don't hike alone. Singing or carrying a bell when hiking often warns the bears away; however, it sometimes attracts them.
• If you notice bear droppings, tracks, or dead animals, get out of the area. Avoid mothers with cubs.
• If you meet a bear, keep calm, slowly back away, or climb well up a tree. Some experts say that if you are attacked, drop to the ground, assume the fetal position, hands behind neck, but this is not necessarily effective.
• Dogs can attract and/or annoy bears. Keep them quiet and leashed. Better yet, leave them home.
• Never feed bears. They'll come to expect it and become a problem. Make sure all uneaten food or garbage is properly disposed of.
• It's easier for humans to adjust their behaviour and protect bears, than it is for Nature to replace "problem" bears that must be destroyed.

Crowsnest Highway

A stopover on the Dewdney Trail in the 1860s, Creston is now an important agricultural area in the Kootenays. Over 12,000 hectares of farmland have been reclaimed in the floodplain of the Kootenay River due to a system of dikes built between the 1890s and the 1930s.

In 1859, Edgar Dewdney, a 24-year-old civil engineer from England, arrived at Governor James Douglas' door in Victoria looking for work. "I possessed a strong constitution and unbounded confidence, and arrived here with a light heart," Dewdney later wrote in his memoirs. Almost immediately, Dewdney began helping Colonel Richard Clement Moody build a trail from Hope to Rock Creek, east of present-day Osoyoos. After working on other road-building projects in the Interior, Dewdney extended the route as far as the town of Wild Horse in the East Kootenay in 1865, and it became

known as the Dewdney Trail.

Today Highway 3 (also known as the Crowsnest route) is the modern version of this early transportation corridor. Some sections of the original trail are still visible from Highway 3. Other parts are being preserved and reclaimed as recreation trails.

Highway 3 starts in Hope (see Trans-Canada Highway section) crossing the southern Interior by climbing up, around, through, and down the Cascade Mountains, the Thompson Plateau, the Okanagan Highland, the Columbia Mountains, and the Rockies, before it reaches the Alberta border near Sparwood. It is a modern, mostly two-lane paved highway that crosses varied terrain. The highest passes are Allison (1342 metres) between Hope and Princeton, Bonanza (1535 metres) between Grand Forks and Castlegar, Kootenay (1774 metres) between Salmo and Creston, and Crowsnest (1396 metres) in the Rockies.

The Interior Salish and Kutenai were the dominant Native cultures in the region and in several places along the route faded images of pictographs still tell their stories.

Rockhounding, gold panning, river rafting, canoeing, kayaking, fishing, swimming, hiking, golfing, wildlife viewing, and biking are just a few of the fair-weather outdoor-recreation possibilities. In the winter, outdoor enthusiasts will find places for alpine and nordic skiing, ice-fishing, skating, and snowmobiling along the route.

Logging and mining are important to many communities along Highway 3, as is agriculture, particularly in the Similkameen, Okanagan, and Creston valleys. Tourism and recreation are becoming increasingly important to local economies.

Hope-Princeton Highway

The infamous Hope-Princeton Highway, the first leg of the Crowsnest route, has always been a difficult stretch of road. Officially opened in November 1949 at a cost of $12 million, for many years it was subject to slides, washouts, and white-knuckle twists and turns. However, work on the road is ongoing, and today the route is a pleasure to drive, with sec-

tions of four-lane highway, passing lanes, easy grades, and spectacular scenery.

Despite the improvements to the highway, the route can be dangerous. Motorists should drive with regard for weather conditions, and bow to the wisdom of slide and avalanche warnings and no-passing signs. Speeders beware: this stretch of Highway 3 is meticulously patrolled by the RCMP.

The Hope Slide

In January 1965, an estimated 100 million tonnes of rock, earth, and trees slid off the face of Johnson's Peak about 16 kilometres east of Hope. The rock and debris travelled across the highway, 150 metres up Mount Coulter on the other side, and back down again. Caused by minor earthquakes, the slide obliterated

In 1965, a series of minor earthquakes dislodged 46 million cubic metres of rock that travelled at speeds over 160 km/h. The slide obliterated Highway 3 east of Hope. Construction of a temporary replacement road took 21 days.

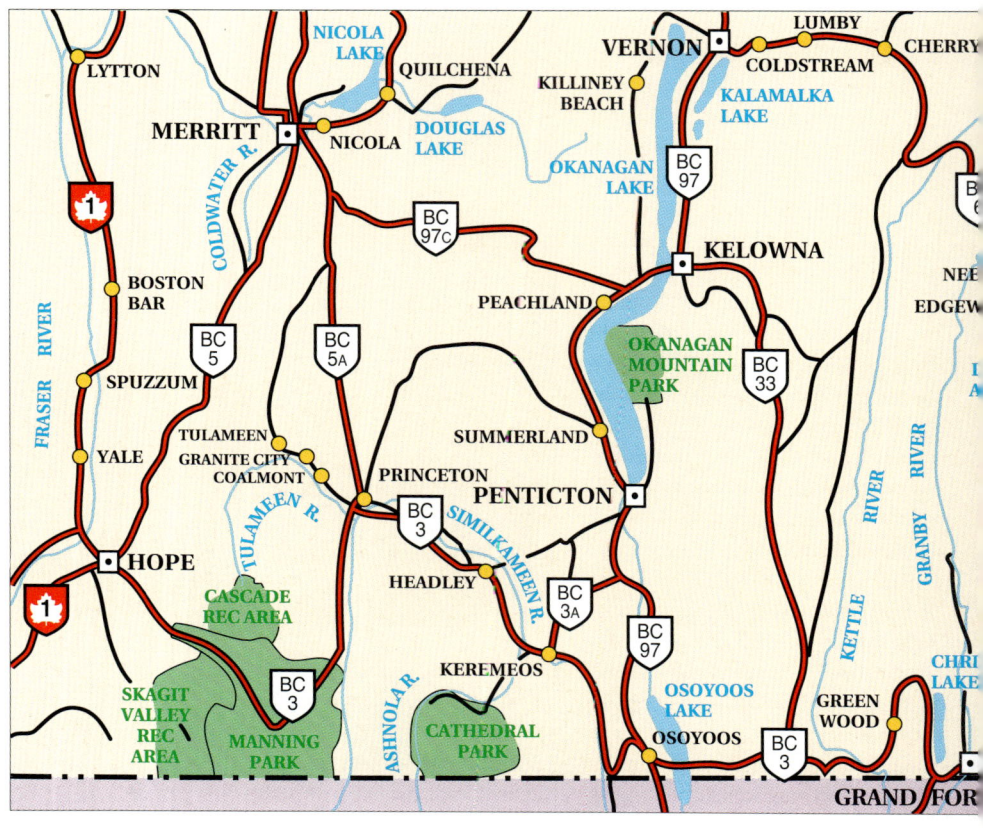

about three kilometres of highway and a small lake. At least four people lost their lives. The road was rebuilt over the top of the rubble, and vegetation is slowly creeping back, but the bare face of the mountain remains.

Historic Trails

Adjacent to Manning Provincial Park's northwestern boundary, **Cascade Recreation Area** is the trailhead for the historic Dewdney, Whatcom, and Hope Pass trails, all built in the 1800s. The parking area is just east of the Rhododendron Flats in Manning Park.

Manning Provincial Park

26 km (16 mi) east of Hope, 48 km (30 mi) west of Princeton.
840-8836

It is the traveller's good fortune that Highway 3 passes through Manning Provincial Park, providing easy access to alpine meadows, sparkling lakes, and wilderness trails. Only three hours from Vancouver, Manning Park is popular year-round.

Along the highway's route through the 66,500-hectare park, the landscape transforms from lush coastal rain forest to the dry forest land of the Interior Plateau. Evidence of the

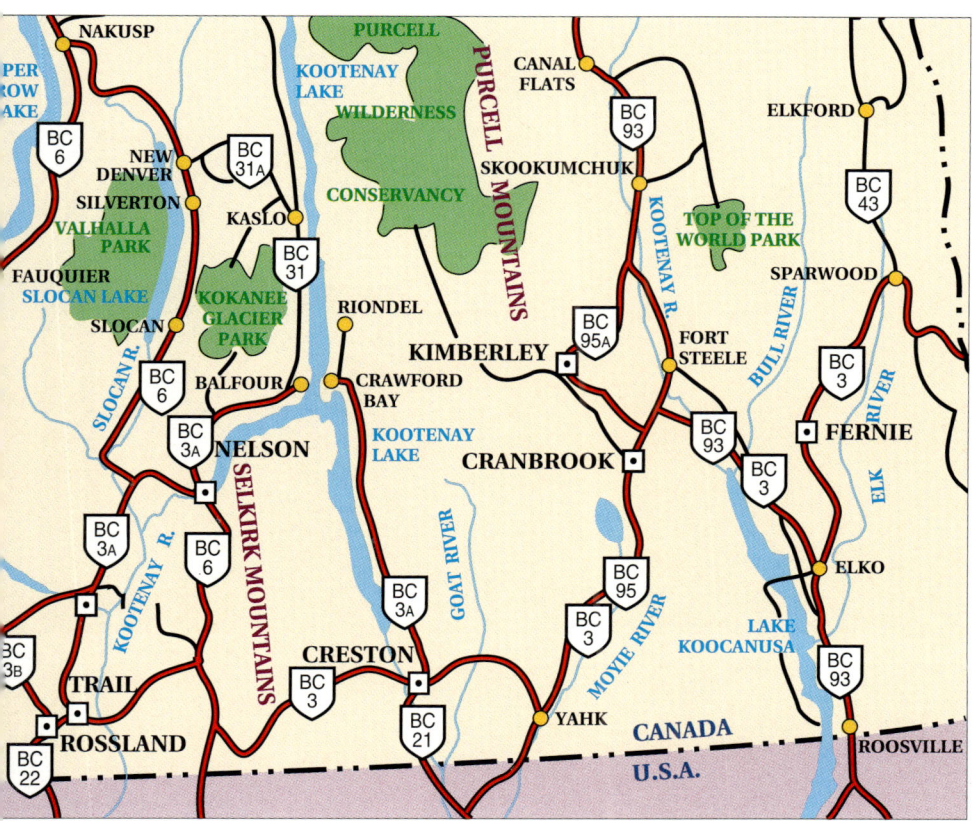

shift can be dramatically found in abrupt weather changes near Allison Pass. Here moody grey rain clouds can, in minutes, change to a bright blue Interior sky. This occurrence repeats across the province. Typically, eastbound clouds release their moisture on the western slopes of the mountain ranges. The eastern-facing slopes thus tend to be dryer.

Motorists may see deer, bear, and coyote from the road or from several wildlife viewing areas. Over 190 species of birds have been sighted in the park. In the spring and summer, picnickers compete with scores of ground squirrels at **Lighting Lakes Day Use Area** (a short drive off the highway at the Manning Park Lodge turnoff). Visitors can also hike around the lakes and rent canoes and horses (840-8844). At **Cascade Lookout** (accessible via a paved road across the highway from the lodge) chipmunks and mountain jays compete with a spectacular view of the towering peaks of the Cascade Mountains and the fast-flowing water of the Similkameen River far below. The **Alpine Meadows** are another nine kilometres up the road. **Beaver Pond Trail** in May and June is also a good viewing site.

Top: The peaks of the Three Brothers in the Cascade Mountains are popular with hikers in Manning Provincial Park.

Bottom: Beaver habitat is visible at several locations along Highway 3 in the park.

The visitor's centre, one kilometre east of the lodge, has maps and information on self-guided nature trails, hiking trails, and special attractions. Particularly appealing are the splashy shows of colour at the **Rhododendron Flats** in May-June, the **Rein Orchid Trail** in June-July, and the alpine meadows' **Heather Trail** in July-August. The trailhead of the **Pacific Crest Trail,** a 4000-kilometre, six-month backpacking route that extends all the way to Mexico is also here, five kilometres east of the visitor centre.

Winter recreation includes downhill runs at **Gibson Pass** (840-8822) or cross-country skiing and snowshoeing on the park's many trails.

Copper Mountain

Thirty-five kilometres past the East Gate of Manning Park, a viewpoint

Edgar Dewdney
Road Builder and Lieutenant-Governor

Englishman Edgar Dewdney was only 24 years old when he arrived in Victoria in May 1859. The energetic civil engineer was never to dig for the gold that had brought him here, but he made an immense contribution to the development of the Interior. Loyal, single-minded, and unafraid of confrontation, he was involved in most of the major transportation projects in the Interior over the next 50 years.

He is best remembered for his work on the Dewdney Trail, begun in 1859, and continued in 1860 with surveyor Walter Moberly (who later found the Eagle Pass through the Selkirk Mountains and did extensive surveying for the CPR). The next year gold was discovered at Rock Creek just west of present-day Osoyoos, and Moberly and Dewdney extended the road there.

From 1862 to 1864, Dewdney was involved in building the Cariboo Wagon Road. When gold was discovered at Wild Horse Creek in the East Kootenay in 1864, Dewdney was contracted to continue the road from Rock Creek east.

"I shall never forget what pleasure and enjoyment I had when walking over the frozen summits on a bright sunshiny early morning, the sun dazzling in the snow, which seemed studded with millions of diamonds, and the air bracing and seeming to give fresh life with every breath you drew," he wrote later.

Other road-building projects included a trail from Lillooet to Bridge River, a road from Savona to Cache Creek, and a trail from Stuart Lake to Omineca. Like Moberly, he did some surveying for the proposed transcontinental railway.

In 1868, Dewdney began a career in government, appointed as provincial representative for the Kootenays in Victoria. In 1872, following Confederation, he became a federal Member of Parliament. In 1879 he was appointed

Indian commissioner for the Northwest Territories and the area's lieutenant-governor in 1881. After another term as an MP, he was appointed lieutenant-governor of British Columbia in 1892.

Upon retiring in 1897, Dewdney returned to engineering, helping to choose the Kettle Valley Railway route. He died in 1916, the year the railway was completed.

Top: The Dewdney Trail as it looks today near Highway 3. Some sections of the trail are maintained for hiking, part of a 1400-kilometre route from Vancouver Island to Banff.

Bottom: Edgar Dewdney's long career in British Columbia included serving as road-builder and lieutenant-governor.

Towering above the Similkameen River, Bromley Rock marks a favourite swimming place east of Princeton.

acknowledges the now defunct mine at Copper Mountain, which operated from 1905 to 1957. Although an elderly Similkameen Native discovered the copper mineral in 1884, a man named "Volcanic" Brown, with grandiose plans for saving the world, filed the claim in 1895. Brown eventually sold his rights for $45,000, but his plans for world harmony shifted inexplicably, and he ended up buying himself some solid gold teeth instead.

When the mine was operating, an average of 1.4 million tonnes of ore was produced per year – mostly copper, with some gold and silver.

Princeton

134 km (83 mi) east of Hope.
Population: 3300. Infocentre: Old Train Caboose at west entrance to town on Highway 3. Chamber of Commerce: 195 Bridge Street, Unit 4, Box 540, V0X 1W0. 295-3103; Fax: 295-3255

At the confluence of the Tulameen and Similkameen rivers, Princeton has a relationship to mining that is ancient. Long before the advent of Europeans, Native people used the site to trade the red ochre of nearby Vermilion Bluffs with distant tribes like the Kutenai and Prairie Blackfoot. *Tulameen* is a native word meaning "red earth," and Princeton was at one time called Vermilion Forks.

Twelve kilometres west of Princeton on Highway 3, **Similco Mines'** (295-6961) open-pit copper mine is a mainstay of Princeton's modern economy, processing 23,000 tonnes of ore per day. Group tours can be arranged .

Princeton is also a ranching town, serving the Nicola and the Similkameen valleys. The **Princeton Museum** (167 Vermilion Avenue, 295-7588) has displays of fossils and Interior Salish, Chinese, and pioneer artifacts.

Just north of town on Osprey Lake Road, stone ruins stand in the trees. What seems to be a medieval castle is in fact the remains of a portland cement factory. The plant actually opened in 1913, but closed almost immediately. The construction cost several million dollars, four years, and several workers' lives. Today romantics speculate about hoaxes, blunders, and swindles, but the more practical minded suggest that a lack of limestone, coal, and financing caused the failure. The site now exists as an RV park.

Local events include the **Spring Fair** and the **Princeton Rodeo,** both in May, **Princeton Racing Days** in July, and the **Fall Fair and Logging Show** in September.

A highlight on Highway 3 east is **Bromley Rock Provincial Park,** a popular Similkameen River camping place for centuries. On summer days daredevils jump off the rock into the deep pools of the river.

The canoe trip along the Similkameen from Princeton to the US border is highly rated and thrilling, but it can be treacherous. Potential paddlers should check at the Infocentre in Princeton for river conditions. The Infocentre will also be able to tell anglers how the fish are biting

Beaver
Castor canadensis

Canada's largest rodents, mature beavers weigh from 15 to 35 kilograms and are found across the country. A nocturnal animal, they are difficult to spot, but it is easy to see evidence of their presence.

Beaver live in lodges up to three metres high, constructed out of mud, twigs, and branches beside slow-moving water. The entrance ways are underwater, but the living quarters are above ground. Beaver don't hibernate; their winter's food supply of leaves, bark, twigs, buds, and other plant material is stored in a large mound beside the lodge.

Canada's national symbol, the beaver is easily recongizable. Its coarse outer layer of red-brown fur covers the soft undercoat that inspired the early fur traders. Felted, this fur was a prestigous lining for mens' hats in 18th and 19th century Europe.

Excellent swimmers, beaver can stay under water for 15 minutes. A beaver tail resembles a thick scaly paddle. When frightened, the animals slap their tails on the water as a warning.

Beaver will often live in colonies of lodges. One lodge will house one adult pair and their newborn and yearling offspring. They usually breed in January or February and give birth in April or May after a 14-week gestation.

On the Old Hedley Road vigilant travellers can spot pictographs, an ancient form of artistic expression. Typically painted with red ochre, the paintings often depict mythological and supernatural motifs. Most pictographs in the Interior are no more than a few hundred years old.

at the approximately 30 good trout lakes within an 80-kilometre radius of Princeton. This is also a good area for rockhounds. Agates, petrified wood, and fossils lie in the hills near Vermilion and McCormack Flats.

Side Trip: Ghost Towns of the Tulameen

About 60 million years ago, the Tulameen area north of Princeton was a shallow lake about 24 kilometres long, filled with plant life that later decomposed to form peat bogs. Over time, coal was formed. The town of **Blakeburn,** established in 1917, once produced one tonne of coal per minute and employed 365 men. Now a ghost town, Blakeburn's story is particularly tragic. In 1930, 45 miners died in an underground explosion, one of the worst mining disasters in BC history. The mine closed in 1940.

Coalmont, about 18 kilometres northwest of Princeton, was founded in 1911. The original hotel is still operating, and the people who live here have retained a sense of humor.

Among the goods for sale at the local store – instant water! Bicycles and boats are available to rent for a closer exploration of the area.

Another two kilometres along the road is **Granite City,** where a cowboy with the fortuitous name of John Chance bent over to get a drink of water in the Tulameen River one day in 1885 and found a gold nugget. By 1886 Granite City was a bustling gold-rush town with 13 saloons and a population of 2000, making it the third largest town in BC. In three years, miners took out $350,000 in gold, but by 1888 the boom was over.

The Similkameen and Tulameen rivers are good places for river panning. You can still find platinum and gold – if you know where to look (Granite Creek area) and when (early spring and late fall). The Infocentre has directions and the Government Agent (295-6957) in Princeton has regulations.

Alternate Route: The Old Hedley Road

Travellers heading east to Hedley and Keremeos may find the **Old Hedley Road** an interesting alternative to Highway 3. (Go through Princeton on Bridge Street, cross the bridge, turn right on Tulameen Ave, and cross Highway 5A to the Old Hedley Road.) This route existed for hundreds of years, long before the fur traders and prospectors came through. Look for Native pictographs on the rocks between 10 and 20 kilometres east of Princeton. Also visible are traces of the **Dewdney Trail,** constructed in the 1860s to connect Hope with the Interior in a bid to minimize US economic and political domination. The Welby Stage ran coaches along this route three days a week from Princeton to Penticton until 1910. Rustic Forest Service camping and picnic spots overlook the river.

Hedley
40 km (25 mi) east of Princeton.
Population: 274

Approaching Hedley from the west, the highway rounds a bend to reveal Lookout Mountain towering 1922 metres above the tiny town. From the highway viewpoint, remains of Nickel Plate Mine's three-kilometre long aerial tramway can be seen – the longest in the world when it was built (ca.1903). The tramway was used to transport ore to a stamp mill at the bottom of the mountain.

One story about the mine's origin says that in 1890 two keen young men on a quest for gold met with some grizzled old prospectors nearby. The greenhorns politely asked the veterans where the best place might be to find gold. One of the oldtimers directed the newcomers to the top of the steepest mountain that he could see. The young men dutifully crawled and clawed their way up the rock face and discovered a rusty red outcrop of rock – and gold. They sold their claim that year for $60,000 and between 1904 and 1955 the mountain yielded $47 million worth of gold, as well as copper, silver, and arsenic. The mining operation currently visible beside Highway 3 east of town reworks old tailings to recover leached gold.

The Hedley Blast, a giant country and western music festival, at-

tracts big-name performers and thousands of fans every year in mid-July.

Hedley to Keremeos: Wildlife Viewing
Between Hedley and Keremeos the highway passes through dry grassland and steep mountain slopes. Motorists can often spot mountain goats, especially in the spring and fall. The route follows the Similkameen River and there are plenty of pull-outs for watching the goats as well as golden eagles, marmots, and other wildlife. The only venomous snake in BC, the Pacific rattlesnake, lives in the dry vegetative areas of the southern Interior, so hikers should watch where they place their hands and feet. (See page 132.)

One of the more unusual ranching operations in the province is found nine kilometres east of Hedley at the **Hubcap Ranch** (499-5492). Owners ride herd on 16,000 of the circular little critters. Visitors are welcome.

In the early 1900s, Hedley was a town of 5000, with six hotels and fashionable stores. The gold, silver, and copper ores played out in 1955. However, gold panners still work the nearby Similkameen River.

Fourth-generation cattle ranchers John and Georgianne Sanders oversee 200 head of cattle and 16,000 hubcaps at the Hubcap Ranch west of Keremeos. The unusual collection attracts callers from around the world.

Cathedral Lakes Provincial Park

494-0321

Three kilometres west of Keremeos is the turn off (south) onto the 23-kilometre access road to **Cathedral Lakes Provincial Park**. The 33,000-hectare park is in the Cascade Mountains and features some truly spectacular rock formations and alpine scenery. Long recognized as a prime wilderness area, Archduke Francis Ferdinand of Austria, whose 1914 assassination triggered World War I, reportedly made a lavish hunting trip to the area in the early 1900s. Hollywood has also discovered the magnificent scenery. Several scenes of the 1986 movie, *Clan of the Cave Bear*, were shot here.

At the core of the park, surrounded by pinnacled peaks, are six turquoise alpine lakes. There is restricted motor vehicle access to a commercial resort (499-5848) on one of the lakes, but otherwise the core is reached only by three hiking routes. Anglers catch cutthroat and rainbow trout in the lakes and streams. Mule deer, mountain goat, and California bighorn sheep are plentiful. Bird-watchers can look for whiskey jacks, Clark's nutcrackers, golden eagles, and ptarmigan. In summer, over 200 species of flowers bloom. Best hiking is from July to October.

Along the same access road, the **Ashnola Mountains Conservation Reserve** is home to one of Canada's largest herds of California bighorn sheep.

Keremeos

29 km (18 mi) east of Hedley.
Population: 900. Infocentre: 415-7th
Avenue, Highway 3, PO Box 452,
V0X 1N0. 499-5225. Seasonal

First learn to say it: care-eh-mee-ose.
Then enjoy the fact that you are in the
"Fruit Stand Capital of Canada." Fruit
and vegetables are available at roadside stands throughout the
Okanagan, but with 25 here (some
open year-round), more just down
the road in Cawston, and the ripening dates earlier than other areas,
Keremeos is a good place to stock up.
(See page 123 for the ripening
schedule.)

Although now primarily known for
its orchards, Keremeos was on the
route of early fur traders like Alexander Ross, the first European to visit
the area in 1811. Taking advantage

of the luxurious golden bunch grass
that once covered the area, the Hudson's Bay Company established a
fort here to pasture oxen, horses,
and cows. The first homestead was
established in the early 1860s and
the first commercial orchard was
planted in 1897 by Frank Richter, a
pioneer cattleman.

The **Keremeos Museum** (at 6th
Avenue and 6th Street) is housed in a
former jail and features pioneer artifacts and police memorabilia. The
Similkameen Valley Museum (2nd
floor of band office on Main Street,
499-5528), run by the Lower
Similkameen Band, specializes in
Native history

The **Old Grist Mill** (Upper Bench
Road, 499-2888), a provincial historic
site, is definitely worth a stop. Built in
1877 by wealthy young Englishman
Barrington Price, the mill is one of the

Horticultural displays
at the 1877 Grist Mill
in Keremeos include
heritage apples,
historic varieties of
wheat, and an
Edwardian herb
garden.

Travellers can see a colourful variety of wild plants along Interior roadways. From top left, clockwise: oxeye daisy, saskatoon berries, mountain ash berries, and tansy.

best examples of its kind in the country. The site includes hands-on interpretive displays, a Victorian garden, a tea room, and a resource centre. (Take Highway 3A east, then follow the signs. Open daily in summer and in winter by reservation.)

The Grist Mill sponsors an annual **Giant Zucca Reunion** in late-August. The zucca, widely grown in the area between 1934 and 1955, was believed extinct until the staff recently tracked down seed from a farmer in the US. The giant fruit can weigh as much as 70 kilograms.

Rockhounds will find Keremeos rewarding. Agate, jasper, and opal are found in the hills nearby. A three-hour hike into **Keremeos Columns Provincial Park** reveals 30-metre natural basalt columns, formed by cooling lava over 30 million years ago. (Travel north on Highway 3A for four kilometres, then east at the cemetery. The pavement ends and a gravel road continues over private land. Ask for permission to cross from residents.)

Wine-tasters will be pleased to note that the first of many Okanagan-area wineries, the St. Lazlo Vineyard (499-2856), is about two kilometres east of Keremeos on Highway 3. Tasters are welcome.

Special events include the **Elks**

Rodeo and a **Native Pow Wow** on the long weekend in May, the **Chopaka Rodeo** on Easter weekend, and **Indian Pow Wow Days** in August.

Spotted Lake

Thirty-five kilometres east of Keremeos, Spotted Lake, on the south side of the road, always attracts attention. The large white rings are formed by magnesium and sodium salts deposited when the lake water evaporates. The curative power of Epsom salts for a variety of ailments is widely accepted. Native people called the lake *Klilok*, "Medicine Lake" and used to soak in its soft mud for relief from rheumatism and arthritis, as well as for spiritual ailments. At present, however, the lake is on private property. Motorists who wish to take photos should do so from the highway.

Mount Kobau is a favourite spot for hikers and amateur astronomers. Access is by a forestry road 11 kilometres west of Osoyoos. **The Mount Kobau Star-Gazing Party** is held annually in August.

Osoyoos

120 km (75 mi) east of Princeton. Population: 3100. Infocentre: junction of Highways 3 and 97 next to the Husky station. Box 227, V0H 1V0. 495-7142; Fax: 495-6161

Like many modern communities along this route, Osoyoos was an important Native camping place for thousands of years. The name comes from the Salish word *soyoos* meaning "crossing point" or "the place two lakes come together," a reference to the natural land bridge that almost

divides Osoyoos Lake in two.

The site was a stopping point along the early Fur Brigade Trail between Fort Okanagan at the head of navigation on the Columbia River and Fort Kamloops, and later it was an important way-station for gold miners. By 1890, cattle ranchers, appreciating the natural grasslands, had taken over, and in 1906 the first orchards were planted. Like Keremeos, Osoyoos boasts the earliest fruit ripening dates in the Okanagan, and there are several roadside stands along the highway. Osoyoos Lake, claimed by locals to be the warmest

Top: The large circles in Spotted Lake are formed when mineral deposits rise to the surface as the water evaporates.

Bottom: Osoyoos lies at the southern end of the Okanagan Valley, a broad glacial trough noted for its warm summer temperatures and fruit and wine industries.

freshwater lake in Canada, has made the town a popular resort and retirement centre.

Canada's only true desert, the **"Vest Pocket Desert,"** is on the northeast side of Osoyoos Lake and accessible from both Osoyoos and Oliver. (See box.)

The **Osoyoos Museum** (495-6723) at Community Park is housed in the 1891 log cabin which was the community's first schoolhouse and later its jail and courthouse. The border crossing south of town is open 24 hours. Special events in Osoyoos include the **Cherry Fiesta**

Vest Pocket Desert

One of the more fascinating natural attractions in the south Okanagan is the "Vest Pocket Desert," Canada's only true desert and an extension of the Great Basin Desert of the United States.

This small geographical anomaly on the east side of Osoyoos Lake between Oliver and Osoyoos, part of which is a designated provincial ecological reserve,supports unique plants and wildlife. Several species are found nowhere else in the country. The desert, which receives less than 20 cm of precipitation annually, supports the largest concentration of birds of prey in the country. Canada's smallest bird, the calliope hummingbird lives here. So does the kangaroo rat, whose body is 65 percent water although it never takes a drink.

The habitat also supports Great Basin spadefoot toads, western skinks (small lizards), western painted turtles, Pacific rattlesnakes, sage thrashers, red-winged kestrels, and praying mantises. Prickly pear cactus and rabbit brush are among the plant life. Native pictographs and remains of *kekuli* can be seen as well. April and May are good times to see desert flowers.

Access from Osoyoos: Follow the signs to the Inkameep Campground (495-7279), run by the Osoyoos Indian Band. They can give permission to travel across their land to the desert. Riding stables next to the campground offer tours during the summer.

Access from Oliver: south of town turn east of Road 22, cross the Osoyoos River, drive north past the deserted Haynes Ranch, and then take a sharp right to the ecological reserve.

Days in April and the **International Waterskiing Championships** in August.

There are a variety of parks and campgrounds in the area. Many local businesses rent boats and other watersports equipment. **Haynes Point Provincial Park** (494-0321; 495-2202), two kilometres south of town and two kilometres north of the US border, is a popular place. The sandspit that makes up the park stretches three quarters of the way across Osoyoos Lake and used to be a favourite shortcut for early ranchers. Now the beachfront campsites are in high demand, making a reservation system necessary.

Okanagan Highland

East of Osoyoos, Highway 3 winds its way around several hairpin turns up **Anarchist Mountain** (summit elevation: 1233 metres). Viewpoints at the top give a panorama of Washington state and the Okanagan Valley. In the spring, the blossoming orchards are an added bonus. The mountain was named after an Irish settler, Richard Sidley, who apparently headed for the hills when his politics were branded too revolutionary for his government employers.

Highway 3 passes through the ranchland and wheat fields of the Okanagan Highland. Many old homesteads are visible from the highway and there are several guest ranches in the area that offer activities such as sheepshearing and gold panning. Tours to the floor of Rock Creek Canyon just east of the bridge, offer explanations of the flora, fauna, and history of the area. Visitors can also rent horses or four-wheel drive vehicles. (Gold Canyon Highlands Tourism Association, RR 1, Rock Creek, V0H 1Y0, 446-2455)

Just west of the bridge is the turnoff to **Mt. Baldy** (498-2262), a family-oriented ski area also accessible from Oliver in the Okanagan. The road also travels by the site of Camp McKinney, one of the earliest lode gold camps in the province. "Boundary Country," stretching from here to Christina Lake, was home to a number of rip-roaring gold mining towns beginning in the 1890s. Cascade, Anaconda, Deadwood, and Eholt are just a few of the places that once housed thousands and no longer exist.

Rock Creek is picturesquely situated in the Kettle River Valley. Prospectors discovered gold here in 1859, and the town still has the flavour of a frontier settlement. Although a massive influx of miners didn't materialize, Governor James Douglas in Victoria anticipated one and contracted 24-year-old Edgar Dewdney to build a trail from Hope to Rock Creek. The Dewdney Trail, surveyed by the Royal Engineers, was pushed through to Princeton in the fall of 1860 and to Rock Creek in the fall of 1861, just as the gold began to peter out.

Highway 33 north of here is an alternate route to Kelowna and Big White ski area along the West Kettle River. The **Kettle Valley Recreation Area,** just north of Rock Creek, is a popular spot for hikers and bikers wanting to explore the old **Kettle Valley Railway** line. The Kettle River offers good canoeing, inner tubing, and fishing.

Special events in the area include

The sole surviving example of the large frame courthouses once found throughout the Interior, this 1902 building is now used as Greenwood's city hall.

the **Bridesville Mounted Sports Day** in August and the **Rock Creek and Boundary Fall Fair** in September.

Midway

50 km (31 mi) east of Osoyoos.
Population: 700. Infocentre: at the CPR Station Museum on the highway.
Box 32, V0H 1M0.
Phone and Fax: 449-2614

"Midway between what and what?" is a common question visitors ask here. This small community is about halfway between Vancouver and the Alberta border.

In 1905, Midway was the site of a railway battle between workers of the CPR and its rival, the US-owned Great Northern Railway (GNR). The feud, based on a bitter conflict between CPR's William Van Horne and GNR's J.J. Hill, occurred when CPR workers blocked the GNR crew's attempt to lay line over CPR ground. The GNR group attacked the barricade and the CPR workers' tent camp. The CPR brought in reinforcements and began ripping up enemy track. GNR rolled out the barbed wire. Both sides

fought off the autumn chill with good stiff drinks, gained courage, and had at each other with fists, shovels, and picks. Luckily no one was killed, and the dispute was settled in court with GN winning expropriation rights over the disputed land. Eventually, however, the CPR gained control of the rail lines west to Hope.

The original station, beside the highway just west of town, houses the Infocentre and the **Kettle River Museum** (449-2614). A police museum is upstairs.

When the Oregon Treaty defined the international boundary as the 49th parallel in 1846, its authors gave no thought to the members of the Okanagan Band who lived on both sides of the border. Some say the **Entwined Trees** (Sixth Avenue and Haynes, follow signs), were joined together as saplings at that time by members of the band to symbolize the spiritual unity of the Okanagan people.

Special events include the **Midway Rodeo** held in July.

Greenwood

13 km (8 mi) east of Midway.
Population: 1000. Infocentre: 214 South Copper Street, Box 430, V0H 1J0.
445-6777; Fax: 445-6166. Seasonal

Greenwood, like most towns in this area, was created by a mining boom that began in 1886. Hidden among the trees on the mountainside are some beautiful turn-of-the-century homes. Their domes, bay windows, and verandas are reminders of the town's more prosperous days. The Infocentre has a driving/walking tour brochure describing over 40 heritage homes and buildings.

The large brick tower standing sentry at the west of town is a remnant of the BC Copper Company smelter. This once-busy facility processed ore from the Phoenix, Mother Lode, and other area mines, employing 400 men from 1901 to 1918. Visitors can tour the eerily beautiful slag piles of **Lotzkar Memorial Park**, which has been described as one of BC's great industrial ruins. (Cross the bridge at Washington Street on the west side of town.)

At one time, Greenwood had a population of 10,000 and along with Phoenix, was considered to be a city of major significance. Although almost a ghost town by 1930, 1200 Japanese-Canadians were interned here during World War II. About 350 remain in the area today.

A map of the outdoor trails around Greenwood is available at the Infocentre for touring old mining sites or backcountry hiking, cross-country skiing, fishing, and camping. The **Greenwood Museum** (445-6355), on Highway 3, is dedicated to the early mining history of the area and has information on ghost towns, including nearby Phoenix.

Jewel Lake, nine kilometres east of Greenwood, is a year-round fish-

Kettle Valley Railway

Of the many railways that appeared during the 1890s and early 1900s, the Kettle Valley Railway is the one that seems to have captured the imagination of railway buffs.

The Crowsnest Agreement of 1897 gave the CPR rights to a rail line from the east across the southern Interior to Nelson. But J.J. Hill was determined to maintain control of the area, by buying and building spur lines which connected to the US. In 1905, workers from the two sides actually came to blows over a right-of-way dispute near Midway.

Construction of the line had to overcome rugged terrain, political and physical battles, declining markets, slides, avalanches, and washouts. The two greatest railway tycoons of the century – Canadian J.J. Hill who controlled the Great Northern Railroad (US), and American William Van Horne who controlled the Canadian Pacific Railway – made the Kettle Valley Railway a personal battleground. Both were vying for control over the lucrative market in the southern Interior, brought about by the mining boom in the Kootenays.

Work finally began on the line connecting Midway to Hope in 1910. Despite a lack of skilled workers, and World War I, the railway was completed in 1916.

It was finally the internal combustion engine that spelled the end of the Kettle Valley line with the opening of the Hope-Princeton Highway in 1948. The railway closed forever in 1964.

"Golden Heights," a Grand Forks landmark, was built by travelling dentist Geoge Averill for his wife Flora in 1895. The showplace home included a carriage house, maid's quarters, a private ballroom, and Michelangelo-style gilt ceilings. The cost was $6000.

ing spot: fly-fishing for rainbow trout in summer; ice-fishing in winter. **Wilgress Lake Rest Area,** 15 kilometres east on Highway 3, is also popular with anglers.

Grand Forks

35 km (22 mi) east of Greenwood. Population: 3187. Infocentre: 7362 - 5th Street, Box 1086, V0H 1H0. 442-2833; Fax: 442-5866

Ideally situated in the "Sunshine Valley" where the Granby and Kettle rivers meet, this broad lush flatland has housed people for hundreds of years.

The huge Granby smelter once dominated the town, processing ore from Phoenix and other area mines in the mining boom of the 1890s. Agriculture and logging are now the major industries.

Visitors driving into town from the west will notice the large brick build-

ings across the highway to the south. This is the remnant of one of many Doukhobor communal settlements, the large farms created by Russian peasants who immigrated to Canada in the 1890s. Although the communal experiment was largely abandoned in 1937 when the community went bankrupt, many Doukhobor people still live in the area, maintaining to varying degrees the customs and traditions of their ancestors. The **Mountain View Doukhobor Museum** (442-8855) on Hardy Mountain Road is a good place to find out more. The Infocentre will have dates of special cultural events such as choir festivals. Typical Doukhobor singing is a capella and the harmonies are extraordinary. Those who prefer learning about a culture through its cuisine, might try the old Yale Hotel downtown, well known in the area for its traditional Russian menu, including borscht, perogis and other typical dishes.

Like Greenwood, Grand Forks has a number of turn-of-the-century homes. The Infocentre has a brochure on a self-guided walking tour. And the **Boundary Museum** (7370-5th Street, 442-3737) houses displays and information about the area's multi-layered history. The **Grand Forks Art Gallery** (7340-5th Street, 442-2211) features local and touring exhibitions and has a gift shop.

The **Grand Forks International Baseball Tournament** held here every year on Labour Day Weekend, hosts teams from as far away as Korea and Japan. Other annual events include the **River Raft Race** in June and the **Sunshine and Borscht Festival** in

July, featuring Doukohbor choirs. Access to **Phoenix Mountain Ski Area** (442-2813) is 21 kilometres west of town on Highway 3.

A backroad drive makes a loop up one side of the Granby River and down the other, through a mining and agricultural area north of Grand Forks. The Infocentre has a map of the 30-kilometre route.

Christina Lake

27 km (17 mi) east of Grand Forks. Population: 1200. Infocentre: Highway 3, PO Box 591, V0H 1F0. 447-6161; Fax: 447-6286. Seasonal

One of the warmest lakes in Canada, Christina Lake is a popular summer recreation centre with a variety of campgrounds, motels, and boat launching sites. Pictographs on the

Doukhobors

In the late 19th century, 7400 Russian peasants known as Doukhobors left their homeland looking for a new place to live. Persecuted from the time they separated from the Russian Orthodox Church in the 17th century, they were condemned as "spirit wrestlers" by an early church official. The Doukhobors adapted the name to mean "those who wrestle for and with the Holy Spirit." Their motto became "toil and peaceful life."

They espoused pacifism, rejecting church liturgy and secular government. An oral culture, their teaching was passed down through a "living Bible" of psalms and hymns.

In 1898, with the aid of novelist Leo Tolstoy and the Quakers, the Doukhobors settled on communal farms in the area now known as Saskatchewan. Although they received special dispensation regarding education and military service, in 1905 this special status was revoked.

In 1908, led by Peter "the Lordly" Verigin, 6000 Doukhobors trekked to BC, rebuilding their communal farms in the Grand Forks and Castlegar areas. But the group's troubles were far from over.

In 1924, Peter Verigin was killed when the train on which he was riding was allegedly bombed. During the 1930s, lending institutions foreclosed and the communal lands went into receivership.

In the 1950s and 1960s, government again put pressure on the Doukhobors, forcing their children into public schools. A radical sect, the Sons of Freedom, gained notoriety through protest methods that included arson and nude marches. Although less active today, Sons of Freedom members still protest what they perceive to be a corruption of the original vision.

Many Doukhobor people continue to live in the West Kootenay. The majority are affiliated with the Union of Spiritual Communities of Christ, led by Peter Verigin's grandson, John. Many use the Russian language and maintain cultural traditions such as pacifism, vegetarianism, and religious customs.

For more information, read *The Doukhobors* by George Woodcock and Ivan Avakumovic (Toronto: McClelland & Stewart, 1977).

rock cliffs at **Texas Creek Provincial Park** on the east side of the lake attest to ancient occupancy of the area. **Ole Johnson Marine Park,** accessible only by boat, has excellent fishing for kokanee, rainbow trout, whitefish, and carp.

Highway 3 (the Blueberry-Paulson), between Christina Lake and Castlegar, climbs to 1535-metre Bonanza Pass through remote forest land of the Monashee Range before dropping back down to Castlegar on Lower Arrow Lake. Old log trappers' cabins can be glimpsed occasionally along the route. Motorists often see deer and black bear.

A variety of forestry and logging roads provide good access to off-road exploration, snowmobiling, and cross-country skiing.

Nancy Greene Provincial Park

Forty-seven kilometres east of Grand Forks, Nancy Greene Lake sits at the junction with Highway 3B to Rossland. The park and the nearby recreation area to the south is named after Rossland's Nancy Greene. (See page 100.)

The park's alpine lake is a great place for a picnic and features a self-guided nature trail, used for cross-country skiing in the winter. No motorized boating is allowed on the lake. Fishing is for rainbow trout. In the summer, an Infocentre is open during the day on Highway 3.

Rossland

28 km (17mi) south of junction with Highway 3 on Highway 3B. Population: 3358. Infocentre: Junction of Highways 3B and 22. Box 26, V0G 1Y0 . 362-7722; Fax: 362-5379

Rossland experienced a major gold rush in the 1890s, and today the main street, combining the town's mining roots with its popularity as a ski destination, is reminiscent of jet-set ski resorts in Colorado – without the jet-set price tags.

During its prime, from 1887 to 1916, Rossland boasted a population of 7000, supporting 42 saloons, 17 law firms, 4 newspapers, 3 breweries, and a daily train to Spokane. It was

Deer

The most abundant big-game animals in North America, deer are members of a family of hooved ruminants (*Cervidae*) that include 40 species worldwide.

The two North American species are the white-tailed deer and the black-tailed deer. The only variety of whitetail in BC is the northwest whitetail, most commonly found in the southeastern Interior and in the Peace River district. The only variety of blacktail in the Interior is the mule deer, found as far north as the Liard River, from the Coast Mountains to the Rockies.

Deer are very common on Interior highways, and at night they can be a genuine hazard. Attracted to headlights, they will leap into the path of oncoming vehicles, causing serious accidents. If you see eyes staring at you from the side of the road, slow down, turn down your high beams, and keep alert.

BC's third largest city in 1897 and produced one-half of the province's gold output. Red Mountain's rich deposits of gold, copper, and silver contributed to the establishment of Cominco, a major Canadian mining conglomerate with a smelter in nearby Trail.

A legacy of the prosperous mining days can be found in the stained glass and other fine detail of the area's heritage homes and buildings. Built in 1897, the **Miner's Hall** (1854 Columbia Avenue, 362-7328) was the first union hall in the province. In the summer, local performers present a light opera production based on Rossland's early days Tuesday to Sunday in the hall.

To skiers, designating the road to Rossland as an "alternate" borders on blasphemy. The historic town is also the site of renowned **Red Mountain** (362-7384; BC Snow Report: 362-5500; 1-800-663-0105). Located in **Nancy Greene Provincial Recreation Area** just north of the city, the area attracts nordic and alpine skiers from around the world to its 850 metres of vertical drop and 30 groomed runs. No johnny-come-lately of the ski world, the first Canadian Downhill Championships were held here in 1897. Besides being the home slope of Nancy Greene, Red Mountain's Kerrin Lee-Gartner was a gold medalist in the 1992 winter Olympics. Other attractions of the recreation area include 2400-metre **Old Glory Mountain,** popular with hikers and berry pickers.

In the summertime, it is possible to take a look at Red Mountain from its dark underside on the **LeRoi Un-**derground **Mine Tour** (junction of Highways 22 and 3B, 362-7722). A number of old mines tunnel below the mountain, and visitors can travel 100 metres below the surface on a guided geology lesson. Although all mining activity ceased in 1929, in its heyday the 548-metre LeRoi shaft was the deepest mine in Canada, producing nearly $75 million worth of gold in its lifetime. Staff say it is the only genuine hardrock gold mine in Canada open to the public. The **Rossland Historical Museum** (362-7722), which houses the **Western Canada Ski Hall of Fame** and a tearoom are also on the site, open from mid-May to mid-September.

Rossland was a booming mining town from 1887 to 1916. Today, Red Mountain's nearby slopes attract skiers from around the world.

At celebrations such as the **Winter Carnival** in January, the **Mountain Music Festival** in June, and **Golden City Days** in September the town is never far from its roots. The **Rossland Light Opera Company** has been presenting Gilbert and Sullivan and other musicals to delighted West Kootenay audiences since the 1890s.

Billing itself the "Mountain Bike Capital of BC," Rossland sponsors the annual **Rubberhead Mountain Bike Festival** (362-7764) each September.

Trail

8 km (5 mi) east of Rossland, 27 (17 mi) km south of Castlegar on Highway 22. Population: 7730. Infocentre: 843 Rossland Avenue, V1R 4S8. 368-3144; Fax: 368-6427

Trail has been a major force in BC's economy for decades. Originally a river port shuttling supplies to miners, in 1895 it became a modest facility to process Red Mountain ore, and later home to Cominco, the largest lead-zinc smelter in the world. Today the smelter processes more than 300,000 tonnes of zinc and 135,000 tonnes of lead annually from mines around the world.

Perched high above the downtown area on the banks of the Columbia River, Cominco's 120-metre-high smokestacks dominate the landscape. The company, and thus the town, is currently suffering from unstable world markets and demands from an increasingly environmentally aware public. Daily tours of the smelter are available. (Contact the Infocentre.)

Many of the men who came to work in the mines and on the railway in the 1890s and early 1900s were Italians who stayed to work in the smelter. Trail's **Silver City Days,** held every May, emphasizes this heritage. Locals claim the city holds the only Italian archives in North America in **Cristoforo Columbo Lodge** (584 Rossland Avenue, 368-9174). Another

Nancy Greene
Gold Medal Skier

"She's great," said US ski team coach Bob Beattie of Nancy Greene in 1967. "She'll fight you to win. I've been trying to get her to defect for five years." Luckily, for Canada, the Rossland-based skier stayed home.

Described by *Sports Illustrated* in 1968 as "friendly but frank," with "the instincts of a Canadian Mountie," Greene was known for her aggressive skiing style. Her nickname was "Tiger."

Born in Ottawa, Greene learned to ski on Rossland's Red Mountain at age three, but didn't begin competitive racing until 1958 when she was 14. She skied in her first Olympics at age 16, in Squaw Valley.

In 1967 and 1968, Greene turned the skiing world on its ear by breaking the stranglehold of the French and Austrians on world championships. Among her awards, two world cups in 1967 and 1968 and Olympic gold and silver medals in 1968. She was named Canada's 1968 athlete of the year.

Greene retired from competitive skiing in 1968. She married her coach, Al Raine, and the coupled opened a hotel in the ski resort of Whistler near Vancouver.

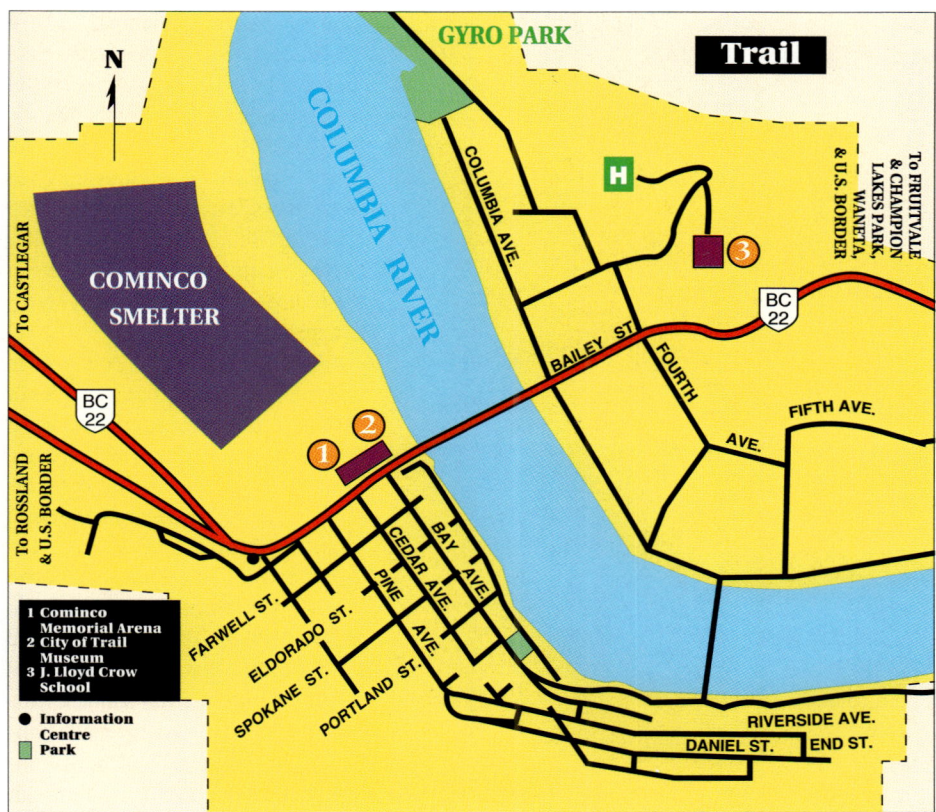

legacy is authentic Italian food – ask locally for the best pasta in town.

The **Trail Museum** (behind City Hall, 1394 Pine, 368-6484) has more information on area history. Hockey buffs might want to search out memorabilia from the Trail Smoke Eaters' world championships in the 1950s and 1960s. **Gyro Park** in East Trail features beautiful gardens and a three-kilometre trail along the east bank of the Columbia River.

Guided tours are offered at Waneta and Seven Mile dams on the nearby Pend'Oreille (pon-dor-eye) River on Highway 22A southeast of Trail. (Contact the Infocentre.)

Waneta's power plant has a capacity of 480,000 horsepower.

Champion Lakes Provincial Park is 12 kilometres east of Trail on Highway 3B. Canoeing, fishing for rainbow trout, and hiking are popular on and around the 1408-hectare park's three small lakes. A summer interpretive service offers information about the park's unique mixed ecological zones. No power boats are allowed.

Alternate Route: Pend'Oreille River

The road along the Pend'Oreille River between Waneta and Nelway is an

Top: This scale model of a 20-metre-high Picasso sculpture overlooks the Columbia River in downtown Trail.

Bottom: Built as a small facility in 1895, the Cominco smelter in Trail now employs about 2500 workers.

excellent wildlife-viewing corridor. Wildflowers, deer, songbirds, eagles, turkey vultures, and osprey can be seen in season. The area is the only habitat for praying mantis in the province outside the Okanagan. (Take the road past Seven Mile Dam.)

Castlegar

94 km (56 mi) east of Grand Forks on Highway 3. Population: 6400.
Infocentre: 1995-6th Avenue, V1N 4B7, next to the Recreation Centre.
365-6313; Fax: 365-5778

Castlegar, like Trail, is primarily an industrial town. But its strategic loca-

tion on a plateau at the confluence of the Kootenay and Columbia Rivers has made it an important settlement site for centuries.

The earliest residents were the Interior Salish, followed by fur traders, miners, farmers, and orchardists. The Columbia River and Arrow Lakes were an early transportation route to Revelstoke for rivermen and sternwheelers.

As in Grand Forks, Doukhobors settled in the nearby communities of Brilliant and Ootischenia in 1904. Here again, the remains of their communal farms and abandoned orchards can still be seen from the highway. The group's spiritual leader, Peter "the Lordly" Verigin, is buried here. **Verigin's Tomb**, on the mountainside above Brilliant, is a local attraction. The **Doukhobor Village Museum** (365-6622) just across from the airport on Highway 3 re-creates a typical communal farm and houses interesting displays and photographs.

Zuckerberg Island was the retreat of a Russian mystic, Alexander Zuckerberg, who came to Castlegar in 1931 to teach Doukhobor children. At the confluence of the Columbia and Kootenay rivers, for 3500 years the island was a camp for Interior Salish, who used to fish for Pacific salmon. Today, there are trails around the two-hectare island, a suspension bridge, and a small museum in the replica of a Russian Orthodox chapel that Zuckerberg built. (Go north toward downtown on Highway 22, turn east at the RCMP station on 9th Street, and follow the signs to the parking lot at 7th Avenue.)

The **Keenleyside Dam,** just north

of town, was built as part of the 1964 Columbia River Treaty, an international agreement between Canada and the US. The controversial document legislated the flooding of the Arrow Lakes for flood control and generation of hydroelectric power.

The **Railway Station CPR Museum** (400 13th Street, 365-6440) was the focal point of Castlegar from 1902 until daily passenger service was discontinued in 1949. The museum was opened in 1988 and continues to expand its displays.

Special cultural events in Castlegar include a **Doukhobor Choir Festival** and the **Castlegar Sunfest** held every June. The **National Exhibition Centre** (365-3337), next to the Doukhobor Village Museum, offers local and touring exhibits of art, history, and science that are changed monthly. A small gift shop features work of local artists.

Castlegar bills itself as the "gateway to the Arrow Lakes" and access to almost 100 kilometres of freshwater fishing and boating. A wildlife-viewing corridor encompasses the area on both sides of Lower Arrow Lake from Castlegar north, including **Syringa Creek Provincial Park** across the lake to the northeast. Rocky Mountain bighorn sheep, elk, white-tailed and mule deer, mountain goats, and a number of bird species inhabit the area.

Salmo

43 km (27 mi) east of Castlegar on Highway 3. Population: 1014. Infocentre: 6919 Highway 6, PO Box 251, V0G 1Z0. 357-9332; Fax: 357-9633. Seasonal

Highway 3 continues east from Castlegar to the village of Salmo with its heritage buildings and stonework

Alexander Zuckerberg built a replica of a Russian chapel on his island retreat in the 1930s. Peter Verigin had invited him to the Castlegar area to teach Doukhobor children.

No longer in use, the Brilliant Bridge is a hand-poured concrete structure, built in the early 1900s by the Doukhobor community. It crosses the Kootenay River.

murals. From the west, travellers pass a small ski hill and the "oldest telephone booth in the world."

The Salmo River, which follows Highway 3 south of here, was known as the Salmon River long before the days of the hydroelectric dams and downstream power benefits. Part

of the Columbia system, today the river has no salmon, but still hosts Dolly Varden trout.

On Sheep Creek Road, eight kilometres south of town, lie the ruins of several old mines with typically evocative names: Kootenay Bell, Reno, and Goldbelt. This and other secondary roads in the area are good for wildlife viewing and cross-country skiing.

The Kootenay Skyway

The route between Salmo and Creston over the Selkirk Range is known as the Kootenay Skyway – it's the highest paved highway in Canada. When the weather is fine, the drive over 1774-metre high Kootenay Pass is spectacular. Snow, avalanches, and limited visibility contribute to frequent closures during the winter. The alternate route

Columbia River Facts

• 2044 kilometres long, 748 kilometres in Canada
• Headwaters: Columbia Lake near Canal Flats in East Kootenay.
• Big Bend Highway, opened in 1940, followed the Columbia River between Revelstoke and Golden. It was the shortest highway route through the Rockies until the Rogers Pass portion of the Trans-Canada Highway opened in 1962.
• Major tributaries include the Kootenay and Okanagan rivers in BC and the Snake River in the US.
• Its drainage basin is 155,000 square kilometres, one of the largest in North America. Over 100,000 square kilometres are in BC.

• Spanish explorers originally named it Rio de San Roque, but it was renamed by early explorer Captain Robert Gray after his ship *Columbia*.
• David Thompson was the first to chart the entire river, arriving at its mouth in 1811.
• The Hudson's Bay Company built a fort at Fort Vancouver on the Columbia (now Vancouver, Washington) in 1824-25, creating the major transportation route from the south into the Interior.
• The Columbia River Treaty with the US was signed in 1964. The controversial terms included a one-time payment for power benefits of $254 million (US). The power benefits are up for renegotiation in 1994.
• The treaty resulted in Duncan Dam (1967) on Kootenay Lake, Hugh Keenleyside Dam (1968) on Lower Arrow Lake, Mica Dam (1973) on the Big Bend, and Revelstoke Dam (1984).

is through Nelson and Highway 3A. Listen to the radio or ask locally for current information.

At the summit, enjoy the pure mountain air at **Stagleap Provincial Park** and picnic at picturesque Bridal Lake. A transition between ecological zones is noticeable. The west side of the Selkirks tends to be more like the coast – wetter, the vegetation thicker – but moving east, the drier vegetation of pine and spruce takes over.

Creston is in the Mountain Time Zone. Sometimes. People in Creston don't like to interfere with time, so in the summer, Creston is on Pacific Time. (See Reference section.)

Creston

83 km (52 mi) east of Salmo. Population: 3929. Infocentre: 1711 Canyon Street, Box 268, V0B 1G0. 428-4342; Fax: 428-9411

Creston is an agricultural and logging community located on a rich floodplain south of Kootenay Lake.

One of the main attractions in the "Valley of the Swans" is the **Creston Valley Wildlife Centre** (428-3260), located on the west side of Creston and south of Highway 3. The Centre is a 6800-hectare project managed by federal, provincial, and private agencies to conserve vital wetlands for migratory waterfowl. Over 240 bird species, including swan, osprey, and hummingbirds, make this a birdwatcher's paradise. On guided canoe tours or self-guided nature walks visitors may glimpse deer, elk, coyote, and moose. Although the interpretive centre is open in the summer only, the site can be toured in

Western Red Cedar
Arbor vitae

There are no true cedars native to North America. The species here are *Arbor vitae*, which means "tree of life."

A mainstay of BC's lumber industry, cedar, while lightweight and brittle, is easy to split, and resistant to rot. It is valued for shingles, posts, and exterior siding.

The tree's tiny scale-like leaves form flat, lacy sprays that are highly aromatic. The cones bear up to 400,000 seeds per pound, making it one of the most prodigious seed producers of the evergreen species.

Mature trees, with their tapered trunks, and shallow, widespread root systems, can reach heights of 60 metres and measure three to four metres in diameter. The largest red cedars are believed to be about 1000 years old.

Native cultures, particularly in the northwest, relied heavily on cedar for housing, totem poles, decorative carving, and dugout canoes. The bark on mature trees was peeled off in strips that were used to make clothing, floor coverings, and baskets.

winter by snowshoe or cross-country ski.

The Kutenai people were the earliest residents, and fur trader David Thompson was likely one of the first white men to visit the area in the early 1800s. Unlike many West Kootenay towns, Creston did not begin with the discovery of a precious metal. It was put on the map by the extension of the Dewdney Trail to the mining town of Wild Horse further east, where gold was discovered in the 1860s. The coming of the CPR and Great Northern lines, and the paddlewheelers that sallied forth from here to communities like Ainsworth and Kaslo made Creston a transportation centre.

Logging was a vital part of the early economy, but no one thought to plant fruit trees on these rich lands until 1908. Today, the fruits, vegetables, and honey sold at roadside stands are a highly valued part of the economy. Creston's two grain elevators are the only ones found in the southern interior.

The **Creston Valley Museum** (219 Devon Road, 428-9262) features the history of agriculture in the Creston Valley as well as a logging display. One interesting artifact is a Kutenai canoe. Its unusual design suggests a link with indigenous people in Russia. Visitors can tour local businesses like the Columbia Brewery, Mountain Stream Trout Farm, and the Kootenay Candle Factory. (Contact the Infocentre.)

Annual events include the **Blossom Festival** on Victoria Day weekend in May and the **Fall Fair** in September.

The Kootenay River is popular with paddlers in the Kootenays. It begins east of here in the Rocky Mountains, heads south into the US, and then comes back into Canada south of Creston. The one- to three-day trip north along the Kootenay River from the US border to Kootenay Lake is a favourite route. Kootenay Lake is a popular recreation area for boating and fishing.

Moyie River

About 36 kilometres east of Creston, Highway 3 intersects with Highway 95. A 24-hour border crossing is 11 kilometres south at **Kingsgate**.

For most of the route to Cranbrook, Highway 3 crosses back and forth over the Moyie River. Forty kilometres east of Creston is a tiny town with the unlikely name of **Yahk,** a booming lumber and railway centre until the 1930s. Some experts say the town got its name from *yaak,* a Kutenai word meaning "bow" referring to the shape of the Kootenay River. Others suggest it comes from the word for arrow, *a'ak.* The town's first hotel, built in 1912, still operates today, and a small museum offers local history. It is here that you can buy the internationally cherished T-shirt, "I've been to Yahk and back."

East of Yahk travellers are definitely in the Mountain Time Zone – Daylight or Standard depends on the time of year.

Moyie, 34 kilometres east of Yahk, is another Kootenay town that had its glory days in the 1890s. Just west of town on Highway 3 travellers can still see remains of the St. Eugene Mine. In 1907 it was the largest lead-silver mine in Canada and employed 400

men. Establishment of the mine in-fluenced the CPR's decision to build its Crownest line across the southern Interior. St. Eugene's consolidation with two Red Mountain mines helped establish Cominco's dominance over the mining industry in this area.

The original discovery was made by a Kutenai man, Pierre, who was awarded a house, cattle, farm imple-ments, and five dollars a month for his share of the claim. Father Coccola, one of Pierre's partners, built churches at Moyie and St. Eugene Mission near Cranbrook with the $12,000 he received. Between 1898 and 1911, the mine produced $11 million worth of ore.

Paddlewheelers once travelled the waters of Moyie Lake. Today travel-lers can stop for a swim, fish for Dolly Varden, kokanee, eastern or brook trout, or examine the intermingling of the dry- and wet-zone ecology in **Moyie Lake Provincial Park** at the north end of the lake. Popular with locals, the park also offers interpre-tive services and hiking trails. David Thompson passed this way looking for the mouth of Columbia River in 1808, and was almost turned back by the swollen waters of the Moyie River at spring runoff.

If you've managed to travel this far through mining country without a touch of gold fever, more power to you. Those who are falling prey to the stories of undiscovered mother lodes, will be glad to hear that rumors still exist of isolated pay streaks in the Moyie River. Gold panners might also try the Negro and Palmer Bar creeks, both tributaries of the Moyie. Ask lo-cally for directions, regulations, and hot tips.

Left: Moyie was thriving in 1907 with 400 people employed at its St. Eugene Mine. Today this quiet town still offers reminders of the days when it was home to the largest lead-zinc mine in the country.

Right: Moyie's original firehall is still standing.

The restored St. Eugene Church near Cranbrook was built from the sale of the St. Eugene Mine claim in the 1890s.

Cranbrook

106 km (66 mi) east of Creston. Population: 15,160. Infocentre: on 22nd Street North, off Highway 3/95, south of the city centre. Box 84, V1C 4H6. 426-5914; Fax: 426-3873

Located in a spectacular setting with the Rockies and Purcells looming in the background, Cranbrook was put on the map when developer/politician Colonel James Baker convinced the CPR to build its Crowsnest line through Cranbrook instead of Fort Steele. Since the Colonel owned a great deal of land in the area, it is likely the CPR decision made him a very happy man.

Not surprisingly, one of Cranbrook's major attractions is the **Cranbrook Railway Museum** (489-3918). The museum currently displays nine carefully restored cars of the Trans-Canada Limited, CPR's luxury "flagtrain" and the Elko Station (ca.1900). Built in 1929, the train served the Montreal to Vancouver route and was known for elegant touches such as exotic inlaid walnut and mahogany panelling.

The museum is constantly adding to its collection. Its directors say it will become the Canadian Museum of Rail Travel in 1998, with the largest collection of its kind in the world. Located downtown at 1 Van Horne Street, the junction of Highway 3/95 and Baker Street, visitors can take the tour and then have tea in the restored dining car. Those lucky enough to be in town in late November and early December, should ask about the formal Christmas dinner galas hosted by the museum.

Some of Cranbrook's finest restored residential and commercial buildings are on the self-guided her-

itage tour, including Colonel Baker's home. Maps and information are available at the Infocentre and the Railway Museum.

Nine kilometres north of town on Highway 95A, at the St. Mary's Reserve (489-2464) on the old airport road, **St. Eugene Mission Church** is the finest Gothic-style mission church in the province. It features priceless hand-painted Italian stained-glass windows, scalloped louvres, pinnacles, and buttresses. Restored in 1983 by the St. Mary's Band and the East Kootenay Historical Society, the church was built in the 1890s with Father Coccola's share

of the sale of the St. Eugene mining claim at Moyie. Native crafts are also for sale at the reserve.

The **Cranbrook Wildlife Museum** (426-5914) in the Chamber of Commerce building (at the Infocentre) displays wildlife species found in the East Kootenay. Rockhounds will be interested in the 500-million-year-old trilobite beds nearby. Ask at the Cranbrook Infocentre for directions and regulations.

Boaters and anglers can enjoy over 100 lakes within 80-kilometres of Cranbook. Special events include **Sam Steele Days** on the third weekend in June which includes a pa-

rade, loggers' sports, and a truck rodeo, and the **Wycliffe Rodeo** in early August.

Just beyond Cranbrook, Highway 95A heads northwest to Kimberley while Highway 93/95 goes to Fort Steele.

Wardner

Nearly nine million fish are caught in BC's freshwater lakes and streams each year. At the once-busy lumbering town of Wardner, 32 kilometres southeast of Cranbrook, visitors to the **Kootenay Trout Hatchery** (429-3214) find out where those fish come from. This facility, the second largest in the BC Fish and Wildlife Branch's operation, raises six million rainbow, brook, and cutthroat trout every year. Their extensive interpretive area, which includes aquariums, educational models and displays, and self-

Top: Classic train cars are being restored at the Cranbrook Railway Museum.

Bottom: Cranbrook owes its prosperity to the railway. When the CPR put its Crowsnest line through the southern Interior in 1897,

Colonel James Baker was instrumental in having the line bypass rival Fort Steele in favour of his town.

guided tours, could very well tell one everything one ever wanted to know about trout.

Lake Koocanusa

Just north of Wardner, the Kootenay River enters the Lake Koocanusa reservoir, which drains south into Montana. The 128-kilometre-long lake was created in 1972 when Libby Dam was built in Montana. Although the word "Koocanusa" may seem like some exotic Native word, in fact it is a merging of "Kootenay," "Canada," and "USA." The lake offers excellent fishing and paddling, and is off limits to power boats.

Kikomum Creek Provincial Park on the east side of the lake and accessible from Jaffray or Elko, connects several small lakes with paved roads making it ideal for cycling. Painted turtles (see box), heron rookeries, and fish-spawning channels are among the other attractions.

From Elko, Highway 93 heads 38 kilometres south to the border crossing of Roosville, open 24 hours a day.

Fernie

87 km (54 mi) east of Cranbrook. Population: 5000. Infocentre: Highway 3 and Dicken Road, PO Box 747, V0B 1M0. 423-6868; Fax: 423-3811

Originally called Coal Creek, Fernie was established in 1898 with the construction of the CPR's Crowsnest route. The town has had a lot of bad luck over the years, which some trace to a curse set on founding father William Fernie.

The story goes that Mr. Fernie met a group of Natives during a prospect-

ing trip and noticed the chief's daughter was wearing a necklace of coal. In exchange for information about the source of the coal, Fernie agreed to marry the young woman. However, once he found out where the coal deposits were, he backed out, and the woman's mother put a curse on the valley.

It may be that some of Fernie's fluctuating fate has had more to do with world markets than bad karma, but among the disasters were an

Western Painted Turtle
Chrysemys picta belli

Commonly seen in the southern Interior, the western painted turtle is always near water, often basking for hours on floating logs. Olive green, with yellow and red markings, the shells can measure up to 25 centimetres.

Turtles eat both plants and animals. Food includes trout fry, tadpoles, water snails, insects, water lillies, and bullrushes.

Nest-building begins in May usually on a southern slope close to water. The female turtle digs a hole with her rear legs, laying about a dozen small (two centimetre) eggs. The young hatch in the fall and stay in the nest until the spring.

explosion in 1902 that killed 128 miners and a fire in 1908 that destroyed 1000 buildings and claimed 10 lives. A flood in 1916 and several mining accidents followed.

In 1964, at the invitation of local citizens, the chief of the Tobacco Plains Band lifted the curse in a special ceremony. It is also worth noting that when Mr. Fernie retired to Victoria in 1906, he remained a bachelor and devoted his life to philanthropic pursuits. Curse or no curse, events like the development of new coalfields in the northeastern part of BC and unstable world prices continue to challenge Fernie's residents.

An interesting architectural feature of the town is the atypical brick and stone, designated as building materials after the fire of 1908. The courthouse, the Leroux Mansion, and the Holy Family Catholic Church are examples of this late-Edwardian style. The Infocentre has a walking-tour brochure. The **Fernie Historical Museum** (corner of Fifth Avenue and Fifth Street, 423-6512) and the **Fernie City Hall Museum** both have displays of early history.

Outdoor enthusiasts have several choices for recreation near Fernie. **Mount Fernie Provincial Park**, three kilometres west of town, offers wildlife viewing, old-growth cedar, diverse vegetation, Lizard Creek waterfall, and places to look for fossils. For alpine and nordic skiers, **Fernie Snow Valley Ski Area** (423-4655) is 14 kilometres west of town, with 730 metres of vertical drop and a season that stretches from November to April.

Rafting companies offer day trips on nearby Elk and Bull rivers.

Sparwood

32 km (20 mi) east of Fernie. Population: 4600. Infocentre: Highway 3 and Aspen Drive, PO Box 1448, V0B 2G0. 425-2423; Fax: 425-7130

Sparwood is a relatively new town, created in 1966 to replace the turn-of-the-century mining communities of Natal, Michel, and Middleton. Billing itself as "the Clean Coal Capital of the World," it sits atop one of the largest soft coal deposits in North America. Sparwood has the largest open-pit mine in Canada (annual output of 5.1 million tonnes) and the world's largest dump truck, the 350-tonne Terex Titan. Be sure to take a look at Dan Sawatzky's giant murals on several downtown buildings. The Chemainus artist created the murals from photos of miners who worked in the area 60 years ago.

The Flathead Valley and the **Akamina-Kishinena Recreation Area** is accessible via secondary road 10 kilometres east of Sparwood on Highway 3. This is isolated wilderness that promises very good wildlife viewing. Grizzly bear, black bear, elk, moose, and deer are among the species. It borders on Alberta's Waterton Lakes National Park to the east and Montana's Glacier National Park to the south. Conditions are primitive and there are no services. Visitors should be well prepared.

Side trip: Elkford

35 km (22 mi) north of Sparwood on Highway 43. Population: 3300. Infocentre: intersection of Highway 43 and Michel Road, PO Box 220, V0B 1H0. 865-4362; Fax: 865-2442

A coal town incorporated in 1970, Elkford bills itself as the "Wilderness Capital of British Columbia." One of largest bighorn sheep populations and the highest concentration of elk in North America live in the area. The Elk River is noted for trout fishing. Elkford has a 40-kilometre interpretive trail system close to town with a variety of hikes and walks. In winter, cross-country skiiers use the same trails. **Wapiti Ski Hill** (865-2020) is the local downhill destination.

The town is also gateway to Elk Lakes Provincial Park, an easily accessible subalpine wilderness in the middle of the Rockies. The trip down the Elk River from Elkford to Elko is a popular outing for experienced paddlers.

Outdoor enthusiasts are concerned about industrial development in the valley. Although mining companies are now required to replant strip-mined areas, at certain elevations it takes a thousand years to rebuild 2.5 centimetres of topsoil naturally.

Alberta Border

The Crowsnest Pass (1357 metres) and the Alberta border are only 19 kilometres east of Sparwood. The Crowsnest Pass is a centuries-old Kutenai route through the Rockies. The Kutenai were closely aligned with the Plains Natives and made the trip through the pass three times a year to hunt buffalo on the Prairies. The Native word for the large rounded mountain in the pass is *Kah, ka-coo-wut-tskis-lun* and means "nesting place of the raven." Another story says the pass got its name when Blackfoot warriors massacred a group of Crow camped here.

Elk
Cervus elaphus

Also known as wapiti, elk are the most highly evolved of the old world deer, crossing over from Siberia during the last Ice Age.

Half again as large as an adult deer, a bull elk stands 1.5 metres tall at the shoulder. *Wapiti* means "white rump" in Shawnee, a marking which helps in identification. The rest of the coat is light brown with darker hair on the neck and legs and a shaggy fringe on the underside of the neck.

Elk are social animals, tending toward open terrain. Females spend most of the year in the valley bottoms with offspring and immature males, sometimes forming herds of 50 or more.

The mating ritual begins in late summer. The males try to attract as many females as possible, and the locking of antlers is a major part of the show. (Elk in rut are very unpredictable; observers should keep their distance.) Gestation is long, up to 240 days. Calves are born in June.

The male's antlers begin to grow in April. The number of points on an antler rack can indicate the age of the animal. Six points, the usual maximum, means the animal is at least four years old. The rack of a mature animal may be as long as 1.5 metres, and as wide as 1.8 metres.

Coquihalla-Nicola

The Nicola Valley boasts some of the finest inland fishing in the country.

With the opening of the Coquihalla Highway (Highway 5) in 1986, the accessibility of this largely ignored area has been greatly increased. The controlled-access highway, with its 110-kilometre-per-hour speed limit, puts Merritt just three hours from Vancouver. Peachland is another hour east over the Okanagan Connector (Highway 97C), and Kamloops another 40 minutes north.

The rolling grasslands and subalpine forests are appealing, however, and travellers will have to steel their hearts to make that kind of time. No hustle and bustle here, the area's quiet allure lies in its lakes, its remoteness, and its fascinating history.

Stretching from the Cascade Mountains in the south to the Thompson Plateau in the north, the region includes a variety of landscapes from coastal rain forest and subalpine slopes to rolling grasslands. On the map, it is roughly the area east and south of Highway 1, west of the Okanagan Valley, and north of Highway 3.

Coquihalla Highway

What with budget overruns and complicated bookkeeping, it is not clear exactly how much this superhighway cost to build, but one estimate puts the 300-kilometre route at over $600 million dollars. The first phase between Hope and Merritt, completed in 1986, has 46 bridges and used more than 20,000 tonnes of steel. The second phase, between Merritt and Kamloops, has only eight bridges, but over 450,000 cubic metres of earth were displaced. During the building of the third "Okanagan Connector" phase, opened in 1990, over 700,000 cubic metres of rock had to be moved. Cost estimates near the 1728-metre-high Pennask Summit on this portion were as high as $3.5 million per kilometre – creating a genuine million-dollar view.

The Coquihalla Highway starts just east of Hope at the junction with Highway 3. The Kawkawa Lake exit is an alternate route to the Othello-Quintette Tunnels, abandoned by the **Kettle Valley Railway** when it closed in 1962. (See Hope.) Several signs displaying a picture of a railway engine with names like Lear, Falstaff, and Juliet appear along the route. These denote former sidings of the Kettle Valley Railway, so named by Andrew McCulloch. As well as being the engineering genius who designed the route, McCulloch had a passion for Shakespeare.

Just before the Coquihalla Summit (elevation: 1244 metres), the massive sheer granite face of **Zopkios Ridge** emerges – truly a magnificent sight. At the toll booth just east of here, cars and recreational vehicles continuing north pay $10.

Merritt

115 km (71 mi) north of Hope on Highway 5, 90 km (56 mi) north of Princeton on Highway 5A. Population: 6010. Infocentre: junction of Highway 5 and 97C, Box 189, V0K 2B0. 378-2281

It is thought that the area's first non-Native resident was a Mexican packer, Juan Garcia, who stopped here with a herd of sheep and cattle on his way to the Cariboo in 1860. Other settlers followed, exploiting the natural grasslands, and developing a ranching industry. When the CPR was built in the 1880s, it was a double blessing to the area – Merritt had an eager market for its coal, and a way to transport its beef to markets farther afield.

Downtown, the **Coldstream Hotel** with its domed copper roof and old-time veranda was a centre for the prosperous and thriving community. "Serving the thirsty since 1908" is the proud motto etched in the sidewalk in front of the hotel today. Built by Murdoch McIntyre for the princely sum of $6000, the hotel was *the* place for honeymooners (bed and breakfast, $1.50). Its rooms with attached

The ranching and logging town of Merritt sits at the hub of several highways. The opening of the Coquihalla Highway in 1986 made it easily accessible from the Lower Mainland, the Okanagan, and Kamloops.

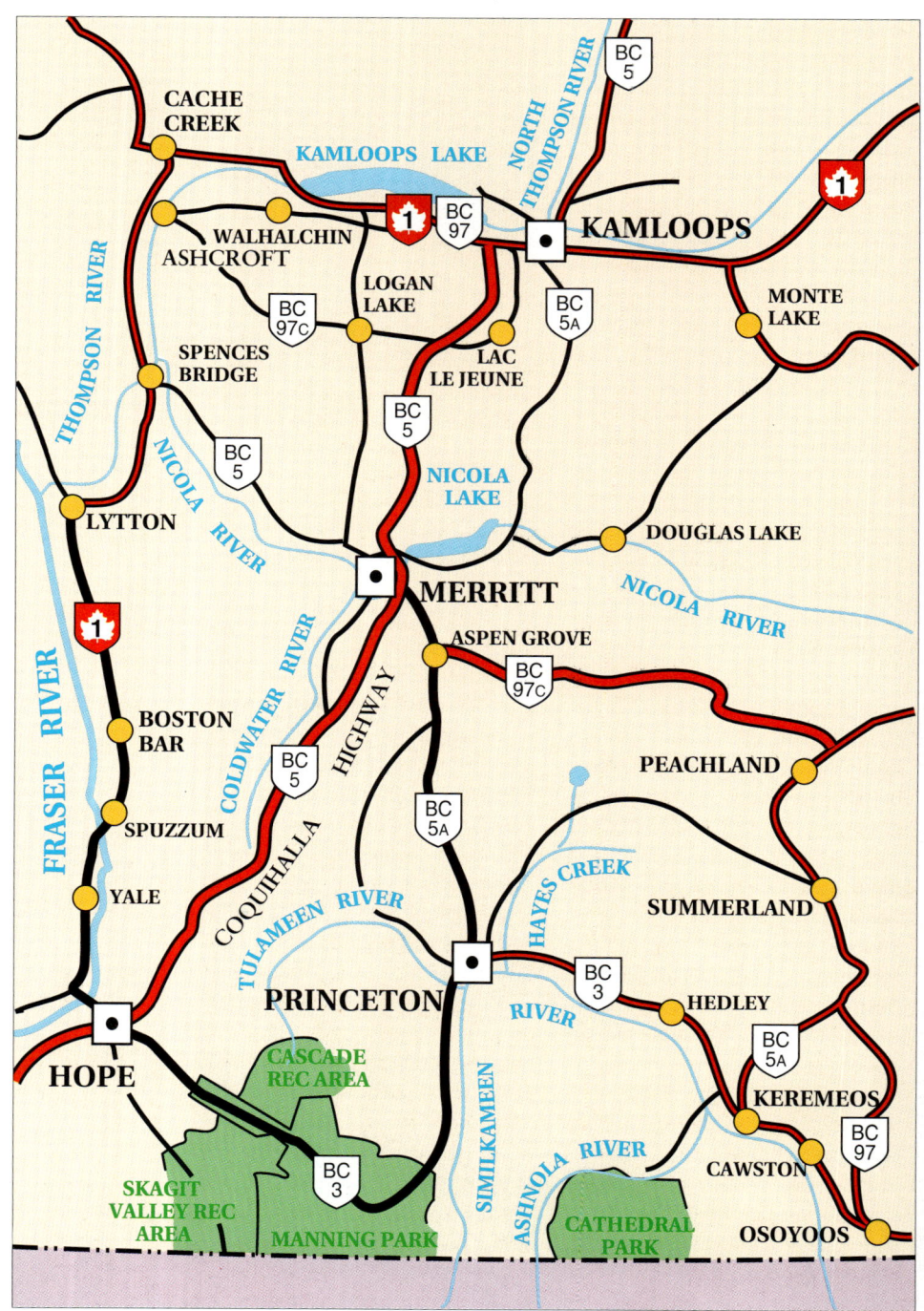

bathrooms made the Coldstream one of the finest establishments in the Interior.

The good times didn't last, however. In 1930, Nicola Pine Mills went bankrupt, and so did the town, remaining in receivership until 1952. The coal mine produced its last lumps in 1946, but the traditional industries of logging, mining, and ranching, along with tourism, are supporting the region again. The **Nicola Valley Museum and Archives** (2202 Jackson Avenue, 378-4145) has displays featuring early mining and ranching history.

Special events include the **Merritt High School Rodeo** in June, the **Lindley Rodeo** in Merritt in July, the **Merritt Horse Show** in August, and the **Fall Fair and Rodeo** on Labour Day Weekend.

Merritt is the hub of activity for the region, with highways spreading out from its centre like spokes on a wheel. Senior citizens volunteer at the Infocentre and they have a wealth of information about places to see, local history, and where to catch the biggest fish. There is an extensive forestry display on the mezzanine. A short nature walk, the **Godey Creek Trail,** starts just behind the centre.

Main outdoor recreation activities are fishing, horseback riding, cross-country skiing, rockhounding, and hiking. Visitors can pursue these activities on their own or at one of the many area resorts and guest ranches. (Consult the Reference section, the Merritt Infocentre, or *British Columbia Accommodations.)*

Nicola Lake Area

The earliest inhabitants of the Nicola Valley were probably the Athapascans who were eventually pushed out or absorbed by the Okanagan and Thompson Salish people. Although initially nomads, about 3000 years ago they became more settled, overwintering in *kekuli* or pit houses around Merritt, Nicola Lake, and Douglas Lake. It is thought that the place name Nicola, is after Chief N'Kwala, who was a Native leader for many years.

Visitors to **Monck Lake Provincial Park** on Nicola Lake can find pictographs and other archeological sites. The park is also a favourite spot for water sports of all kinds, including wind surfing.

In the old town of Nicola, **Murray Church**, built in 1876, is one of the

Heritage Hiking

During the first half of the nineteenth century, fur brigades – great clanging processions of men, women, and horses – carried supplies and furs in and out of the Interior. In 1846, the Hudson's Bay Company established the first fur brigade trail to lie entirely within the province, through the Cascades and into the Nicola Valley. Some of the original blaze marks still exist and historians and hikers are working to identify and re-establish those early trails.

The **Kettle Valley Railway** operated from 1916 to 1962 between Midway and Hope. Outdoor enthusiasts are hoping to claim all of its 500 kilometres of abandoned railroad bed as a hiking and biking trail. At present, only portions are dedicated for this use. Infocentres at Merritt, Princeton, and Hope will have updates on the status of these trails. Or write the Okanagan Similkameen Parks Society, PO Box 787, Summerland, BC V0H 1Z0.

Rodeos are popular events in the Nicola Valley. Cowboys have been working area ranches since the 1860s.

oldest in the province, and, locals claim, one of the most photographed structures in British Columbia. On Highway 5A toward Kamloops, the beautiful old **Quilchena Hotel** (378-2611), built in 1908, is still open for business. Ahead of its time, the hotel implemented a drinking-and-driving policy well before breathalyzers. The test was simple. There were no chairs in the bar – if a cowboy fell over, he'd had too much. Lunch may be seasoned with more stories of early life in this ranching area.

Along the Douglas Lake Road not far from Quilchena, is the 200,000-hectare **Douglas Lake Cattle Ranch** (350-3344), the largest working cattle ranch in Canada. The land was originally homesteaded in 1872, but the company expanded with the construction of the CPR in the 1880s.

The railway no doubt made early cowboys like Dan McGinnis very happy. McGinnis' job was to drive about 150 head of cattle from Douglas Lake to Hope twice a month, on a road so narrow in places that the animals could barely walk single file. "On one side rose a wall of rock, and on the other side was a sheer drop of 300 feet," the 19-year-old cowboy wrote in 1886. "I lost as many as eleven steers in one trip."

Currently running up to 17,000 head of cattle in the summer, the ranch offers tours of the spread via four-wheel drive jeep and has several fishing resorts on its property.

Around Douglas Lake visitors can also notice the path of retreating glaciers. Erratics, eskers, drumlins, moraines, and the north-south direction of the lakes were created by the moving and melting ice sheets.

Over 150 small lakes dot the terrain, making the Nicola Valley the preferred destination for 50 percent of BC's freshwater anglers. "A lake a day as long as you stay" is the local promise. Many experts feel the best fishing is in the area roughly east of Highway 5 and north of the Coquihalla Connector. Dolly Varden, kokanee, rainbow, mountain whitefish, and freshwater ling cod are among the major species in area lakes and streams.

The Nicola, Coquihalla, and Coldwater rivers are also important salmon-spawning tributaries of the Fraser River system.

A seasonal road south of Quilchena travels to 1450-metre- high **Pennask Lake Provincial Park,** highly recommended for rainbow trout fishing. The Pennask Lake trout are considered so superior that their eggs are used for the provincial trout-stocking program. Other good lakes along the road are Hope, Roche, and Chataway. Ice-fishing is a popular wintertime activity.

Special events include the **Spahomin Wild Horse Roundup** at Douglas Lake in June and the **Spahomin Rodeo** at Quilchena in August.

Logan Lake

42 km (26 mi) north of Merritt. Population: 2130. Infocentre: PO Box 1060, V0K 1W0, 523-6322; Fax: 523-6983. Seasonal

Lava from early volcanos, fossils found pressed into the sedimentary rock, and coal beds are part of the geology of the Coquihalla region. Besides coal, metals such as gold, silver,

lead, iron, zinc, copper, and molybdenum have traditionally been mined. The mother lode that supports metal mining is the Guichon Creek Batholith, 200-million-year old granitic rocks that stretch from Merritt to Cache Creek. The batholith contains some of the largest deposits of low-grade copper and molybdenum in the province.

Visitors can tour one of the largest open-pit mines in the world, **Highland Valley Copper** (575-2443), near Logan Lake. The mine employs almost 1200 local residents. In 1991, it processed an average of 126,000 tonnes of ore per day.

Murray Church was built in 1876 at Upper Nicola. The earliest settlers in the valley arrived in 1867.

The above reward will be paid for the arrest and detention of **WILLIAM (Bill) MINER**, alias Edwards, who escaped from the New Westminster Penitentiary, at New Westminster, British Columbia, on the 8th August, 1907, where he was serving a life sentence for train robbery.

DESCRIPTION:

Age 65 years; 138 pounds; 5 feet 8½ inches; dark complexion; brown eyes; grey hair; slight build; face spotted; tattoo base of left thumb, star and bullet girl right forearm; wrist joint-bones large; moles centre of breast, 1 under left breast, 1 on right shoulder, 1 on left shoulder-blade; discoloration left buttock; scars on left shin, right leg, inside, at knee, 2 on neck.

Communicate with

LT.-COL. A. P. SHERWOOD,
Commissioner Dominion Police.

Bill Miner
"The Grey Fox"

Bill Miner, "the master criminal of the American West," began his career in 1859 as a 16-year-old searching for fortune in California. Broke, Miner and three companions robbed a stagecoach, netting $75,000. Bill was hooked.

Credited with originating the expression "Hands up!" Miner spent the next 55 years alternately robbing stagecoaches and serving time in prison. His victims always described him as a gentleman – soft-spoken, courteous, apologetic. To the slew of police and Pinkerton men who pursued him, the elusive Miner became known as "the Grey Fox."

After 34 years in and out of San Quentin, Miner was released in 1903, aged 60. Bungling his first attempt at train robbery, he "retired" to BC's Nicola Valley as grey-haired, mild-mannered George Edwards. During this time, several train robberies occurred in the Pacific Northwest. All the while genial George Edwards charmed small children and grandmothers in the Nicola Valley.

On May 8, 1906, Miner's luck ran out. He robbed the wrong CPR train near Kamloops and found only $15. While escaping, Miner and his companions lost their mounts. Confronted by the police, the engaging George Edwards had almost convinced his accusers of their mistake when one of his companions panicked and opened fire. The photograph above shows Miner on his way to the Kamloops jail.

Miner was sentenced to life imprisonment in the penitentiary at New Westminster. However, as a newspaper reporter noted at the trial, "He claims to be 63, but looks like a man of 50, and moves like one of 30." Fourteen months later the Grey Fox escaped and took up where he left off.

He was arrested and imprisoned three times more, escaping twice. The years finally took their toll, and on September 2, 1914, Bill Miner died in prison, aged 71.

Lac Le Jeune is a popular recreation area 26 kilometres east of Logan Lake on Highway 5. **Lac Le Jeune Provincial Park** is known for its sandy beaches, excellent rainbow-trout fishing, and hiking trails. In winter, 56 kilometres of groomed trails appeal to beginner and intermediate skiers. Lac Le Jeune Resort (372-2722) has modest downhill-skiing facilities.

Wildlife viewing opportunities exist for a variety of species including mule deer, elk, moose, yellow-bellied otter, and badgers. Careful birdwatchers may see osprey, hawks, owls (including the endangered burrowing owl), eagles, falcons, and 200 species of other migratory birds. Highway 5A to Kamloops is a prime wildlife viewing corridor.

Highway 5A South

South of Merritt, Highway 5A travels to Princeton through an area rich in history. Aspen Grove, at the junction with 97C to Peachland, is where quiet, genteel George Edwards lived in the early 1900s. Edwards' friends and neighbors assumed he was independently wealthy until he was arrested for train robbery in 1906. It was then they learned he was the notorious outlaw Bill Miner, one of America's most-wanted bad guys.

Cross-country skiers will appreciate **Kane Valley,** 18 kilometres south of Merritt. The area has 40 kilo-

Sunset at 1728-metre Pennask Summitt on Highway 97C.

metres of trails for beginning and intermediate skiers with covered rest areas along the routes.

The highway also passes by several old homesteads and ghost towns like Granite City, Tulameen, and Coalmont. (See Princeton.) **Kentucky-Alleyne Provincial Park** is noted for its trout fishing and turquoise lakes, but also has a "kame and kettle" topography. These hills and depressions are yet more evidence of ancient melting glaciers. Wildlife include black bear, coyote, deer, and birds such as hawks, falcons, and grebes.

Okanagan

Locals claim Osoyoos Lake is the warmest in Canada. The resort town attracts thousands of visitors each summer.

With its semi-arid landscape, 2000 hours of sunshine a year, and many kilometres of sandy beaches, the Okanagan has a definite California ambience. The population doubles and even triples between June and September as vacationers enjoy its water sports, cycling, hiking, wildlife viewing, and rockhounding. Golf season stretches from March to November, sometimes year round. Several communities host rodeos. Culture-seekers enjoy galleries, museums, and theatre performances. In the wintertime, skiers flock to three major facilities –

Apex Alpine in Penticton, Big White in Kelowna, and Silver Star in Vernon.

The 160-kilometre-long Okanagan Valley is a glacial trough on the Interior Plateau containing 145-kilometre-long Okanagan Lake and several smaller lakes. The Okanagan River system drains southward into the Columbia River in Washington state. The main route through the valley is Highway 97.

Human history includes early residence by Okanagan and Shuswap Natives, followed by fur traders, missionaries, miners, and ranchers. Fur traders established a brigade route in the early 1820s that ran from Fort Okanagan at the junction of the Columbia and Okanagan rivers to Fort Kamloops and beyond to Fort Alexandra on the Fraser River. Although it was not in the interests of the fur companies to encourage settlement, both Westbank (in the Kelowna area) and Osoyoos were favourite stopovers.

In the late 1850s, the Okanagan Valley became a route for American miners to the Fraser and Cariboo goldfields. Some entrepreneurs, realizing that they could make a better living supplying the miners than digging for gold, established ranches and farms in the fertile valley instead.

The orchard industry began in the 1860s when Father Charles Pandosy planted the first fruit trees. In the 1890s Lord and Lady Aberdeen harvested the first commercial apple crops, precipitating a land boom that made Penticton, Kelowna, and Vernon prominent centres. Land that sold for a dollar an acre in 1898 was snapped up for a thousand dollars an acre in 1910. Today, the Okanagan produces a fifth of Canada's commercial peach crop, a third of its apples, half of its cherries, pears, and plums, and all of its apricots. In season, roadside stands along the highway sell fresh fruits and vegetables.

Vintners from around the world recognize the quality of Okanagan wine. The entire valley celebrates the **Okanagan Wine Festival** (490-8866) every fall, but most wineries offer tours and sampling year round.

Despite its value as an agricultural area, the Okanagan is the fastest growing region in the province. In 1991, 5000 people moved into the valley – an average of 14 a day. In Kelowna, the annual growth rate is about 7 percent. (Vancouver's growth rate is 3 percent. At the height of the oil-boom years in the 1970s, Calgary's growth was 5 percent.)

As in almost every other part of the province, logging is an important part of the economy, particularly in the central and northern Okanagan.

Okanagan Fruit and Blossom Schedule

Fruit	Blossom	Ripening
Apricots	Apr 7 to 30	Jul 15 to Aug 10
Cherries	Apr 15 to May 10	Jun 25 to Jul 20
Peaches	Apr 15 to May 10	Jul 30 to Sept 1
Pears	Apr 20 to May 16	Aug 15 to Sept 15
Prunes	Apr 20 to May 16	Sept 1 to 20
Apples	Apr 25 to May 20	Aug 1 to Oct 10
Grapes	Apr 25 to May 20	Sept 5 to Oct 10

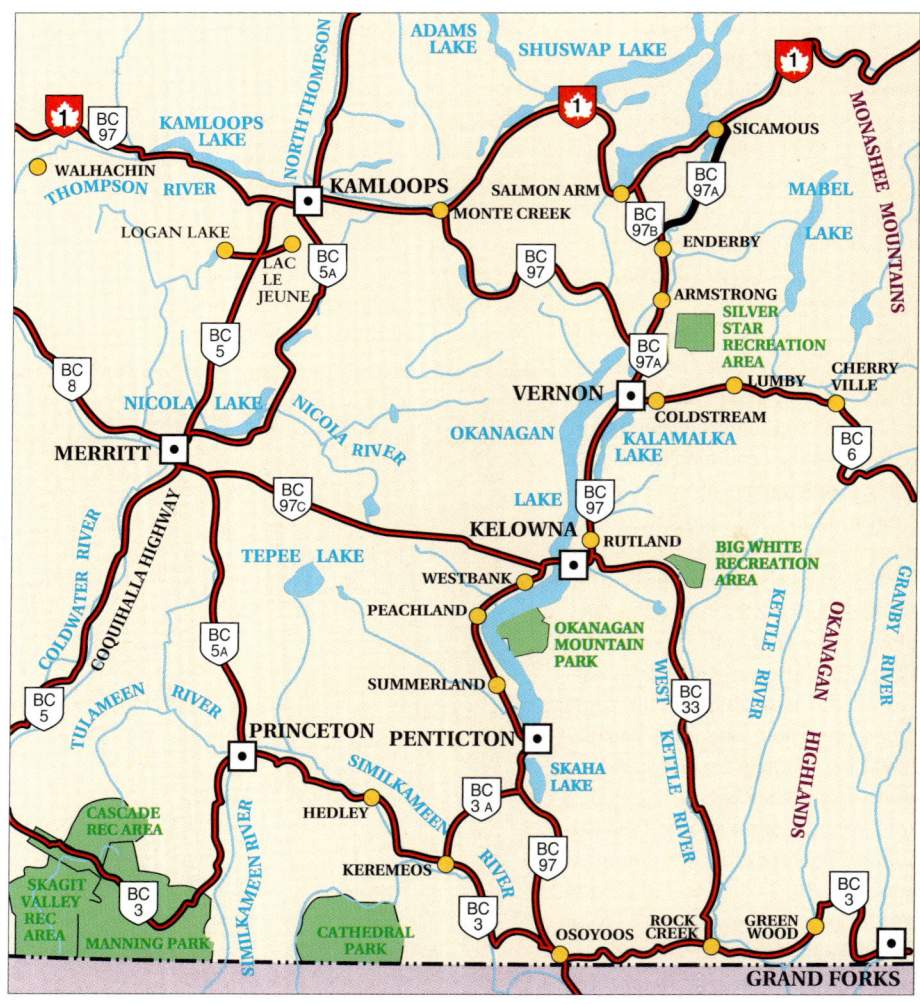

Osoyoos Oxbows

East of Highway 97 on Road 22
north of Osoyoos.

Located between Osoyoos and Oliver, the **Osoyoos Oxbows** area is good for wildlife viewing. Just north of Osoyoos Lake, this marshland provides a dramatic contrast to the otherwise semi-arid landscape – one of the hottest and driest areas of Canada. The habitat supports songbirds, waterfowl, western painted turtles, and a variety of small mammals. On the east side of the Osoyoos River, the deserted buildings of the Haynes Ranch still stand. Judge John Haynes was the earliest customs officer in the area and the patriarch of a prominent early ranching family.

Past the ranch site, signs mark a wildlife habitat reserve and the access road to the provincial **Haynes Lease Ecological Reserve** which protects a portion of the "Vest Pocket Desert." (See page 92.) About three kilometres north along Black Sage Road, look for signs on the west side of the road marking the **Burrowing Owls Enhancement Area**. The Ministry of Environment has imported burrowing owls here from Washington state in an effort to restore this endangered species.

Oliver

20 km (12 mi) north of Osoyoos. Population: 2135. Infocentre: Box 460, V0H 1T0. 498-6321; Fax: 498-3156

"Honest John" Oliver, the premier of BC from 1918 to 1927, is the namesake of this town. Remembered for his progressive irrigation policies, Oliver's foresight has served the Okanagan well.

Mining enjoyed a frenzied, but brief prominence. Today, an interpretive sign and a cross mark the site of **Fairview** (five kilometres southwest on the Oliver-Cawston Road), the greatest gold mining camp in the Okanagan from 1892 to 1902. A few

The "vest pocket desert" between Osoyoos and Oliver is one of 131 ecological reserves in the province established for research, preservation, and education. Some of them are open to the public, including the Haynes Lease Ecological Reserve shown here.

original buildings remain, but none are marked. Once a busy saloon, an old log building with a sagging roof sits in a field about three kilometres past the site. Modern miners still probe the area.

The **Oliver Museum** (106 West 6th Avenue, 498-4027) is in the police building. The original **North West Mounted Police Building**, brought from Fairview, is next door. Oliver also has a partly paved, 18-kilometre walking and biking trail along the river.

Area skiers pass by another once-thriving gold-mining town, Camp McKinney, on the road to **Mount Baldy** ski area (498-2262). Thirty kilometres east of town, the ski area has 12 runs, two T-bars, and 550 metres of vertical drop.

There are four wineries in Oliver, and they all offer tours and tastings. Bright's Wines (Highway 97 South, 498-4981); Gehringer Brothers Estate Winery (Road 8, 498-3537); Okanagan Vineyards (Road 11 West, 498-6411); and Divino Estate Winery (Road 8, 498-2784).

North of town on Highway 97, **McIntyre Bluff and Canyon** was the site of an early battle between the Shuswap and Okanagan people. Today the bluff offers a panoramic view of the valley and Vaseux Lake. Paddlers and hikers will be rewarded by Native rock paintings at the base of the bluff. The bluff is accessible from Sea Crest or River roads.

Motor boats are not allowed on seven kilometre-long **Vaseux Lake** (15 kilometres north of Oliver on Highway 97), thus providing an opportunity for quiet canoeing. A fed-eral bird sanctuary and wildlife viewing area, the lake hosts over 200 species of birds at different times of the year. Rare trumpeter swans and chukar partridge, songbirds such as canyon wrens and lazuli buntings, and water fowl are among the viewing possibilities. On the hillsides above the highway, California bighorn sheep are prevalent during the fall rutting season. Seven species of snake and fifteen species of bat also live in the area. **Vaseux Lake Provincial Park** has camping facilities. The **Wildlife Centre** at a pull-out on Highway 97 has a good interpretive display.

Okanagan Falls

20 km (12 mi) north of Oliver. Population 1100. Infocentre: Highway 97, Box 295, V0H 1R0. 497-8222

In the 1890s, a man named Snodgrass dreamed of making this pretty town – then called Dogtown – the centre of the Okanagan. (Neighboring Skaha Lake was called Lac du Chien; *chien* is French for "dog.") He built the first steamboat on Skaha Lake and the Okanagan River, but transportation problems proved too complicated, and his dream died. The area was used primarily as ranch land until the 1930s. Then orchards were planted and a tonier name, Okanagan Falls, was chosen.

Bassett House Museum (1145 Main Street, 497-5308) is located in an authentically restored and refurbished mail-order house, built in 1909. The **Memorial Rose Garden** on Highway 97 beside Centennial Park has 190 hybrid tea roses.

Tucked away in rustic White Lake

Valley, the space-age National Research Council **Dominion Radio Astrophysical Observatory** (497-4708) is north on Highway 97. (Follow signs at White Lake Road.) Scientists at the observatory study radio signals (electromagnetic radiation) through extremely powerful telescopes. Visitors can take a guided tour on summer Sundays from 2 to 5 PM, or a self-guided tour at other times. **White Lake** is also a popular bird-watching spot.

Christie Memorial Provincial Park on Skaha Lake is a popular swimming area, and **Okanagan**

Eighteen-Hole Golf Courses in the Okanagan

Kelowna
- Gallagher's Canyon Golf Resort. RR #3, McCulloch Road, V1Y 7R2. 861-4240; Fax: 861-1852
- Kelowna Golf and Country Club. 1297 Glenmore Drive, V1Y 4P4. 762-2531; Fax: 868-3360
- Kelowna Springs Golf Club. 480 Penno Road, V1X 6S3. 765-8511
- Mission Creek Golf and Country Club. 1959 KLO Road, V1W 2H8. 860-3210
- Shadow Ridge Golf Course. Highway 97. Box 1046, Stn A, V1Y 7P7. 765-7777
- Sunset Ranch Golf and Country Club. 4001 Anderson Road. 765-7700; Fax 765-7733

Oliver/Osoyoos
- Fairview Mountain Golf Club. On Golf Course Road. PO Box 821, Oliver, V0H 1T0. 498-3521; Fax: 498-3077
- Osoyoos Golf and Country Club. West Bench. PO Box 798, V0H 1V0. 495-7003; Fax: 495-3511

Peachland
- Ponderosa Golf and Country Club. Ponderosa Drive. PO Box 336, V0H 1X0. 767-2149;
  toll free in BC: 1-800-663-6110

Penticton
- Penticton Golf and Country Club. On West Eckhardt Avenue. PO Box 158, V2A 6K8. 492-8727

Summerland
- Summerland Golf and Country Club. 2405 Mountain Avenue. PO Box 348, V0H 1Z0. 494-9554

Vernon
- Hillview Golf Club. 1101-14th Avenue, V1B 2S6. 549-GOLF or 549-4653
- Predator Ridge Golf Resort. 360 Commonage Road, V1T 6M8. 542-3436; Fax: 542-3835
- Spallumcheen Golf and Tennis Club. On Highway 97N. PO Box 218, V1T 6M2. 545-5824; Fax: 549-7476
- Vernon Golf & Country Club. 800-23rd Street, V1T 6V2. 542-9126; Fax: 542-5468

Westbank
- Shannon Lake Golf Course. Shannon Lake Road V0H 2A0. 768-4577

Bird-watching is popular throughout the Okanagan. At the north end of Skaha Lake, Canada geese fly overhead while herons and loons (foreground) stay close to the water.

Falls Provincial Park west of town on Green Lake Road is a unique ecological zone in an otherwise arid landscape. The lush vegetation includes deciduous trees that attract a large variety of insects. At night, bats and nighthawks provide aerial acrobatics as they feed on the bugs. Other wildlife include beaver, muskrat, snakes, and waterfowl.

Le Comte Estate Winery (497-8267) and Wild Goose Vineyards and Winery (497-8919) are local vineyards.

The area is good for rockhounding. Okanagan Falls has several jade shops.

Penticton

20 km (12 mi) north of Okanagan Falls. Population: 25,970. Infocentre: 185 Lakeshore Drive, V2A 1B7. 1-800-663-5052, 493-4055; Fax: 493-4066

Many towns in BC are at the confluence of two rivers, but Penticton is a meeting place of two lakes: Okanagan and Skaha. The deep blue waters of Skaha Lake were once part of Okanagan Lake. Over time, silting built up the delta that is the present site of Penticton.

When Tom Ellis came here in 1866, it had been an Okanagan Native settlement for centuries. The

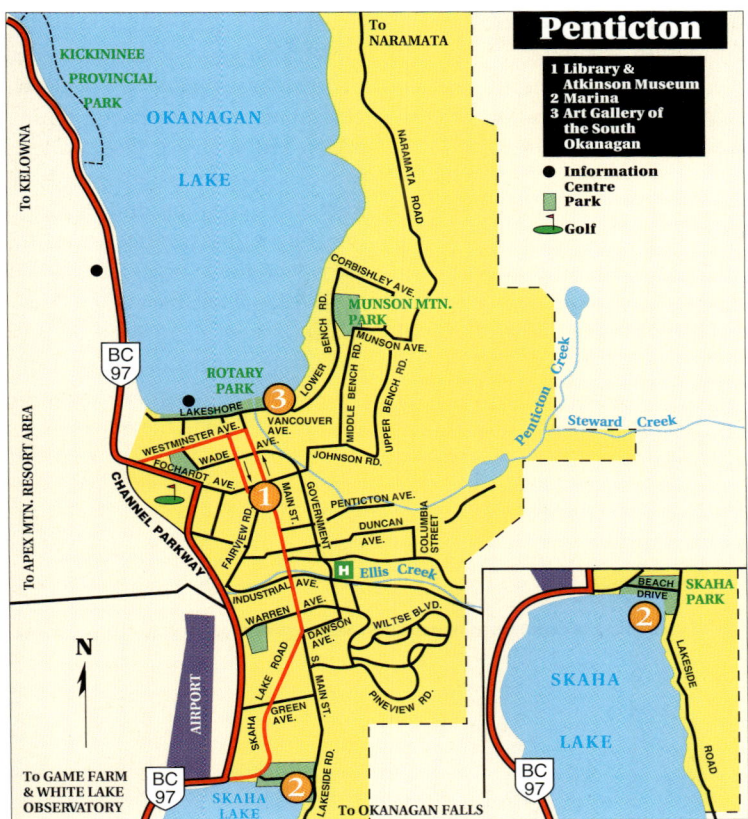

Penticton

1 Library &
  Atkinson Museum
2 Marina
3 Art Gallery of
  the South
  Okanagan

● Information
  Centre
▨ Park
⛳ Golf

Natives called it *Pen-tak-tin*, "a place to live forever." Mr. Ellis agreed and built a ranching empire encompassing 12,000 hectares. His round-up covered the area from Naramata to Osoyoos, and he drove his cattle all the way to Hope over the Dewdney Trail. Most historians credit Ellis with planting the first fruit trees in the area, but one early account says he was only copying the Natives who cultivated wild species.

The townsite was laid out in 1905 when the Southern Okanagan Land Company bought the Ellis holdings. By 1910 only 400 people had settled in the area, despite the elegant CPR paddlewheelers launched in 1892 to attract touist dollars. Rumors of the Kettle Valley Railway caused a land boom in 1912. Twenty-two real estate firms set up shop selling land at up to $3000 an acre. By 1915 the railway was completed.

The **R.N. Atkinson Museum** (785 Main, 492-6025) features the largest collection of Western Canadiana in the Interior, and it is well worth a visit. Displays include the Okanagan Natives, early settlers, the Kettle Valley Railroad, mining, orcharding, and natural history.

Many art galleries exist in Penticton that show the work of local artists, including the **Art Gallery of the South Okanagan** (on the lakefront, east of the Infocentre, 493-2928). The **En'owkin Cultural Centre** (257 Brunswick Street, 493-7181) has art shows from time to time, an archives and library of Native history, and the first, if not the only, Native publishing house in Canada, Theytus Books.

The **Okanagan Summer School of the Arts** (220 Manor Park Ave. Box 22037, V2A 8L1, 493-0390), operating since 1960, holds classes each July. Distinguished faculty have included Robert Silverman, Tony Onley, W. O. Mitchell, Jan Rubes, Ingrid Suderman, Ann Mortifee, and Judith Dampier.

Penticton's two lakes provide almost 3000 metres of beaches and a variety of water sports are possible. Several marinas rent boats, houseboats, and supplies. Wind surfers love Skaha Lake's 30-knot winds in August. Parasailing and bungee-jumping opportunities exist for those who thrive on adrenalin.

The **Penticton River Channel** between Okanagan and Skaha lakes is popular for inner-tubing and wildlife viewing, and there is a walking/cycling path along the bank.

Over 100 different species of imported and native wildlife inhabit 224 hectares at the **Okanagan Game Farm** (497-5405), overlooking Skaha Lake south of Penticton.

S.S. *Sicamous*

One of the original CPR paddle-wheelers on Okanagan Lake, the luxurious S.S. *Sicamous* now sits in Lakeshore Park in Penticton.

Steamboat service began on the lake in 1886. But when the CPR trunk line was completed from Sicamous to Vernon in 1892, the CPR began operating a regular service on the lake. Its luxury paddlewheelers attracted tourists, and the agricultural community found a way to transport their produce. The economy was changed forever.

Meaning "shimmering waters" in Shuswap, the S.S. *Sicamous* was launched in 1914, replacing the S.S. *Aberdeen*. Able to carry 500 passengers plus freight, the ship's deluxe embellishments included stained glass skylights, brass chandeliers, Burmese teak, and Australian mahogany. Passengers had access to 40 staterooms, four salons, a smoking lounge, and observation lounges. Dinner was tastefully served in a 20-metre dining room by uniformed waiters.

Despite their romantic associations, sternwheelers have a long and valiant history in the Interior, providing basic transportation when there were no roads or railroads. In April 1931, the CPR terminated sternwheel service on the lake. The *Sicamous* is currently being restored by the Kettle Valley Railway Association.

Rockhounds should have a field day in this area. Evan G. Cameron, an Okanagan geologist, claims that "all of the common and uncommon types of rocks existing in the world are found within a radius of approximately 40 miles (65 km) of Penticton." Ask at the Infocentre. A display at the R.H. Atkinson Museum also pinpoints good rockhounding areas.

Wineries in the Penticton area are Cartier Wines (2210 Main Street, 492-0621) and Hillside Cellars (1350 Naramata Road, 493-4424).

Jeanette Armstrong
Director, International School of Writing, En'owkin Centre, Penticton-Okanagan Band

I guess I'm biased like everyone else about where they grew up. I think this is probably the most beautiful area in the country. I am so familiar with it, I feel like it's very much a part of my internal landscape.

When I have tried living in other cities, I have felt a huge loss.

I stay here principally because I am Okanagan, and I define myself as that. I have very strong close ties to the land here and very strong ties to the community, the language, the body that makes up my whole self, which is my family. Without that around me I'm not whole.

I grew up on the Penticton Indian Reserve. My early years were spent on the reserve in a very different lifestyle than people in the non-Native community. I really didn't participate in the non-Native community other than high school.

It did create problems for me and others because we weren't easily accepted, we were different. But I came from a strong family background that had a lot of pride in being Native, and I didn't see anything wrong with my culture.

The Penticton-Okaganan people and the Okanagan Native people in general have always had a great pride in their culture. Our understanding, which is ingrained in our cultural teachings, is that every person has the right to be what they are, and every culture has the right to be what they are. We seek to create peace and harmony as a result of that value. Every time there is debate, confrontation, conflict, or whatever, the Okanagan people have risen as the peacemakers.

I like to define myself as an activist in a creative sense, rather than as a writer. Principally I see my creative arts as a way to activate change in my community and in the wider community.

For the local community, the En'owkin Centre is a source of pride and recognition for ourselves of what is possible. We are one of the leading Native organizations in the country, in terms of future development in the literary arts. So we've become a measurement, a standard, in excellence. That's a real source of pride.

The En'owkin Centre was formed in 1979 to house the activities of the Okanagan Indian Education Resource Society, representing all Native organizations in the Okanagan valley.

Locals celebrate the importance of the fruit industry with the **Penticton Blossom Festival** in April and the week-long **Penticton Peach Festival** in July. In August, athletes from

Pacific Rattlesnake
Crotalus viridis oreganus

The Pacific rattlesnake, the only poisonous snake in BC, is found in the dry areas of the southern Interior, usually near cliffs and talus slopes. Normally about 80 centimetres long, this species can grow up to 1.5 metres. The distinguishing feature is the segmented tail or rattle.

The venom of the Pacific Rattlesnake is dangerous, but this species is not aggressive. If given a choice, they'll retreat rather than attack. However, if surprised or stepped on, they'll strike without rattling a warning. When hiking in dry areas of the southern Interior, always watch where you place your hands and feet, and listen for the rattle. Wear long pants and sturdy footwear.

If bitten, keep calm and still, and get to a hospital. Penticton Hospital is equipped to treat snake-bite patients.

Although Pacific rattlers are not social creatures, they do spend the winter in communal dens in talus slopes or caves. As many as a hundred rattlers might live in one den which they will likely share with other creatures.

The snakes go into the den in mid- to late-September, and they are out in late March or early April. They mate in late summer, and the young are born in September.

around the world come to compete in Penticton's **Ironman Canada Triathlon**.

One of the Interior's top ski areas, **Apex Alpine** (292-8222; 1-800-663-1900) is a half-hour drive west of Penticton.

Side Trip: Naramata

16 kilometres (10 mi) northeast of Penticton. Population: 850

A visit to Naramata provides a chance to stay near the lake but get off the crowded highway. This is where Canadian filmmaker Sandy Wilson spent her childhood and the adolescence she depicted in the feature film *My American Cousin*, which was shot in the area.

Robinson House, a hotel built in 1910, is named after a prominent land promoter who also established Summerland and Peachland. John M. Robinson named the town after a Sioux Indian chief visited him during a seance and spoke of the love of the chief's life, Narrramatah.

The stretch from the Okanagan Highland down to Penticton was one of the most difficult challenges facing Andrew McCulloch when he was surveying the Kettle Valley Railway (KVR). He solved the problem by creating a series of switchbacks on the mountain above Naramata, creating the longest 2.2 percent grade in Canada. Portions of the now-defunct line have been planted over, but hikers can walk to old station sites like Arawana, Glenfir, Adra, and Chute Lake. Ask locally or follow the road to Rock Ovens Park, a former KVR construction camp, four kilometres past the old Glenfir station.

The Lang Vineyards in Naramata (496-5987) offer tours daily during the summer.

Okanagan Mountain Provincial Park

The longest undeveloped shoreline on Okanagan Lake and an opportunity to explore a northern desert await travellers at **Okanagan Mountain Provincial Park.** Accessible by road north of Naramata or south of Kelowna, no thoroughfares cross the 10,462-hectare park. It has 24 kilometres of hiking trails, some of them former fur-brigade routes. As always when hiking in the Okanagan and Similkameen regions, beware of rattlesnakes. They are not aggressive, but hikers must watch where they put their hands and wear sturdy shoes. (See page 132.)

Summerland

16 km (10 mi) north of Penticton. Population: 8765. Infocentre: Highway 97, Box 1075, V0H 1Z0.
494-2686; Fax: 494-4039

Back on Highway 97 north of Penticton, **Giant's Head Mountain,** a once-active volcano resembling the profile of a man, towers over the orchards and vineyards of Summerland. Since the Native word "Okanagan" derives part of its meaning from the word "head," some surmise that similar shapes on rock faces up and down the valley may be how the area got its name. The mountain is a popular place for hiking and affords a spectacular panorama of the Okanagan Valley.

Summerland also owes its existence to John M. Robinson. An owner

of several Manitoba newspapers, he came to the Okanagan looking for mining opportunities in the late 1800s. After tasting local peaches, he developed an irrigation scheme instead and sold land parcels claiming "Heaven on earth with summer weather forever!" By the early 1900s, Summerland boasted the first hydroelectric plant in the valley, its own light and telephone system, and orchards containing a million fruit trees.

The **Summerland Trout Hatchery** (Lakeshore Drive, 494-0491) one of eight provincial facilities, raises rainbow and eastern brook trout. Although tours are not normally available, the public can view the site and a small display.

The **Federal Agricultural Research Station** (494-7711) is just off the highway opposite Sun-Oka Provincial Park. The development of the Spartan apple is one result of the centre's research. Scientists here also were responsible for discovering the importance of the trace element boron in the health of fruit trees. Current projects include de-

Summerland, an agricultural community since the turn of the century, is increasingly popular with tourists and retirees.

velopment of a sterile insect program as an alternative to insecticides. The centre offers tours and has a small museum. Outside, the ornamental garden is popular for picnics. One of the largest steel girder bridges of its kind in North America crosses Trout Creek Canyon here. The 200-metre high, 500-metre-long structure was part of the Kettle Valley Railway.

Visitors more interested in the hedonistic side of agriculture can tour the Summerland Sweets Factory (497-0377), maker of the jams, candies, and fruit leathers that are found for sale in many Okanagan roadside stands. Sumac Ridge Estate Winery has tours during the summer (Highway 97, 494-0541).

The **Summerland Museum** (9521 Wharton Street, 494-9395) features local history, and an art gallery upstairs has work of local artists.

Ogopogo

Ogopogo, the Loch Ness Monster of Okanagan Lake, is considered tourist hype by some, but there are many people who take its existence very seriously. In 1990 and 1991, a Japanese television network sent film crews and an underwater submersible to prepare documentaries on the legendary creature.

The manager of the Chamber of Commerce, Gerry Frederick, says he wasn't a believer until an NBC film crew was in Kelowna preparing for an *Unsolved Mysteries* segment on the "monster." In order to get as much mileage out of the event as possible, Frederick organized a local crew to film the American crew filming their search.

"The lake was glassy clear," he says, describing classic sighting conditions. "There was no wind, and there were no other boats in the area. And all of a sudden the NBC cameraman shouted, 'There it is,' and starting zooming in on it with his camera. The phenomenon lasted for about 15 or 20 seconds. There was this dark movement in the water about 20 or 30 feet long; the wake moved with it. It was very exciting." He couldn't make out details like a head or tail, but the experience convinced him. 'Up till then I was just going along with it," he says. "Now I'm a believer."

He's not alone. Okanagan Natives described N'ha-a-itk, the lake monster that lived in a cave near Squally Point, to early pioneers such as Susan

Peachland

25 km (16 mi) north of Summerland. Population: 3053. Infocentre: on the Okanagan Connector (Highway 97C) for eastbound traffic. 767-6677

More than two kilometres of public beach line the main street of this orchard community, making it a popular summertine destination. The **Peachland Museum** (5890 Beach Avenue, 767-3441), an unusual, eight-sided structure that used to be a church, sits on the same street. Local history and old photos of the Kettle Valley Railway are featured in the museum's displays.

From downtown, boaters can set out for **Okanagan Mountain Provincial Park,** directly across the lake. The park's Squally Point is one of the places where the legendary Ogopogo has repeatedly been sighted. A difference of opinion exists about whether or not the creature is real, but boaters should be vigilant, just in case.

Trepanier Creek, at the north end of town, reportedly got its name Allison in the mid-1800s. Since the monster often came out of the water during storms and claimed lives, the Natives carried small animals to sacrifice when approaching the point.

In 1914, Mr. F.M. Buckland, a prominent Okanagan citizen, was among a group of campers on the lake who discovered the decomposing remains of a strange animal they'd never seen before. He described it as close to two metres long and weighing about 200 kilograms. The neckless creature had a thick hide, tusks, and flipper-like arms. Apparently bones from the animal were on display for several years in the area. One scientist who examined them concluded they belonged to a prehistoric creature. Unfortunately, the bones have since disappeared.

Although skeptics still claim Ogopogo is an invention of the tourism industry, some scientists take the creature seriously.

The International Society of Cryptozoology, based in Washington, DC, is dedicated to the investigation of "all matters related to animals of unexpected form and size or unexpected occurrence in time and space."

Just because the existence of an animal seems impossible, they say, it doesn't mean it is impossible. No one believed that the two-metre-long fish, the coleacanth, still existed until it was caught off the South Africa coast in 1938. Or that a clam without a digestive system could exist until John Reid discovered it off Vancouver Island in 1979.

Comparisons with Scotland'sLoch Ness monster are inevitable. People have postulated that Nessie is a plesiosaur, an aquatic reptile, thought to be extinct for 65 million years. It is possible Ogopogo is too.

Another explanation involves a huge creature that was sighted off the Oregon coast in the 1930s, possibly an extinct whale. Some theorize that this creature could have travelled up the Columbia River to the Okanagan.

In the early-1980s the Okanagan Similkameen Tourist Association offered a one million dollar reward for evidence of the creature's existence. Many people submitted photographs to local Ogopogo expert Arlene Gaal, but she didn't find any of them conclusive. (The offer was withdrawn in 1985 when the insurance premiums reached $100,000.)

"Look at it this way," says Frederick. "No one has ever been able to prove Ogopogo's existence. But no one has been able to disprove it either."

For fmore information read Arlene Gaal's book, *Ogopogo* (Surrey, BC: Hancock House, 1985).

Peachland sits across from Okanagan Mountain Provincial Park and Squally Point, home of the legendary Ogopogo.

from the surgical procedure of trepanning, cutting a hole in the skull. The story goes that while hunting in 1817, Chief Short Legs' scalp was badly torn by a grizzly bear. The chief was not recovering, so after several days, fur-trader Alexander Ross operated, removing several pieces of bone from the chief's skull. "In fifteen days by the aid of Indian medicine he was able to walk around," Ross wrote. "And at the end of six weeks from the time he was wounded, he was on horseback, again at the chase."

Today, Trepanier Creek Road is where wine tasters will find Hainle Vineyards Estate Winery (767-3370), A & H Vineyards (767-9250) and Chateau Ste. Claire (767-3113).

A good place to view spawning kokanee salmon in the fall is **Antler's Beach** at the south end of town.

Eneas Lakes Provincial Park and **Darke Lake Provincial Park** are good fishing spots. **Hardy Falls** is a popular local hiking destination.

Three kilometres north of Peachland, the Okanagan Connector (Highway 97C) is the fastest route to the Lower Mainland or Kamloops via the Nicola Valley.

Kelowna
60 km (37 mi) north of Penticton. Population: 70,720. Infocentre: 544 Harvey Avenue (Highway 97), V1Y 6C9. 861-1515; Fax: 861-3624

The view of wild waves to the north and calm waters to the south often greets travellers crossing Kelowna's famous Floating Bridge on Okanagan Lake. The paradox may typify the heart and soul of modern Kelowna.

Attracted by the legendary good

weather and laid-back lifestyle, people from across the country are flocking to the Okanagan, and Kelowna particularly. Experts estimate the city's population will have doubled by the year 2000. Some fear the increase will bring about changes that will alter the community's essence. Already the increased demand for housing is encroaching on orchard land.

Luxury homes now dot prime lakeview lots, but they are a far cry from August Gillard's earth home in 1862. Apparently, when the red-bearded, gruff-mannered Gillard emerged from his half-buried dwelling one day, he reminded his Native neighbors of a crotchety bear after a long hibernation. They called the man and the place *kim-am-tou-che* (brown bear), which was later refined to grizzly bear, *kelowna*.

When Princess Margaret opened the 1400-metre-long **Floating Bridge** in 1958, it was the first of its kind in North America. The unusual 640-metre-long pontoon structure floats up and down with lake levels.

Guisachan Heritage Park (Cameron Avenue, just off Gordon Drive) is a popular attraction – the site of a ranch built in 1861 by Hudson's

---

WAC "Wacky" Bennett: Hardware Premier

"The finest music in the country is the ringing of cash registers," according to William Andrew Cecil Bennett, BC's longest-reigning premier.

The Kelowna-based politician was premier of BC during a time of general prosperity. And his tenure from 1952 to 1972 was a time of major development in the Interior, including the expansion of the road system and the provincial railway (now BC Rail), and the construction of hydroelectric projects on the Peace and Columbia rivers. Bennett was the first premier from a Social Credit party that was to dominate provincial politics for 50 years. He survived disastrous political scandals and several colourful cabinet ministers during his years in office.

Born in New Brunswick in 1900, young William was raised in a strict Presbyterian family. At the end of World War I, he moved west to Edmonton, married, and opened a hardware store. When the Depression came, he moved to BC, first to Victoria, then to Kelowna.

In Kelowna he started another hardware business, and, as author Derek Pethick notes, in *Men of British Columbia*, "pondered the paradox of poverty in a land of plenty."

Elected to the provincial legislature in 1941, Bennett became premier in 1952. Because of his leadership, the Social Credit Party was to become a major force in BC politics until 1991.

Although WAC Bennett was defeated in the polls in 1972, his son Bill became premier in 1975. WAC Bennett died in Kelowna in 1979.

Bay Company trader John Mc-Dougall. The Earl and Countess of Aberdeen bought it in 1890 and oversaw the first large-scale planting of fruit trees and hops in the central Okanagan. The Earl and Countess were very busy people – she was the founder of both the World Council of Women and the Victorian Order of Nurses and he was Governor General of Canada from 1893 to 1898. In 1902 they sold the ranch to the Cameron family who lived at Guisachan until 1983. Today, the elegant bungalow, reminiscent of those in Great Britain's colonial India, operates as a first-class restaurant (862-9368 or 764-4770).

Benvoulin Heritage Church, on Benvoulin Road, is the oldest standing church in Kelowna, built in 1892 by Lord and Lady Aberdeen.

The **Kelowna Museum** has a variety of displays including a *Tyrannosaurus rex* skull. The **National Exhibition Centre** (470 Queensway, 763-2417) mounts several special exhibits each year. The **Provincial Orchard Industry Museum** (1304 Ellis, 763-0433), was Kelowna's first restored heritage building. Its displays include aspects of orcharding from irrigation to canning.

Kelowna's professional company, **Sunshine Theatre,** performs contemporary plays during the summer months at Kelowna Community Theatre (Water Street and Doyle Avenue, 763-4025).

There are several wineries in the Kelowna area. In Westbank: Quail's Gate Vineyard (3303 Boucherie Road, 769-4451) and Mission Hill Vineyards (1730 Mission Hill, 768-7611). In Kelowna: Cedar Creek Estate Winery (5445 Lakeshore Drive, 764-8866) and Calona Wines (1125 Richter, 762-3332). In Okanagan Mission: Summerhill Estate Winery (764-8000); St. Hubertus Vineyard (764-7888); and Cedar Creek Estate

Pandosy Mission

Established in 1860 by Father Charles Pandosy (above) and colleagues from the Oblate order, the Pandosy Mission was the first permanent European settlement in the valley and the first non-Hudson's Bay Company settlement in the province. The Oblate Fathers spent their first winter on Duck Lake, north of present-day Kelowna in 1859, but almost starved and froze to death. In the spring, the group established the mission on its present site, with a garden and cattle, chickens, ducks, and geese. The Oblates are also credited with planting the first vineyard and orchard, and building the first school. Three of the original log buildings are still standing: the chapel, the root house, and the living quarters. The mission now operates as a provincial heritage site and is open year-round, weather permitting. (Benvoulin and Casorso roads, 860-8369)

Kelowna

1 Benvoulin Heritage Church
2 Guisachan Heritage House
3 City Park
4 Father Pandosy Mission
5 The Kelowna Museum
6 Orchid Industry Museum
7 City Park
8 Mission Creek & Sutherland Hills Parks

● Information Centre
▮ Park
⛳ Golf

Winery (764-8866). North in Okanagan Centre: Gray Monk Cellars (766-3168).

A number of other local industries offer tours including BC Packers (763-7003); Okanagan Orchard Tours (769-4719); Sun Rype (860-RYPE); and the McCulloch Forest Tour. Ask at the Infocentres.

Over 60 parks, totalling 240 hectares, are in the vicinity of Kelowna. **Knox Mountain Nature Park** at the north end of Ellis Street gives first-time visitors a great view of the city and a sense of where things are. The park also has nature trails, a nature pavilion, and a picnic area.

Downtown, 14-hectare **Kelowna City Park** is very popular on hot days. The S.S. *Fintry Queen*, one of last paddlewheelers to travel the lake, now operates as a tour boat and restaurant from the park (763-2780).

Not far from Orchard Park Shopping Centre, the clear waters of Mission Creek run through **Mission Creek Regional Park** and neighbouring **Sutherland Hills Provincial Park**. Attractions include spawning kokanee in the fall and 100 species of flowering plants between April in August. (From downtown, turn south off Highway 97 to Springfield Road on Cooper. Follow Springfield

Visitors to Kelowna have access to a variety of water sports downtown at City Park.

Road east to the parking lot.)

The most spectacular section of the old Kettle Valley Railway Line is between Ruth and Myra stations with its 16 trestle bridges through **Myra Canyon.** "Never saw a railway built on any such hillside as this," was what chief engineer Andrew McCulloch had to say about this portion of the line. Now used by hikers and bikers, access is about 18 kilometres east of town on McCulloch Road and the Myra Creek Forest Service Road. During the week logging trucks use the road, so check locally. Ask at the Infocentre for a map and information about 20-kilometre Crawford Hiking Trail.

Okanagan Mountain Provincial Park (see also page 133) is accessible south of town via Lakeshore Road. The hike to **Wild Horse Canyon** is very popular. Other parks with hiking or nature trails include **Lions Nature Park** in Rutland along Mission Creek, **Scenic Canyon Regional Park** off Field Road in East Kelowna, and the **Woodhaven Nature Conservancy Park** at the end of Raymer Road in Okanagan Mission.

Big White, 54 kilometres from Kelowna, is a major ski destination in the Interior, offering two high-speed quad chairlifts, 625 metres of vertical drop, a lift capacity of 11,500 skiers per hour, and a fully developed ski village (765-8888; 1-800-663-2772). Cross-country skiers can use Big White's 25 kilometres of nordic trails or try the **Telemark Ski Area** across the lake near Westbank on marked Forest Service trails. **Postill Lake,** 19 kilometres east of the airport, has over 100 kilometres of trails including a biathlon route.

Okanagan Lake is much used for canoeing and fishing. Other popular lakes are McCulloch, Idabel, and Woods. Fishing in the area is mostly for rainbow, cutthroat, and kokanee.

The North Okanagan

The north Okanagan enjoys slightly cooler temperatures and lusher vegetation than the south. Although early attempts were made to duplicate the soft-fruit orcharding success of the southern Okanagan, farmers realized the land was better suited to dairy farming and hardier fruits and vegetables.

A secondary road travels the west side of Okanagan Lake to Vernon via Fintry and Westside Road. Highway 97 travels north past Duck Lake, Wood Lake, Oyama, and Kalamalka Lake through picturesque country alternating dry grasslands with irrigated orchards.

Approaching Vernon from the south, **Kalamalka Lake** is dazzling on a bright cloudless day. One interpretation of its name is "lake of many colours." Glacial deposits at several places along the shore cause the water to shimmer and shine in an array of blues and greens. Access to **Kalamalka Lake Provincial Park** is south of Vernon on the east side of the lake.

Vernon

55 km (34 mi) north of Kelowna. Population: 21,140. Infocentre: 6326 Highway 97 North, Box 520, V1T 6M4. 545-1415; Fax: 542-3256

Vernon sits at the centre of four valleys (Priest, Pleasant, Coldstream, and Mission) within easy reach of two large lakes. Although early fur

Agricultural needs and housing needs are increasingly in conflict in the Okanagan, the fastest-growing area in the province. These orchards are in Rutland, north of Kelowna.

traders discouraged settlers, once gold fever hit, the friendly climate and lush natural grasslands made this an attractive settlement area.

Originally called Priest's Valley, after Oblate Father Durieu who built a cabin in the area in the 1860s, the city of Vernon was eventually named after early rancher Forbes Vernon. Along with brother Charles, Forbes founded **Coldstream Ranch,** one of the largest in Western Canada. In 1891, Lord and Lady Aberdeen bought out the Vernons and planted the first orchard in the area. The CPR had been completed north of here in 1885, so when a branch line was extended to Sicamous in 1892, fruit marketing became feasible. The town incorporated that same year.

Although at one time it was a major hop grower in the province, Coldstream Ranch became one of the largest producers of fruit in the British Empire. In 1917, the orchards produced 800 boxcars of apples and 200 boxcars of other fruit which were shipped to England at a value of over a million dollars.

Others attracted to the area's good agricultural land included Cornelius O'Keefe and Thomas Greenhow who, while driving cat-

tle from Oregon during the Cariboo gold rush in the 1860s, were so impressed with the knee-high bunch grass, they decided to stay. The restored **O'Keefe Ranch** north of town is a major area attraction.

Many Chinese miners opted for the wealth of the soil rather than the elusive promises of gold, and they number among early settlers as well.

Agriculture remains an important part of the economy of the North Okanagan. In season, travellers can sink their teeth into juicy red strawberries and other fresh produce at Western Canada's largest outdoor farmer's market, held Mondays and Thursdays from April through October in the **Vernon Recreation Centre** parking lot.

Paddlewheel Park was the site of the terminal of the Shuswap-Okanagan Railway. Visitors now can visit the retired steamship S.S. *Naramata* and the Okanagan Landing Railway Station (on Okanagan Landing off 25th Avenue), vital transportation links dating from the 1890s. One of Vernon's earliest buildings, Luc Girouard's cabin, is located in **Polson Park,** a picturesque place in the middle of the city with a meandering stream complete with swans.

The **Greater Vernon Museum and Archives** (3009-32nd Avenue, 542-3142) includes displays about the semi-nomadic Interior Salish, early fur traders, miners, and cattle ranchers, chronicling the town's growth from a cowtown to a modern city.

Vernon is a hive of cultural activity. Housed in a former power plant, Vernon's nationally ac-

Idyllic Polson Park is in the centre of Vernon, the Interior's oldest incorporated city.

Kalamalka Lake is the site of the Interior's only underwater marine park, Ellison Provincial Park.

claimed **Powerhouse Theatre** (542-6194) offers a full season of classic and contemporary theatre during the year. A unique cultural experience is offered by **Sen 'Klip Native Theatre** (542-1247) who perform Native legends every weekend from July to September, one hour before dusk at Komasket Park off Westside Road. In late summer, members of the Okanagan Nation (542-4328) gather at the park for canoe and horse races, games, and dancing.

Over a dozen galleries exhibit the work of local artists. The *Vernon Visitors Guide* lists forty painters, weavers, photographers, potters, quilters, printmakers, sculptors, and jewellers who will open their studios to visitors for viewing and chatting. (Contact the Infocentre.)

The only brewery in the valley, Okanagan Spring (542-2337), pro-

duces a highly rated beer and offers tours.

Annual events include the **Vernon Winter Carnival** (largest in Western Canada) in February, the **Head of the Lake Rodeo** in May, the **Bella Vista Triathlon** in July, and the **Old Time Fiddlers Competition** in August.

Rockhounds can look for opal and agate. (Contact the Infocentre.)

Kalamalka Lake Provincial Park

South of Vernon, across the lake from Highway 97, the virgin grasslands of 890-hectare **Kalamalka Lake Provincial Park** give a sense of how the landscape seduced early ranchers like the Vernons and Cornelius O'Keefe. It used to be like this all the way to Osoyoos, 140 kilometres to the south.

In order to protect the fragile ecosystem, some areas of the park are restricted, but there is much to enjoy including spectacular views of the lake and colourful wildflowers in spring. The turquoise water makes swimming particularly exotic at Jade, Juniper, and Cosens bays.

Four distinct ecological zones exist in the park: arid grassland, woodland, forest, and wet areas, containing ten plant species rare in BC. Pacific rattlesnakes also live here but they are shy creatures that prefer to be left alone. (See page 132.) Other hazards include unexploded bombs left over from target practice during World War II – a military base is just across the lake. (Metal objects along trails should be left undisturbed and reported to RCMP.) Please stay on the paths.

Ellison Provincial Park

Ellison Provincial Park southwest of Vernon on Okanagan Lake has Western Canada's only freshwater underwater marine park, which will rate it high on scuba divers' lists (equipment rentals: 549-2040). Fans of the park also claim it has the best beaches in the Okanagan. Regardless, its location is beautiful, with the Okanagan Highland to the west across the lake, the peaks of the Monashee to the east, and a delicate whiff of pine hanging in the air.

Silver Star Provincial Recreation Area

Silver Star Ski Area (542-0224; 1-800-663-4431) is located in **Silver Star Provincial Recreation Area** where a privately owned gaslight theme village hosts some of the best skiing in

Commerical orcharding began in the Okanagan in the 1890s. Today, BC Tree Fruits, a cooperative that represents a majority of Okanagan growers, markets 450 million pounds of Okanagan fruit to more than 40 countries annually. Apples are the dominant crop, representing 80 percent of total fruit grown.

the province: 59 alpine runs with 760 metres of vertical drop and 70 kilometres of groomed nordic trails. The chairlift operates year round and offers magnificent views of Kalamalka and Okanagan lakes. In the summer, visitors hike the alpine meadows or bike the Mile High Descent, which covers 25 kilometres over a 1535-meter vertical drop. The good part is you can take the chairlift up and rent bikes for the downhill ride. On the way to Silver Star, visitors can try Vernon's version of the **Magnetic Hill**. Ask locally for directions.

Ken Mather
Manager
O'Keefe Ranch
Vernon

I came here in 1984. I'm just somebody who has worked in heritage sites for a long time, appreciates what they represent, and loves the work. I've been doing it for 19 years.

There's a field across there that we've just planted to oats. In August we'll thresh that with the old binder. We'll tie up the stooks and we'll stook it all up and then we'll use horse-drawn wagons and load up the bundle wagons. We've got a great big steam tractor that has a long belt attached to it,

I've been at O'Keefe eight years. And I'm probably stuck here because it's a really hard place to leave. It's beautiful. We live right here on the site. I have two little boys, and my wife and I, we have our own milk cow, we have our own chickens. It's awfully hard to say, "Well gee, I'm going somewhere else for better money." I mean the fact is you'll never find a style of life like this in what I do. It's very much a love.

What I'd like to see here is the real traditional ranching practices. I'd like to see a selection of cattle that showed people the traditional breeds that would have been here in the early days – Texas Longhorns, lots of shorthorns, before Herefords even appeared. I'd like to see cutting horse demonstrations, roping demonstrations. We're not really a working ranch right now. We just have some farm animals as part of the attraction.

and we'll actually thresh-out the old way. There was a lot of wheat grown on O'Keefe Ranch because the Okanagan was the breadbasket for a long time, before the Prairies took off. So those sort of activites are more and more what we want to do.

There seems to be a resurgence of interest in this sort of thing. Part of it is the search for something genuine in an age that tends to be fairly artificial. People are looking at the whole cowboy thing and liking what they see. In the States people are scouring the country for old cowboy gear. If you could find an old pair of boots or something like that, they'd sell for hundreds of dollars. And a good pair of angora chaps is worth thousands of dollars. Because it's heritage, it's nostalgia, but also people are seeing a real value to it.

Swan Lake

North of Vernon at the junction of Highways 97 and 97A, Swan Lake Bird Sanctuary is a good place to view blue herons, white geese, swans, Canada geese, and many other species, although access is confusing. The Infocentre at the south end of the lake can provide directions.

O'Keefe Ranch

At the north end of Swan Lake, Highway 97 heads west to Kamloops, past the **O'Keefe Ranch** (542-7868), a lovingly restored history lesson and a major attraction. Established in 1867 by Cornelius O'Keefe and Thomas Greenhow, the ranch was totally self-sufficient, with a church, store, and a still-functioning blacksmith shop. The buildings date back to the 1870s and some, like the mansion, contain original furnishings. A working ranch until 1977, Cornelius' son Tierney still visits from time to time to make sure everything is as it should be. The facility is now operated as a historic site and hosts an annual cowboy poets' jamboree each May. (See page 197.) Open for viewing during the summer months, the ranch has a year-round restaurant.

Highway 97 continues on a very scenic drive through **Falkland** (Infocentre: Box 92, V0E 1W0) and **Monte Lake** to Kamloops. Among the special events are the **Falkland Stampede and Rodeo** held annually on May long weekend and the **International Dog Sled Races** in January.

Highway 97A travels north of Vernon through Armstrong and Enderby and meets the Trans-Canada at Sicamous or Salmon Arm.

Armstrong

23 km (14 mi) north of Vernon.
Population: 2845.
Infocentre: Box 118, V0E 1B0.
546-8155; Fax: 546-8868

Armstrong's history is wrapped up in agriculture and railroading. The first settlers called the settlement Aberdeen, honoring the illustrious couple who introduced commercial orcharding to the Okanagan. But the town was renamed when William Heating Armstrong's London banking house helped finance the Shuswap and Okanagan Railway.

Historically "the bread basket" of the northern Okanagan, Arm-

St. Anne's Church was built at O'Keefe Ranch in 1889. With its original pews, furnishings, and pump organ still intact, today it is a popular place for weddings.

strong is actually located in the Spallumcheen Valley, and is well-known for its hardy fruits, asparagus, and celery. Local dairy cows provide the milk for the famous Armstrong cheese. If you arrive on Monday, Thursday, or Saturday, you can tour the **Armstrong Cheese Factory** (Pleasant Valley Road, 546-3084).

Armstrong has an old cowtown feel to it with its wide main street, railway running down the middle, and turn-of-the-century architecture. The **Armstrong Hotel**, built in 1892, still operates. The **Armstrong-Spallumcheen Museum** (Railway Avenue, 546-8318, seasonal) depicts local history.

The **Caravan Farm Theatre** (546-8533) is located just outside of

---

Nick Hutchinson
Artistic Director Caravan Farm Theatre Armstrong

I live here for two reasons: art and potatoes. It's difficult to do just one of those, but both – it's impossible.

People come and expect to have a wonderful theatre experience in this funky old place. We've done a whole gamut of plays from *Animal Farm* to *Romeo and Juliet*, to *Strange Medicine* (a musical), to *The Mystery Cycle*. I mean, *the* gamut.

When I was in my early twenties and onwards, I was really trying to find my own place. I went to theatre school in France, and then I came back to England. But then I needed to get away because having a mother who was the top actress in England [Dame Peggy Ashcroft, who died in 1991] didn't make it easy for someone who was full of having to prove himself. I was trying to find a place where I could work as me.

I became really politically involved and that landed me up somehow in Montreal in 1970 and then in BC, where I bought a horse, rode in the Chilcotin, and was doing my cowboy dream. And then at some point along that line, Paul Kirby, who was the guy who started the Caravan, needed an artistic director and so [in 1976] I rode my horse from Pemberton to Salmon Arm – and that was that.

This place has a generative power. There's a clan of about 200 people who have worked with the group off and on over the years who come back, and then there are new people who are sort of questing for something else – looking for a different way of working, for living in a different kind of way. And there's a whole generation of our kids, too, who come back all the time.

My mother adored it. She came out lots of times and actually performed with the Caravan, in the Bill Miner show, touring on the road for a few days.

I'm not sure what it is, because it's sixteen years that I've been doing this. I'm not sure how much of me relates to what part of it. Part of me is really happy when I'm just farming with the horses.

Armstrong (watch for direction signs downtown). Many of Canada's finest artists join the company each summer to present original work and classics from Brecht to Shakespeare in an unusual outdoor setting. During the winter, company members conduct sleigh rides as well as special Christmas productions.

Other special events in Armstrong include the annual hot air **Balloon Rendezvous** on Thanksgiving weekend, the **Kinsmen Rodeo** in August, and the **Interior Pacific Exhibition** in September.

Outdoor recreation includes hiking on Mount Rose and Mount Swanson and birdwatching at **Otter Lake Wildlife Preserve**.

Enderby

13 km (8 mi) north of Armstrong on 97A. Population: 1825. Infocentre: Shuswap River Park, Old Vernon Road, Box 1000, V0E 1V0. 838-6727; Fax: 838-2144. Seasonal

The Shuswap River has long been important to area residents. Natives used the river as a transportation route. Lambly's Landing, near the present site of Enderby, used to be the head of navigation for steamers coming from Sicamous on Shuswap Lake. Farmers soon planted grain on the rich soils of the flood plain and a grist mill was built in 1887. Today farmers raise dairy cows and other crops, and agriculture, along with logging, continues to be important to the economy.

The **Enderby Museum** (on Highway 97 in the city hall complex, 838-7170), features changing displays

The Armstrong Hotel, built in 1892, is still operating.

The spectacular beauty of Rainbow Falls at Monashee Provincial Park is only for backpackers or fly-ins. The wilderness park has no road access.

of the area's farming, logging, and transportation history as well as artwork of local artists

There are a lot of horse people in the north Okanagan, among them the Sawatzky family, who operate **Birch Meadows Farm** (five kilometres north of Enderby on the Enderby-Grimrod Road). The Sawatzkys raise Morgans, the giant work horses who helped build the province, hauling logs and freight in the early days. They have about two dozen horses at present, among them a ten-year champion. Visitors are welcome.

The **Enderby Cliffs**, the highest in Okanagan, provide a spectacular view of the valley. Ask for directions at the Infocentre. **Mabel Lake** is accessible to the east of Enderby. Pictographs on the western shore of the lake and warm sandy beaches are among the attractions. The **Shuswap River** has appeal for paddlers of all levels, with the most difficult sections closest to the headwaters. The **Kingfisher Community Fish Hatchery and Environmental Interpretive Centre** (Mabel Lake Road, 838-6569) raises about 250,000 salmon and trout each year. Survival rate for fish here is 15 percent, compared with a provincial average of 0.4 percent.

Hidden and Bard lakes are good for trout fishing.

Sidetrip: The Monashee Highway

Highway 6 east of Vernon, the Monashee Highway, travels through an area rich in history. **Lumby** (Infocentre: Box 534, V0E 2G0, 547-2300), considered the logging centre of the North Okanagan, attracted settlers from Quebec in the late 1800s. Originally called White Valley, the town was renamed after an early miner and farmer who came to BC in 1862, settling in the Spallumcheen area in 1870. Moses Lumby became vice-president of the Shuswap and Okanagan Railway and Vernon's government agent in 1891.

Inspired by stories of gold in Barkerville, miners were in the **Cherryville** area as early as 1863. Farming and logging took over in the 1880s but mining continued until the 1930s. Travellers who look closely will see the remains of the Chinese workings and water canals along the river. And if they look really closely, maybe they'll see something glinting and beckoning in the water of Cherry Creek – the mother lode was never found.

The **Shuswap River Hatchery** (547-6673) is north of Lumby on Mabel Lake Road near Shuswap Falls. **Mabel Lake Provincial Park,** with its warm water and good fishing, is just enough off the beaten track to provide relief from the Okanagan crowds. Its temperate cedar and hemlock forests provide a contrast to the drier landscape of the Okanagan Valley.

The remote **Monashee Provincial Park** is also accessible from Highway 6. Although trail access to this 7513-hectare wilderness area is limited to experienced hikers, the many alpine lakes, rock formations in Valley of the Moon, and 3000-metre peaks have a strong appeal.

Highway 6 past Lumby and Cherryville is a beautiful but winding drive east through the Monashee Mountains to the Arrow Lakes. A free ferry takes travellers across the lake from Needles to Fauquier. North is Nakusp, Revelstoke, and the Trans-Canada Highway. East of Nakusp, Highway 6 continues south through the Slocan Valley.

Outdoor enthusiasts have reclaimed the old Kettle Valley Railway line for hiking and biking.

One of the most spectacular sections is the trestle bridge over Myra Canyon east of Kelowna.

West Kootenay

Glacier-fed Kootenay Lake is over 120 kilometres long and features record-sized rainbow trout, Dolly Varden char, and Kokanee salmon.

The West Kootenay region has often hosted people who were "different." The earliest inhabitants were the Kutenai, more closely allied to the Plains Natives than to the Interior Salish. The Kutenai regularly crossed the Rocky Mountains to hunt buffalo.

In the early 1900s English orchardists settled around the Kootenay and Arrow lakes, growing prize-winning cherries and apples while beating the wilderness back with parasols. At the same time, Doukhobors settled around Castlegar, escaping persecution in Russia (and Saskatch-ewan) for their pacifist views. During World War II, hundreds of Japanese-Canadians from coastal BC were forced to relocate to internment camps here. And today there are pockets of homesteaders and artisans throughout the area, pursuing alternative lifestyles.

David Thompson travelled this way on his route to the Pacific in 1808, but the West Kootenay didn't receive much attention from Europeans until the discovery of copper and silver at Toad Mountain near Nelson in 1886. Then prospectors filed claims throughout the "Silvery Slocan" Valley and Kootenay Lake region, and settlers and business people built towns and railways. In the mid-1950s logging became viable on a large scale in the Interior, and forestry became important to the economy.

The West Kootenay is made up of several valleys encompassing three north-south river systems: the Arrow Lakes/Columbia, the Slocan, and the Kootenay. Throughout the southern Interior, the natural corridors provided by the rivers, lakes, and valleys encouraged north-south trade with the Americans, a worry to early politicians such as Governor James Douglas. In early mining days, the American Fourth of July was as common a holiday as the Queen's Birthday. The building of the Dewdney Trail in the 1860s and the Crows Nest rail line in the 1890s were attempts by business and political leaders to prevent American dominance.

The cold temperatures of the glacier-fed lakes and abundant precipitation have prevented the West Kootenay from becoming a major tourist destination like the Okanagan or Shuswap regions. But out-

Osprey

Members of the hawk family, the migratory osprey are found throughout the Interior from early spring to autumn near lakes, rivers, and sloughs. The Nelson-Creston area supports about 140 pairs of nesting birds, one of the largest concentrations in the world.

Dark brown on the upper body with white forehead, chin, neck, and underparts, the average osprey weighs about 1.5 kilograms with a wingspan of 160 centimetres.

Their distinctive nests are often seen on dead trees, telephone poles, pilings, or other manmade structures. Made of twigs, branches, and sticks, the bulky structures range from a half metre to 2.5 metres in diameter and can be up to two metres high.

Although it is not uncommon for osprey to commandeer the nests of other species such as Canada geese and great horned owls, in the Kootenays, one osprey pair was observed returning to the same nest 11 consecutive seasons.

Osprey usually lay two to four eggs in May and June; the young hatch in five to six weeks and remain fledglings for six to eight weeks.

Sometimes known as the "fish hawk," osprey are unique among hawks in their ability to capture and handle fish. A bird may dive from 10 to 20 metres for a fish swimming one metre under water. Tenacious creatures, they have been known to drown rather than release a fish that is too big to lift from the water.

At the top of their food chain, osprey can serve as indicators of environmental problems. In the 1960s, the population underwent a serious decline in some areas because of the presence of organochlorine pesticides such as DDT. Since restrictions of such substances have come into effect, osprey populations have increased.

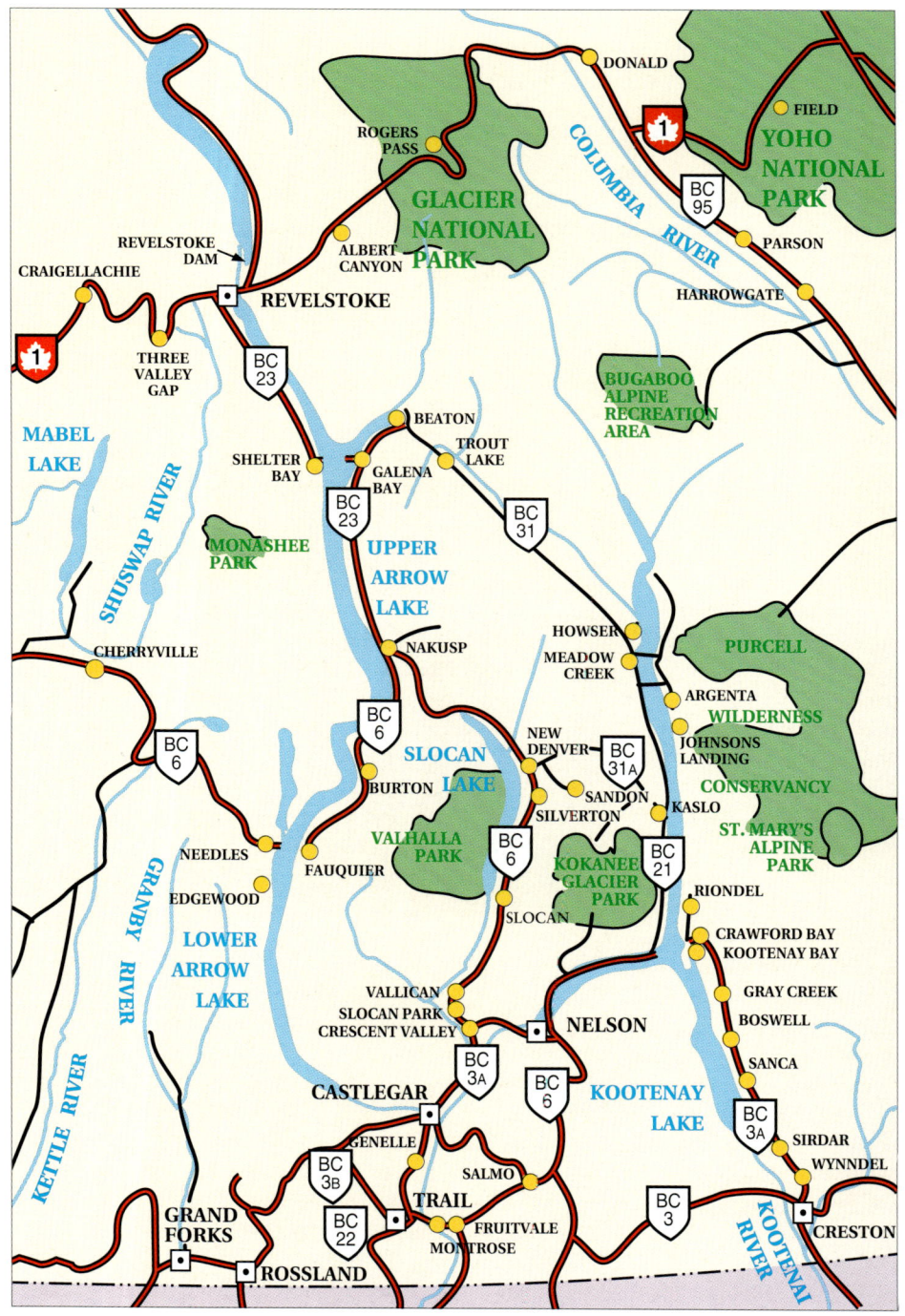

Dams and Osprey: Castlegar to Nelson

Travelling east from Castlegar, Highway 3A follows the Kootenay River, a major tributary of the Columbia. The headwaters of both rivers are in the Rocky Mountains, but they flow in opposite directions – the Kootenay south to Montana, the Columbia north around the Big Bend – finally joining together at Castlegar.

There are several dams and power plants along this stretch of highway that keep all our electric lights and pizza warmers humming. Old-timers in the area tell stories about pulling big salmon out of the Kootenay, Slocan, and Columbia rivers before the hydroelectric projects were installed. Tours of the newest facility, BC Hydro's **Kootenay Canal Generating Station**

door enthusiasts appreciate the area's wide range of recreational activities. They come to swim, ski, hike, paddle, bike, fish, hang-glide, spelunk, and soak in the hot springs.

Exploring the West Kootenay is not a straightforward journey. *SuperGuide's* route heads east from Castlegar to Nelson, north beside Kootenay Lake to Kaslo, west to the Slocan Valley, and south to Highway 3A. Then the tour heads back to Nelson, crossing Kootenay Lake via the free ferry at Balfour and travelling down the east side of the lake to Creston. However, there are circle tours within circle tours in this area, including the Lardeau Valley and Nakusp. All kinds of permutations are possible.

Corra Linn is one of six dams and seven power plants on the 45 kilometres of the Kootenay River between Castlegar and Nelson.

The city of Nelson was founded when the Hall brothers discovered silver in 1886 on nearby Toad Mountain. Today it is known for its large population of artists and its restored heritage buildings.

(359-7287), are available. Others are operated by West Kootenay Power and Light and the city of Nelson. Several pull-outs along the road have interpretive signs and impressive views. The **Bonnington Falls** are the reason the river was unnavigable between the Kootenay and Columbia systems. But it was a favourite salmon fishing spot for Natives, who likely were camping here 4000 years ago.

Just past **Taghum,** the road crosses the river. The big piles of twigs on top of telephone poles are osprey nests. In the spring, it is possible to see little beaks flapping over the edge demanding lunch. Osprey sometimes return to the same nest year after year. When the bridge was being built in the 1980s, crews had to replant one of the poles so as not to disrupt the tenants' breeding habits.

Grohman Narrows Provincial Park, four kilometres west of Nelson is a day-use park with a short trail beside a small marsh.

Nelson

43 km (27 mi) east of Castlegar. Population: 8510. Infocentre: 225 Hall Street, V1L 5X4. 352-3433; Fax: 352-6355

When the Hall brothers discovered silver on Nelson's Toad Mountain in 1886, it attracted the attention of prospectors and mining syndicates. Other discoveries quickly followed from Greenwood to Kimberly.

The town was incorporated in 1897, and, calling itself the "Queen City," soon grew to prominence as a cultural, transportation, and business centre. In the 1980s, a major heritage revitalization program was launched, restoring over 350 homes and office

buildings. Hollywood, always quick to spot a pretty face, chose the town as the location for two movies in 1987, *Roxanne* and *Housekeeping*.

The Infocentre has two brochures on self-guided heritage tours. **Cottonwood Falls was** the site of the first hydroelectric generation plant in the province, opened in 1896. The **Provincial Courthouse** (Vernon and Ward Streets) was designed by Francis Rattenbury, the British architect responsible for both the parliament buildings and the Empress Hotel in Victoria. When it opened in 1899, Nelson's electric streetcar system was the only one in the West outside of

Vancouver and Winnipeg – and the smallest in the British Empire. A restored car sits on the waterfront at the mall. The beautifully restored **Capitol Theatre** (421 Victoria, 352-6363) is the centre of cultural activity in Nelson with local, national, and international programming.

The **Nelson Museum** (402 Anderson Street, on the way to the Kootenay Lake Ferry, 352-9813) is the place to go for displays and information on local history. Some say there are more artists and artisans per capita living in the Nelson area than anywhere else in Canda. The craft shops and galleries on and

S.S. *Nasookin*

Paddlewheelers of all shapes and sizes were an integral part of the transportation system in BC's early days, and the Kootenays relied heavily on these sturdy ships. The first sternwheeler chugged up the Arrow Lakes in 1865, but when mining and settlement boomed in the 1890s, the railway companies began a fierce competition for supremacy in freight and passenger service, adding more and more vessels on the lakes and rivers. Between 1897 and 1957, a fleet of 11 of these ships plied Kootenay Lake alone.

In 1913, as part of a plan to develop the tourist trade on Kootenay Lake , the CPR launched the 1869-ton *Nasookin* on Kootenay Lake with a 15-gun salute. The ship was the largest of BC's sternwheelers and one of the most elegant – with mahogany and wicker furniture, Wilton carpets, electric lights, coloured skylights, and fine dining. All that remains of the ship today is the pilot house and observation deck, restored as a private home, visible on west side of the highway, four kilometres north of Nelson.

near Baker Street have a variety of interesting and authentic souvenirs for the folks back home. In the summer months, an organized **Artwalk** tours the galleries (352-2402).

The Kootenay Lake Summer School of the Arts (352-2402) is another popular summer activity.

Ask for directions to **Gyro Park** (you can see its gazebo from Baker Street). Getting there is complicated, but the park has lovely gardens, a swimming pool, and a great view. **Lakeside Park,** right beside the big orange bridge, is popular with windsurfers, swimmers, and picnickers.

In winter, skiers head for **Whitewater Ski Area** (354-4944), 19 kilometres south of Nelson off Highway 6. Even in times of a province-wide snow drought, there is usually snow here. **Morning Mountain Ski Area,** five kilometres west of town on Granite Road in Blewett, is popular with families. Many area residents cross-country ski. There are trails at Whitewater but many more at local parks and logging roads. Ask at the Infocentre.

Other recreational activities include water sports, hiking, biking, fishing, and hang gliding. Annual events include the **Sno Fest** in February and the **Curling Bonspiel** in July.

West Side of Kootenay Lake

Nelson is a good base camp for side trips and recreational activities on 120-kilometre-long Kootenay Lake. The water is a little cold for swimming, but there are several sandy beaches that prove the exception. Kaslo and area are best for boat rentals and charters. Besides fishing, water skiing, and paddling, visitors can look for the several rock faces on the lake that display Native rock paintings.

northeast of Nelson. Spawning kokanee salmon are a major attraction in the fall. A 16-kilometre access road to Kokanee Glacier Provincial Park also starts here.

Kokanee Creek Provincial Park

One of the area's nicest beaches is at 257-hectare **Kokanee Creek Provincial Park** (825-4723), 19 kilometres

Kokanee Glacier Provincial Park

This 32,000-hectare wilderness area is very popular with local residents for both winter and summer use.

Robert Inwood
Heritage Revitalization
Consultant
Nelson

I started off as a carpenter, working on renovation and restoration projects in downtown Nelson. I've always enjoyed Victorian architecture, so I tended to gravitate toward the design end of things.

The initial steps for the Nelson program came from the BC Heritage Conservation Branch which had just done a survey of the province. Because the mall had just been put in, the merchants were looking to do something with the downtown. I ended up being in the right place at the right time.

I coordinated the program for five years, starting in 1980, working with a partner from Heritage Canada. It was a long process. There were some people who were gung-ho right from day one, and others that dragged along. But one of the reasons Nelson is such a success story is that we had amazing participation – 90 percent in the first five years. Since then virtually every store in Nelson has been renovated in some fashion. That's why it looks so good.

It's a popular program. I've worked with

dozens of other BC communities: Rossland, Revelstoke, Trail, Kaslo, New Denver, Hazelton, Keremeos, Port Hardy, Port Alberni, McBride, and Fort St. John.

There have been some real big success stories. If you drive into Nelson and try to find a parking place, you'll see the town is just going crazy. It was about to dry up and blow away ten years ago.

I enjoy the work. Heritage revitalization gets people's mindsets turned around so they see the history of the community from a positive vantage point, rather than a bit of the past that needs to get shoved out of the way to make way for the future. The town takes pride in itself, people appreciate the historic fabric of their community more, they learn about it and talk to their friends about it. There seems to be a general deepening of their awareness of the whole history of the area.

I don't see the interest in heritage revitalization slowing down. People's appreciation of historic buildings seems to be on the upswing. And I'm already working on renovations of my renovations. Time marches on; it's a fact of life.

Kokanee Creek drains 1981-metre-elevation Kokanee Lake. Its glacial waters flow into Kootenay Lake at Kokanee Creek Provincial Park.

Trails enter the park from several directions, but Gibson Lake, from the Kokanee Creek road, is a pleasant day-hike to subalpine terrain. There are 30 lakes in this rugged area, many of them stocked with cutthroat trout, and most lying between 1700 to 2100 metres elevation. Attractions include glaciers and wildlife. At times grizzly bear warnings are posted: read the signs and sing loudly as you go. Off key is fine. (See Bears, page 77.)

Ainsworth

16 km (10 mi) north of Balfour.
Population: 57

At the tiny town of Ainsworth, it is easy to imagine yourself back in a simpler time, when mining was king and a fortune was over the next rise.

The first settlement here in 1882 was overshadowed by developments elsewhere, and the town was destroyed by fire in 1896. However, silver mines like the Pearl Lulu, Skyline, Highland, Jeff Davis, and Mile Point contributed to its recovery and Ainsworth boomed until the turn of the century. The Silver Ledge Hotel, built in 1896, still stands, although it does not operate as a hotel.

Nowadays people flock here for the 40°C to 43°C pools and the eerie caves at **Ainsworth Hot Springs** (229-4212). The hot springs are just off the highway, beside Kootenay Lake, and there are motels if you can't imagine moving another inch once you've had your soak.

Cody Caves

Travellers who enjoy dark subterranean places should turn off Highway 31 five kilometres north of Ainsworth. **Cody Caves Provincial Park** (825-4421) – and 800 metres of explorable passage – is 16 kilometres along a seasonal gravel road. The impressive underground display includes stalactites, stalagmites, soda straws, tunnels, and galleries formed millions of years ago. There is a guide service and equipment rental at the cave in summer, and a year-round interpretive display. Wear warm clothing and take a flashlight.

Kaslo

32 km (20 mi) north of Balfour.
Population: 845. Infocentre: 4th Avenue and A Street, Box 329, V0G 1M0. 353-7323. Seasonal

Dubbed "the quintessential Rocky Mountain town" by *National Geo-*

graphic (and it's not even in the Rockies), this is another Kootenay town that's survived the ups and downs of mining, lumbering, and orcharding. Galena ore was discovered in 1892, Kaslo was incorporated in 1893, and for a while it was a hive of activity with paddlewheelers coming and going, 20 hotels, 14 barbershops, a sawmill, and banks. It even had its own railroad, the indomitable narrow-gauge Kaslo and Slocan line. A fire and a flood in 1894 slowed the town down, but it gave the people a legacy of survival that carries through to this day.

The **Langham Centre** (353-7425), once a rough-and-ready hotel, then a bank, and eventually an internment centre during World War II, is now restored as an arts centre with a small theatre and gallery. The **Kaslo-on-the-Lake Summer School of the Arts**

is held at the Langham each July and August (353-7425). **Kaslo City Hall** (353-2311), in use continuously since 1898, is a designated national historic site. The Infocentre has a walking-tour brochure.

On the lakefront sits the S.S. *Moyie*, the oldest of five remaining historic sternwheelers in Canada. Built in 1898, the boat logged over two million miles in her lifetime, carrying miners, settlers, tourists, and business people up and down the lake. The visitor's centre (353-2525) has interpretive displays and tours.

Kaslo Bay is one of the best fishing spots on Kootenay Lake. Four- to six-kilogram Dolly Varden are not uncommon, and one lucky angler reeled in a record Gerrard trout weighing over 15 kilograms. There are several marinas, resorts, and guiding outfits in Kaslo and vicinity.

Originally the mining town of Ainsworth had five hotels, but the Silver Ledge, built in 1896, is the only one remaining.

The S.S. *Moyie*, now a museum in Kaslo, was the last commercial sternwheeler to operate in BC. The vessels had shallow drafts that allowed them to dock on beaches, making them an important means of early transportation in the Interior.

The annual **May Day** celebrations have been going on since 1893 and include such diverse activities as the traditional maypole dance and logging sports.

Sidetrip: Lardeau Valley

North of Kaslo, partly paved Highway 31 gives access to Meadow Creek, the **Duncan Dam,** and the Lardeau Valley. Southeast of Meadow Creek, the road travels to the Quaker community of Argenta and the trailhead for the **Purcell Wilderness Conservancy** and **Fry Creek Canyon Recreation Area**.

Highway 31 travels up the Lardeau River, by Trout Lake, past the sites of old mining towns like Poplar, Ferguson, and Trout Lake City. There are few amenities, but the scenery is unbeatable and the fishing is great.

The Lardeau River is the spawning place for Gerrard trout and a wildlife management success story. During the 1950s there were only about 50 rainbow spawning here each year. Now the annual run numbers a thousand.

At Galena Bay a free ferry travels across the Upper Arrow lake to Shelter Bay where Highway 23 connects to Revelstoke and the Trans-Canada Highway. Self-guided tours are offered at **Hill Creek Spawning Channel and Hatchery** (eight kilometres east of Galena Bay on Highway 31). During spawning season it's a great place to view black bear, osprey, eagles, mink, and otter. South of Galena Bay, Highway 23 leads to Nakusp.

Ghost Town Highway

Highway 31A west of Kaslo continues to the "Silvery Slocan" Valley. This area was a frenzy of mining activity in the 1890s – "silver, lead, and hell" were raised in the Slocan, the saying goes.

Although towns like Nelson and Kaslo survived the boom-bust cycle, many didn't, and along this road the former towns of Retallack,

Ada Robichaud
Manager, Tin Cup Cafe, Sandon

I like the balance of living here and going to university. I originally came up here to do work in the archives. But I never got to it.

There's interesting things going on here. I think of the buildings as dream homes because somebody's dreams are locked up in them. People keep coming back – the Japanese who were here, and the miners.

A Japanese woman came through a few weeks ago and I was showing her around this house. She looked at the wooden bathtub in the back room and said she remembered taking baths in that. Her uncle had built it. She'd lived in the house next door during the internment.

I think ghost towns attract eccentrics. It's not your waterslide crowd. Many people have the

sense that they've been here before or they'd like to stay.

People ask if I've seen ghosts. That doesn't happen to me. I'm not afraid of dark places. I feel comfortable with ghosts. But people want there to be ghosts here.

I lived for a long time in Ferugson in the Lardeau – same time, same era. It went until the First World War and then never recovered. There were 3000 people there and now you can't tell where any of them lived. It just looks like a meadow.

Left: An old building in Sandon displays embellishments of the past. Restoration continues, but many original buildings have been destroyed by flood or fire.

Right: The Tin Cup Cafe, one of the few remaining original buildings in Sandon, is open during the summer months.

Zincton, and Three Forks, stand as skeletons today. Retallack (sometimes called Whitewater), at 1085 metres elevation, yielded over a million dollars in rich galena ore.

One of the most famous of the ghost towns is Sandon. (The turnoff is at Three Forks junction, 34 kilometres west of Kaslo.) In 1891 prospectors discovered a rich outcropping of ore here that led to the establishment of claims like the Noble Five, the Slocan Star, and the Payne Boy. Sandon boomed and the Silvery Slocan became one of the richest silver regions on the continent.

By 1898 Sandon had 5000 residents, 23 hotels and saloons, several banks, two newspapers, an opera house, three breweries, a hydroelectric plant, and two railroads. The town was rebuilt after a fire in 1900, but declining markets put it on a downhill course. The Sandon Historical Society is presently restoring two of the old buildings. Two other original buildings house the **Sandon Museum** (358-2247) and the **Tin Cup Cafe** during the summer. The hydroelectric plant is still operating, and mining continues.

The seven-kilometre **Three Forks-Sandon** Trail is on the railbed of the former Kaslo and Slocan Railroad and good for cross-country skiing.

The road to **Idaho Lookout**, a favourite day trip of local residents, is on the south side of Carpenter Creek in Sandon. Ask locally about current conditions. This 12-kilometre gravel mountain road is not for the faint of heart, but it winds almost to the top of Idaho Mountain with its glorious alpine meadows, usually in full flower in August. The panoramic view from the fire lookout (2280 metres elevation) includes Slocan Lake, Kokanee Glacier, and the Valhallas. The area is popular with bears as well as hikers. (See Bears, page 77.)

New Denver
47 km (28 mi) west of Kaslo.
Population: 596. Infocentre: 803 Kildare Street, Box 398, V0G 1S0.
358-2631; Fax: 358-7998

Descending into New Denver alomg Highway 31, travellers see the sparkle of Slocan Lake and look right across to New Denver Glacier in **Valhalla Provincial Park**. Early explorers called this town Lucerne, for its similarity to the Swiss landscape, and later a romantic with big expectations named it Eldorado. As mining in the area boomed, and the mother lode turned out to be silver, not gold, the town named itself yet again. New Denver carved out a niche for itself as a supply and service centre, assuring its survival, but a walk down its main street clearly speaks to its mining past.

To the south of Carpenter Creek is "the orchard," one of several sites in the Slocan Valley where hundreds of Japanese-Canadians were interned during World War II.

The Silvery Slocan Museum (358-2201) on the main street of town is open June to October and features several interesting displays including a Japanese room.

Directly across the lake, Valhalla Provincial Park lines most of the eastern shore. Access from this end of the lake is by boat, and there are local guides. Ask at the Infocentre.

The abandoned Nakusp-Slocan rail line north of town is used by bikers and hikers.

Sidetrip: Nakusp

52km (32 mi) north of New Denver.
Population: 1270. Infocentre:
92 West 6th Avenue, Box 387, V0G 1R0.
265-4234; Fax: 265-3808

The town of Nakusp sits on Upper Arrow Lake, a continuation of the Columbia River. Here the mountains – the Monashees on the west side of the lake, the Selkirks behind – are a little gentler, less imposing than those to the east.

As part of the Slocan mining boom, entrepreneurs were planning to build a smelter in Nakusp, and the Nakusp-Slocan Railway was built in 1893. But when Trail's smelter operation expanded, the

Japanese-Canadian Internment

In December 1941, Japan attacked Pearl Harbour. Eight weeks later, in February 1942, the federal government invoked the War Measures Act and ordered the removal of all Japanese and Japanese-Canadians living on BC's coast. Most were given only 24-hours notice.

Many of the 22,000 men, women, and children labelled as "enemy aliens" had been born in Canada and spoke no Japanese. About 13,000 were "relocated" to internment and work camps in BC's Interior; others were sent east of the Rockies.

While many of the men were sent to work camps, women, children, and elderly were often settled in the almost-ghost towns of Greenwood, Sandon, Kaslo, Slocan, and New Denver. A special camp was built at Tashme, in the mountains west of Hope. The largest number of internees (4800) were housed in the Slocan Valley south of New Denver at Lemon Creek, Passmore, and Crescent Valley.

In some places, people were housed in old buildings, such as the Langham Hotel in Kaslo, the hockey rink in Slocan, or even tents. But the most common housing were the rows of uninsulated one-room shacks that housed two or more families.

Writer Joy Kogawa and popular scientist David Suzuki are two prominent Canadians who spent part of their childhoods in the camps.

In 1986, the federal government formally apologized and offered financial compensation to surviving internees.

plan was dropped. Agriculture, logging, and transportation became the economic mainstays.

Nakusp was an important stopover on the busy sternwheeler route

Hot Springs

Nakusp Hot Springs is one of several soothing natural spas found in the southeastern Interior. In BC, hot springs seem to follow two major paths. One stretches along the coast from the Yukon to US border, and the other is more closely connected to the Rocky Mountain Trench making a path from northwest to southeast.

Hot springs occur when surface water finds its way underground through rock fractures and is heated by hotter rock closer to the earth's core. The temperature of the water increases approximately 1°C for every 33 metres it descends. At 2.5 kilometres beneath the earth's surface the temperature is hot enough to boil water. Ground water that reaches this depth percolates back to the earth's surface via other crack systems.

On its journey, the water absorbs minerals which some feel gives it therapeutic properties. The medicinal value is debatable, but hot springs are a wonderful way to ease weary muscles.

For more information, consult the Reference section. Also see Jim McDonald's *Hotsprings of Western Canada* (Vancouver: Waterwheel, 1991).

up and down the lakes until the 1950s. In the 1960s, much of the surrounding land was flooded as part of the Columbia River Treaty, a controversial development that wiped out entire towns and destroyed much of the farmland.

Local history can be studied at the **Nakusp Museum,** (next to the Infocentre, 265-3323). A walk along the lakefront by the old Leland Hotel is also a pleasant diversion. The town is proud of its recreation potential and boasts excellent fishing nearby for rainbow trout, Dolly Varden, and kokanee salmon.

Naksup Hot Springs (352-4033), 12 kilometres northeast of town, is popular with residents throughout the West Kootenay. (Watch for the sign one kilometre out of town.) Nestled among the trees in **Nakusp Hot Springs Provincial Park,** the hot springs are an ideal place to soak after a good workout on the surrounding cross-country ski and hiking trails. Both skis and bathing suits are for rent at the facility, which is operated by the Village of Naksup. A campground and chalets are nearby.

Three undeveloped hot springs, Halfway River, St. Leon, and Halcyon, are north of town on Highway 23. St. Leon and Halcyon were popular resort areas before the flooding of the lake – remnants of the pools and buildings can still be seen. One source claims the Kootenai and Colville tribes fought battles over the Halcyon waters.

Summit Lake Ski Hill offers family skiing 10 kilometres south of Naksup, and Summit Lake is popular for ice fishing in the winter.

Highway 23 connects with the Trans-Canada Highway at Revelstoke. The Galena Bay-Shelter Bay ferry is free, but check the schedule before you leave Nakusp. The ferry does not operate between midnight and 5 AM Highway 6 continues south of town, crosses the Lower Arrow Lake on the free ferry from Fauquier to Needles, and then heads west to the Okanagan. The Needles-Fauquier ferry runs every half hour and is available on a shuttle basis from 10 PM to 6 AM.

Silverton

5 km (2 mi) south of New Denver.
Population: 246

From New Denver, Highway 6 heads south along Slocan Lake through the picturesque mining town of Silverton. The **Silverton Gallery and Mining**

Mattie Gunterman

Born Ida Madelaine Werner in La Crosse, Wisconsin in 1872, Mattie Gunterman is well known among Canadian photographers for her photographs of pioneer life in the Interior.

Gunterman moved to Seattle as a teenager; an uncle there taught her to use a camera during the early Kodak craze. Diagnosed with tuberculosis and told by doctors she hadn't long to live, in 1897 she left Seattle, and along with her husband Will, their five-year-old son Henry, their dog Nero, and their horse Nellie, walked 800 kilometres to Beaton on the Arrow Lakes in the Kootenays. (The photo above, taken by Gunterman, shows the family possibly on the Dewdney Trail in 1898.)

In 1898, the Lardeau was a vital mining area, part of the West Kootenay mining boom. Will worked as a logger and miner in the camps around Beaton, and Mattie worked as a cook. Her photographs show ordinary activities of the community and contain a sense of humor and a spontaneity that contrast with the more formal portraiture popular at the time.

Hard times hit the mining communities in the Lardeau during the early 1900s and the Gunterman family suffered as well. While working in Alberta in 1927, a fire destroyed the Gunterman home, all her original prints, and much of her equipment. She continued to live in the Lardeau area, and died of a heart attack in 1945 at age 73.

In 1961, when Ron D'Altroy of the Vancouver Public Library was travelling through Beaton, he met an old trapper who told him about some photographic plates that he had stored in a shed. The trapper was Henry Gunterman. The 300 glass negatives were all that remained of Mattie Gunterman's photographs. Carefully restored, they are now part of the photographic archives of the Vancouver Public Library and a remarkable record of pioneer days in the West Kootenay.

The Slocan Valley near Slocan City offers a spectacular view of the Valhalla Range of the Selkirk Mountains. Although the Slocan area saw a mining boom in the 1890s, the Valhallas have never been known for mineral deposits.

Museum (358-7788) is in a 1917 schoolhouse. An outdoor mining display features both 19th- and 20th-century mining equipment from the area. The gallery features performances and displays.

The town's pebble beach is a good place to watch the clouds go by. The lake is deep, the water is cold, and hordes of tourists are unheard of.

Motorists should watch carefully for wildlife – there are lots of deer along this route, and too many of them are killed by unattentive motorists. Black bear, especially around Red Mountain, are not uncommon. The lookout south of Silverton provides a memorable view of Slocan Lake and Valhalla Provincial Park.

Valhalla Provincial Park

Valhalla Wilderness Society, Box 224, New Denver, BC V0G 1S0.
BC Parks: 825-4421

Numerous alpine lakes dot the upper reaches of this 49,600-hectare wilderness area, and a hike up one of several creeks passes through a variety of forest, subalpine, and alpine terrains. The lakes are stocked with trout, and in July and August the blueberries are sweet and juicy. Wildlife such as bear, mountain goat, deer, cougar, and mountain caribou live on the slopes, and eagles soar overhead.

The park is accessible by boat or logging road from several locations, including a trail from Slocan City that winds along the shore of the lake – an easy and enjoyable day trip. The parking area for the trailhead is two blocks west of the main street at the head of the Slocan River. The trailhead is across the bridge and up the road a hundred metres. The park is also accessible via Drinnon Lake in the Little Slocan Valley. The turnoff is 20 kilometres south on Highway 6.

Boaters can reach the park from several places along the east shore. At Slocan City, put in at the beach beside the mill and paddle up the lake. On both sides, pictographs tell mysterious stories on the rock faces. The lake is cold for swimming, but on a hot day, it's very refreshing.

Slocan City

19 km (11 mi) south of New Denver.
Population: 280.
Infocentre: Box 50, V0G 2C0.
355-2282; Fax: 355-2666. Seasonal

Slocan City is a quiet mill town today, with one hotel and a handful of stores, but in the 1890s it was a wide open mining town. Slocan was at the end of the rail line, and sternwheelers carried miners and supplies up and down the lake from here to Silverton and New Denver. Slippery gamblers plied their trade at the 16 hotels and saloons that lined the main street, and more than one miner lost a hard-earned fortune in a card game over a bottle of whiskey. Unfortunately, there aren't many of the old buildings left and the evidence of Slocan City's colourful past is relegated to museums and history books.

Slocan Valley

There is evidence that people have lived in the Kootenays for 7000 years, with at least 14 Native villages on the Slocan River alone. Native groups have not lived in the valley for many years, but a plan to relocate the highway over an ancient burial ground in the late 1980s brought a renewed interest in local Native history from both Natives and non-Natives. Declared extinct by the federal government in 1965, descendants of the Sinixt people have been returning to Vallican, at the confluence of the Slocan and Little Slocan Rivers, over the last few years. The modern Sinixt claim that their people lived permanently in the valley, and they were not nomadic as historians and archeologists report. The Vallican archeological site is on the backroad south of Winlaw. Ask locally.

Once a raucous mining town with a population of 6000, Slocan City is now a logging town of a few hundred.

At Balfour, travellers can take "the longest free ferry ride in the world" across Kootenay Lake.

The Slocan River empties into the Kootenay River just west of the junctions of highways 3A and 6. But our route heads east, back to Nelson for the completion of the tour.

Free Ferry across Kootenay Lake

Balfour, 34 kilometres northeast of Nelson on Highway 3A, used to be a stop on the paddlewheeler routes up and down Kootenay Lake. Today, the small community is a popular resort area and a terminus for the "longest free ferry ride in the world." The schedule depends on the time of year, so check the times locally. The crossing to Kootenay Bay takes about 45 minutes, and as the ferry pulls away from the dock, travellers may catch a glimpse of an osprey dive-bombing the water in search of breakfast or an eagle carefully circling overhead.

Kootenay Lake East Shore

Infocentre: Box 4, Gray Creek, V0B 1S0. 227-9267; Fax: 227-9449

The east shore of the lake was also part of the 1890s mining boom in the Kootenays. The old chimney at **Smelter Bay**, visible as the ferry approaches Kootenay Bay, was part of a plant that employed 200 men in the early part of the decade. The smelter processed ore from the rich Blue Bell Mine in Riondel that supported a town of one thousand. But when the Hall Smelter opened in Nelson in 1896, the Pilot Bay Smelter was no longer economical, and it closed down.

Riondel, north of Kootenay Bay, is now a retirement community, but

Non-Native settlement began with the mining boom in the 1890s. Other settlers homesteaded during the early 1900s. When the Doukhobor communities near Castlegar dissolved during the 1930s, many families established farms in the Slocan Valley.

The **Slocan River** is popular with kayakers and canoers. Floating along the current on inner tubes is a favourite summer pastime of local residents. Depending on the time of year, the rapids at Winlaw are a minor or major whitewater thrill and there are other hazards such as log jams on certain portions. Ask about river conditions locally. Whether visitors travel down the river or down the highway, they will pass by picturesque farms and old log buildings. Although speeding chip trucks heading for the pulp mill in Castlegar present a hazard, the relatively light traffic on Highway 6 has made it a favourite bicycle touring route.

its **Blue Bell Mine** was a going concern until 1957. Robert Sproule first staked the claim in 1882, but had to travel all the way to Fort Steele to make it official. While he was away, Thomas Hamill found the claim, and because he happened to be on a hunting trip with the gold commissioner, gained ownership. Hamill was shot on the site in 1885, and Sproule was hanged for the crime in 1886, although he steadfastly proclaimed his innocence.

The east side of the lake was the Crowsnest Highway until the construction of the Salmo-Creston Skyway in 1963. This scenic route is dotted with resorts, bed and breakfasts, and campsites. Year-round fishing on the lake is for Dolly Varden, kokanee, rainbow, and whitefish, although some restrictions may be in effect. Check locally. Boats and guides are available.

At **Crawford Bay**, historic **Wedgewood Manor** (227-9233) has an international reputation and offers memorable meals or a cup of tea in a park-like setting. The **Crawford Bay Fall Fair,** a popular event since 1910, is held annually in late August.

Pilot Peninsula is an interesting place for exploration. A hike up to the lighthouse reveals an impressive view of the lake. Paddlers can view 600-million-year-old rock formations along the shore. A unique camping experience is offered by a local nonprofit group, The Guiding Hands Recreation Society (227-9555). They hold outdoor-education programs at a teepee camp on the peninsula .

"Kootenay Lake's largest and oldest general store" in **Gray Creek** was opened in 1913. The owners claim it is "the most interesting store you've ever seen," supplying everything from organic food to chain saws. The **Gray Creek Sailing Regatta** is held every Labour Day Weekend.

There are tales of buried treasure in this area. One story tells of three men who in 1892 came across a huge gold nugget in these mountains, estimated then to be worth $650,000. While attempting to lower it into their row boat near Gray Creek, the rope broke and the nugget disappeared in 60 metres of water. The nugget has yet to be discovered.

From Gray Creek, seasonal Highway 44 (opened in 1991) leads to Kimberley in the East Kootenay. (Ask at Gray Creek about the road conditions.) Gray Creek is "metric-free" so the summit at the pass is 6800 feet, and it's 55 miles to Kimberley.

South of Gray Creek, **Boswell** is home of the famous Glass House (223-8372). This unique free-form structure was constructed by a retired funeral home director out of 500,000 embalming bottles which he collected from across the country.

The scenic drive continues along the lakeshore for another 50 kilometres through the old mining town of **Sanca**. At **Kuskanook** – a Kutenai word meaning "end of the lake" – the popular Métis poet Pauline Johnson enthralled audiences with her mesmerizing stories on one of her crosscountry tours in the 1890s.

Just before Creston there is a viewpoint at the junction of Highways 3 and 3A, which takes in the south end of the lake, the Creston flats and the Selkirk Range.

East Kootenay

The fertile bottomland of the Rocky Mountain Trench is geologically unique. Visible from space, it stretches 1600 kilometres from north to south, ranging from 16 kilometres width in the south to three kilometres in the north.

At the same time that Simon Fraser was battling the turbulent waters of the river that was eventually to bear his name, David Thompson was viewing the quiet beauty of the Kootenay Valley for the first time. "It resembles a large basin, surrounded by lofty mountains which form a vast amphitheatre and present a picturesque sight," wrote Thompson in 1808. Although the area had long been inhabited by Kutenai and Shuswap Natives, Thompson was the first European to cross the Rockies and explore the Rocky Mountain Trench area with its semi-arid grasslands, plentiful game, and mystical hot springs.

When Thompson made his observations, he was here (as was Fraser) on behalf of the North West Company. The fur-trading company was anxious to find the mouth of Columbia and exploit the river as a supply route before the Americans could. Thompson lost the race to John Jacob Astor's Pacific Fur Company by just a few weeks. But he is responsible for charting most of the Columbia River's watershed between 1807 and 1812. He established Kootenae House near Invermere in 1807 and several forts in Washington and Idaho.

The discovery of gold at Wild Horse Creek near present-day Fort Steele in 1864 opened up the area to settlement. When claims were staked on the Big Bend of the Columbia River in 1866, the valley became a major transportation route with stern-wheelers bustling up and down the waterways. The construction of the CPR through the Rogers Pass in the early 1880s, the discovery of rich ore deposits near Kimberley and coal in the Elk Valley in the 1890s, and the completion of the CPR's Crowsnest rail line in 1898, further stimulated development and settlement.

The East Kootenay seems a world apart from the rest of the Interior. Perhaps this is because the region is so far from the provincial centres of power on the coast. Or perhaps it has to do with the towering peaks of the Purcell and Rocky mountains standing sentinel on either side of the valley. As with the Kutenai who resided here before the arrival of the fur traders, today's residents enjoy an easier alliance with the area east of the Rockies and the American states to the south than with the rest of BC.

The mild temperatures and varied landscape make the East Kootenay region a popular outdoor recreation destination. Vacationers can enjoy mountain climbing, alpine fishing, whitewater rafting, canoeing, swimming, and water skiing within hours of each other. Some of the best golf courses in the province are at Fairmont and Radium. Panorama Resort and Fernie Snow Valley are popular ski areas, and Bugaboo heli-skiing is world famous.

Founded by mining, Kimberley increasingly relies on Bavarian-style hospitality and top-notch skiing for its economic well-being.

Highway 93/95 travels north from Cranbrook through the wide valley of the Rocky Mountain Trench to Radium Hot Springs. One fork, Highway 95, continues north beside the Columbia River to Golden on the Trans-Canada, the other, Highway 93, through Kootenay National Park to Alberta. The two highest mountain passes on the route are both on Highway 93: Sinclair Pass (1486 metres) and Vermilion Pass (1639 metres).

Kimberley

32 km (20 mi) north of Cranbrook on Highway 95A. Population: 6015. Infocentre: 350 Ross Street, V1A 2Z9. 427-3666; Fax: 427-5378

Historically, Kimberley has depended on the riches beneath its mountains. The Sullivan Mine was for many years the world's largest producer of lead

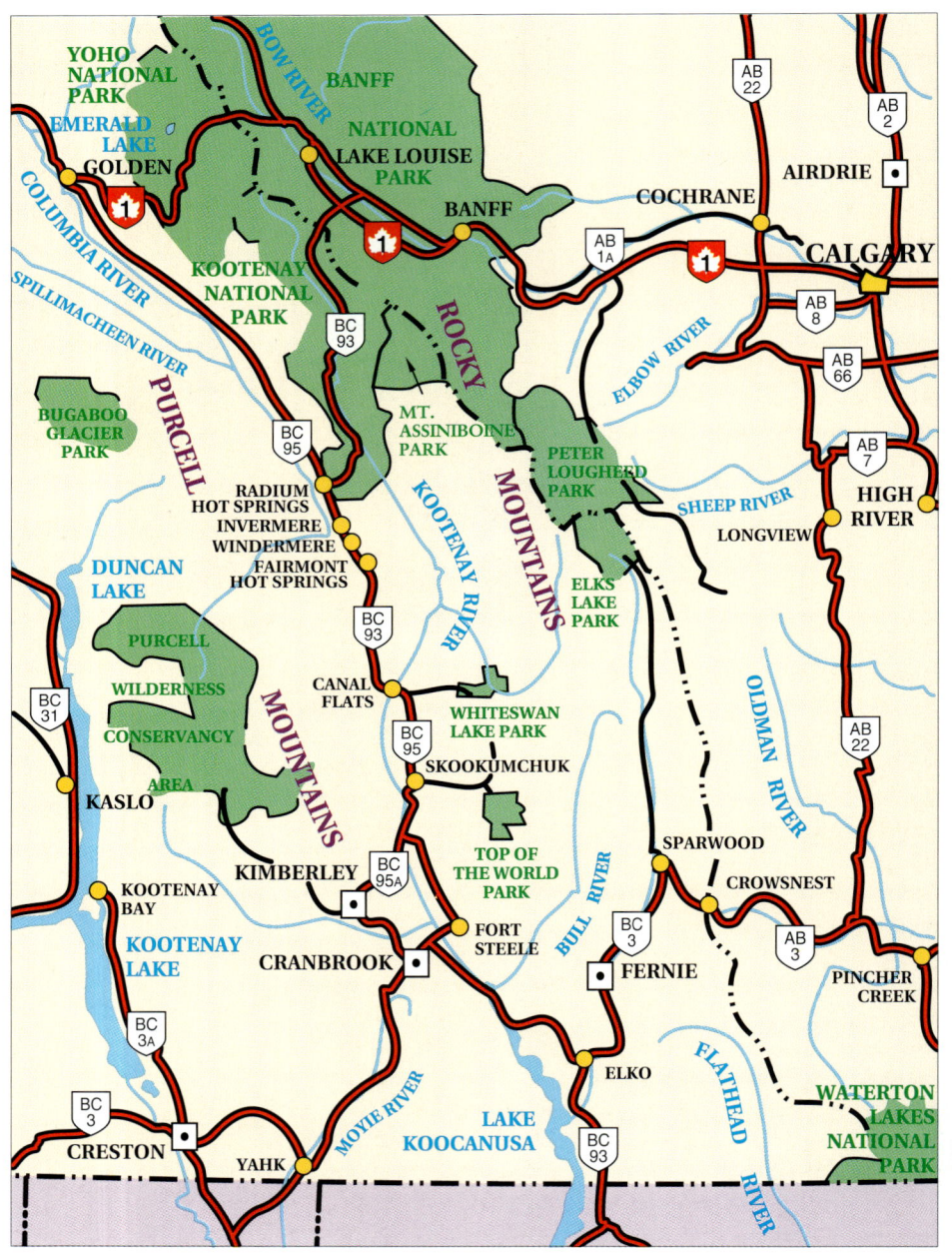

and zinc ore. The Sullivan discovery was made in 1892 with the first shipment to the smelter in Trail in 1900. Cominco took over the Sullivan in 1910, and it was the economic mainstay of the area for several decades. But nowadays, with world markets less and less reliable, the town is shifting its economic base to the riches on top of the mountains – scenery, snow, and ambience. Although several hundred workers currently depend on the mine and concentrator, the facility is scheduled to be shut down by the year 2000.

Kimberley is nestled between the Purcells and Rockies, overlooking the Valley of a Thousand Peaks. At 1117 metres above sea level, this is one of the highest cities in Canada, so it makes sense that the town adopted a Bavarian theme in 1972. The move transformed it from a drab mining town to "BC's Oom-Pah-Pah Capital," and tourism is now the number-two industry, attracting 300,000 visitors annually. Many European tourists, impressed by the clean air and other alpine attributes, have settled in the area. What began as a marketing idea now has authentic ingredients. **The Old Bauernhaus Restaurant** is a prime example. Two German families looking for a new place to live dismantled a 400-year-old family home in Germany and rebuilt it here in 1989.

South of town on Highway 95A, **Marysville** was scheduled to have the Sullivan's smelter in 1898, but plans were abandoned with the development of the smelter at Trail. Today an easy five-minute nature walk along a

The 400-year-old Bauernhaus was dismantled in Bavaria in 1987 and reconstructed in Kimberley in 1989. Today it is a family-run restaurant offering authentic German cuisine.

boardwalk and a gravel trail attracts visitors to the **Marysville Waterfalls**. Wild roses and other wildflowers are an added bonus in June.

In town, the **Bavarian Platzl** on Spokane Street is the centre of everything. Attractions include the world's largest cuckoo clock, European restaurants and delis, and in the summer, wandering minstrels. At the end of the Platzl the **Heritage Museum** (427-7510) emphasizes mining, but also has an interesting archival collection of photographs and newspapers. Within walking distance on Fourth Avenue is the one-hectare **Cominco/Kimberley Gardens**, showcasing 48 varieties of flowers and over 50,000 plants.

The **Bavarian Mining Railway** on Gerry Sorensen Way offers a 2.5-kilometre train trip with a view of the city, the Rocky Mountains, and the Sullivan Mine. Depending on production schedules, visitors can take underground tours of the mine. (Contact the Infocentre, 427-3666.)

The **Kimberley Ski Resort** (1-800-667-0808) on North Star Mountain is

Workers at Fort Steele Provincial Heritage Site maintain machinery and equipment that existed at the turn of the century.

a major ski destination in the Interior with 34 runs on 1200 acres and a vertical drop of 701 metres. Operated by the city of Kimberley, North Star is also the home slope of 1982 world downhill champion Gerry Sorensen.

Special events include the **Old Time Accordian Championships** in July and the **Winterfest** in February.

Hikers can reach the Purcell Wilderness Conservancy and St. Mary's Alpine Park via Highway 44 west of Kimberley. This seasonal highway climbs over the Purcells and leads to Gray Creek on Kootenay Lake.

Alternate Route: Fort Steele Provincial Heritage Site

16 km (10 mi) northeast of Cranbrook on Highway 3/95. 489-3351

With the discovery of gold at **Wild Horse Creek** in 1864, miners rushed to the area from Montana, Washington, and Idaho. Some, like John Galbraith, realized there was more

profit in tending to the needs of the prospectors than actually doing the backbreaking work of gold mining. For the hefty price of $10 per pack horse and $5 per person, Galbraith allowed the prospectors to cross the Kootenay River on his cable ferry to reach the banks of the creek. Galbraith's success encouraged brother Robert to move west, and the pair opened a store and established a packtrain to Walla Walla, Washington. Soon Little Lou, Axe Handle Bertha, Wildcat Jennie, and Gunpowder Sue opened up a "finishing school" in the settlement. A town was born.

By the 1880s the gold rush was long over, and the population of several thousand gold seekers at Galbraith's Ferry had dwindled to a few hundred. But in 1887, there was conflict between the Kutenai Natives and the white settlers. A detachment of 75 North West Mounted Police headed by Superintendent Sam Steele set up a post, staying long enough to settle the dispute. The citizens of Galbraith's Ferry, grateful for the peaceful handling of the matter, renamed their town Fort Steele.

With the resurgence of mining activity in the Kootenays in the 1890s, Fort Steele once again became a centre of activity. It was a bitter blow to the community when the CPR's Crowsnest line went through Cranbrook farther to the south in 1898. Residents left for more prosperous ventures elsewhere, and the bustle faded to a faint rustle.

Today there are over 60 restored and reconstructed buildings on the site. In the summer months history comes alive as costumed staff recre-

The Valley of a Thousand Peaks: Three Mountain Parks

ate life in Fort Steele as it was in the 1890s, hosting wagon rides, live stage shows in the Wild Horse Theatre, and a variety of special events. Fort Steele is open year round, but the peak season is mid-June to Labour Day.

The Fort Steele Infocentre has a pamphlet that gives directions to the graveyard at Wild Horse townsite and "the last mile" of the **Dewdney Trail**. This historic route was hacked through the bush from Hope in the mid-1860s in a successful attempt to maintain British sovereignty over the area. The portion here is a two-hour hike, passing the old mining site of Fisherville, the Chinese graveyard, and Wild Horse Creek.

Birdwatching areas nearby are **Bummers Flat,** nine kilometres north of Fort Steele and **Wasa Slough Wildlife Sanctuary**, 14 kilometres north.

Wasa Lake, just south of the junction of Highways 95A and 93/95, is one of the most popular recreation areas in the East Kootenay. **Wasa Lake Provincial Park** has several beaches, an interpretative program, and self-guiding nature trails.

The scenery continues to be spectacular as Highway 93/95 winds north through grasslands and pastures and the peaks of the Rockies loom overhead. Turn east at the pulp mill town of **Skookumchuk** for access to **Premier Lake Provincial Park** and excellent trout fishing. Fisheries staff from the hatchery in Wardner collect eggs here for distribution to lakes throughout the province. Wildlife includes Rocky Mountain bighorn sheep, elk, and deer. Blue heron, eagle, and os-

Popular attractions at Fort Steele are the Clydesdale horses and authentic (no shock absorbers) wagon rides.

Looking north at Top of the World Provincial Park. Natives have visited this area for at least 9000 years, mining its prized chert.

prey also populate the area.

Hot springs are a major attraction in the Kootenays, with two major resorts north of here. But those who like to do their soaking in isolation, might want to explore **Ram Creek Hot Springs,** located in a 121-hectare ecological reserve. Turn off Premier Lake Road before the park and head 11.5 kilometres up Sheep Creek Road

A little farther north on Highway 93/95, a sign indicates the access roads to **Whiteswan Lake Provincial Park** and **Top of the World Provincial Park.** Whiteswan Lake, 16 kilometres off the highway, has good trout fishing in its two lakes and the added bonus of rustic **Lussier Hot Springs'** several pools.

Top of the World Wilderness Park is another 38 kilometres along the road. The dominant peak of this 8791-hectare park is Mount Morro, 2912

metres in elevation. (Most of the park is above the 1800-metre level.) Kutenai Natives used to mine chert here, a highly prized hard blue-grey rock which they traded or fashioned into tools and weapons. There is big game, but one of the most popular activities is the trout fishing. Bird-watchers at Fish Lake may see Clark's nutcrackers, Steller's and gray jays, sandpipers, loons, eagles, and osprey. The park's many trails attract hikers in summer and skiers in winter.

Although the creeks in this area have been well-worked by prospectors since the 1860s, gold panning is still a possibility. Findlay Creek, just south of Canal Flats, is one such place. Others include Boulder, Wild Horse, and Perry creeks. The area around Skookumchuck Creek is good for rockhounding.

Canal Flats

117 km (70 mi) north of Kimberley.
Population: 824

The **Columbia River** begins its 2044-kilometre journey to the Pacific Ocean at **Columbia Lake**, just north of Canal Flats. And the **Kootenay River**, with headwaters in Kootenay National Park, passes within a kilometre of Columbia Lake south of here.

In 1882, a colourful Englishman named William Adolph Baillie-Grohman, hatched a scheme to build a canal that would connect the two bodies of water. In 1889, 200 workers dug the two-kilometre-long canal – 14 metres wide and 3 to 4 metres deep. But the plan fell apart. Baillie-Grohman returned to England in 1893 and spent the rest of his days writing accounts, some say embellished accounts, of his adventures in the wilds of the Kootenays.

The Kootenay River offers a scenic canoe/kayak trip through novice to intermediate whitewater from north of Canal Flats to Fort Steele. **Canal Flats Provincial Park** has boat-launching facilities, and a bighorn sheep-enhancement area is nearby. The winds on Columbia Lake make it a favourite with windsurfers.

Fairmont Hot Springs

112 km (69 mi) north of Cranbrook

The healing powers of Fairmont Hot Springs have been attracting people for centuries. The Kutenai Natives revered the springs for their mystical origins. As European settlement advanced, they became a rest stop for stage coach travellers. In 1922 a re-

sort was established which has grown into an international tourist destination.

The hot pools – open to everyone, not just hotel guests – are the largest natural hot pools in Canada, made doubly attractive because they are fed by a calcium spring and there is no sulphur odour. Above the hotel, is the simpler "Indian Pool" where a soak in one of the stone bathtubs, a paddle in one of the small pools, and the view are free. Temperatures in the hot pools range from 43°C to 48°C.

In addition to the main resort, there are a number of motels and

Dramatic hoodoo formations stretching several kilometres along Dutch Creek are visible from Highway 93/95 south of Fairmont Hot Springs.

Kootenae House was built near present-day Invermere by fur-trader David Thompson in 1808. This replica of the fort was built in 1922.

campgrounds nearby, as well as a golf course and **Fairmont Ski Area** (345-6311; 1-800-663-4979) with 304 metres of vertical drop, 12 alpine runs, and 22 kilometres of nordic trails.

Invermere

24 km (15 mi) north of Fairmont Hot Springs. Population: 2075. Infocentre: 6th Street and 7th Avene, Box 2605, V0A 1K0. 342-6313; Fax: 342-2934

This picturesque town on **Lake Windermere** is only a three-hour drive from Calgary and popular as a summer resort with Albertans. But it attracts historical interest as the site of Kootenae House, the first fur-trading fort in eastern British Columbia.

David Thompson was the explorer who mapped the Columbia River system in the early 1800s. In 1807 the North West Company learned their rivals the Pacific Fur Company were

about to establish a fort at the mouth of the Columbia River. Accompanied by his young Métis wife and their three children, Thompson crossed the Rockies and built a post between the present site of Invermere and Athalmer. For the first few months Peigan Natives, with whom he had been friendly, became angry at his foray into Kutenai territory and laid siege to the fort. The Peigan and Kutenai were sworn enemies and the Peigan were fearful that Thompson would be trading knives and guns for furs with the Kutenai. The Peigan eventually gave up their vigil and Thompson was able to successfully chart the river, but was beaten to the coast by his rivals. There's no trace of the fort today; a stone cairn marks its approximate location.

The **Windermere Valley Pioneer Museum** (342-9769) is a 19th-century log complex featuring the his-

tory of the upper Columbia Valley and Banff and Kootenay national parks. One of the more impressive parts of the collection is a copy of David Thompson's journal, a limited edition of 500. The main building is the former Athalmer train station.

When the CPR moved its divisional point to Revelstoke from Donald (near Golden on the Trans-Canada Highway) in 1897, many of Donald's buildings were torn down and moved to Revelstoke, along with its people. However, when the townspeople were ready to move the church, they discovered it was gone. A local couple, not aware of the plans for the church, had disassembled it, barged the logs down to Windermere, and rebuilt it. **St. Peter's Stolen Church** (342-9400) is located on Kootenay Street and Victoria Avenue in Winderemere, just south of Invermere.

Panorama Ski Resort (342-6941; 1-800-663-2929) 18 kilometres west of Fairmont Hot Springs, features a 1158-metre vertical drop for alpine skiing, 28 kilometres of groomed nordic trails, and heli-skiing. In the summer the area is open for hiking, horseback riding, and rafting. The Panorama road also accesses the northern boundary of the **Purcell Wilderness Conservancy** and the 61-kilometre trail over 2256-metre Earl Grey Pass. Lake Windermere is popular with wind surfers.

Radium Hot Springs

16 km (10 mi) north of Invermere.
Population: 450.Infocentre:
St. Joseph's Street, Box 225, V0A 1M0.
347-9346; Fax: 347-6459. Seasonal
Radium Hot Springs is both a town and a hot springs. The town is a small logging community at the junction of Highways 93 and 95. The hot springs

Built in 1887, St. Peter's "Stolen" Church in Windermere has an unusual history.

Between 1886 and 1914, fifteen paddlewheelers travelled the Columbia River between Columbia Lake and Golden. Today, the wetlands provide a superb wildlife habitat and gentle paddling for canoers.

is at the Aquacourt in Kootenay National Park, just east of the townsite.

Travellers have hard decisions to make. To the northwest, Highway 95 leads through the scenic Columbia wetlands to Golden. To the east, the Kootenay Parkway (Highway 93) travels north through Kootenay National Park to Alberta. There are many motels and campgrounds in this area which make it an excellent base for forays in either direction.

Radium's two 18-hole golf courses are among the best in the Interior.

Highway 95: The Columbia Wetlands

Radium Hot Springs is about halfway along the 180 kilometres that make up the only remaining undeveloped portion of the Columbia River. (Just north of Golden, the Columbia widens into man-made Kinbasket Lake, created when Mica Creek Dam was built at the Big Bend in 1973.) Thirteen additional hydroelectric power projects dam the water along the rest of the Columbia's 2044-kilometre journey to the Pacific Ocean, with dozens more on tributaries.

The 26,000-hectare natural wetland between Canal Flats and Golden houses a variety of marsh, river, and woodland habitats, supporting several species of flora and fauna. The majority of wintering elk in the Columbia River basin can be found here. With the spawning of kokanee in October, golden eagles soar overhead. Dozens of species of waterfowl, including Canada Geese, ducks, osprey, and swans, breed here.

Between 1866 and 1914, paddlewheelers travelled the river between Columbia Lake and Golden. Today, this portion of the Columbia River is one of the best canoe routes in the province for novices. The trip between Athalmer and Golden takes about 7 days. (Information: 347-9505.)

Bugaboo Glacier Provincial Park and Alpine Recreation Area

At Brisco, 27 kilometres north of Radium, a gravel road provides seasonal access to 358-hectare **Buga-**

boo Glacier Provincial Park and the adjoining 24,624-hectare **Bugaboo Alpine Recreation Area,** 45 kilometres to the east. (Beware of logging trucks. Travel with your lights on, and pull over when necessary – they have the right of way.)

There are over 200,000 mountain climbers in North America, and many of them come to this rugged wilderness area. Part of the Purcell Range, the Bugaboos contain the range's largest icefield, and its peaks, many over 3000 metres, are for experienced mountaineers only.

The Purcells may be just across the valley from the Rockies, but they are much older. The sedimentary rocks of the Purcells originated 1.5 billion years ago, when algae was the dominant life form. The geological turmoil caused by the development of the Rockies about 70 million years

ago allowed the intrusions of molten rock in the Purcells. Over time uplift and the erosive forces of wind, water, and glaciation removed the weakened outer layers of its peaks, creating the dramatic granite spires seen today. A privately run lodge, which is a headquarters for heli-skiing and heli-hiking, is located just outside the park boundaries.

Kootenay National Park

The boundary of Kootenay National Park lies immediately east of the town of Radium Hot Springs. The only park in Canada with both cactus and glaciers, it encompasses 1406 square kilometres of diverse topography, flora, and fauna. The varied habitat is home to 993 plant, 92 bird, 58 mammal, 4 amphibian, and 3 reptile species.

Bugaboo Glacier Provincial Park and Alpine Recreation Area contains the largest icefields in the Purcell Mountains. Here a climber inspects the Vowell Glacier below 3398-metre Howser Spire.

As in all Canadian national parks, if you're in a motor vehicle and you plan to stop in the park, you must obtain a permit. Ticket booths are right on the highway. Permits are good in any Canadian national park for the duration of the permit. The park information centre just past the west gate (or the Marble Canyon Information Centre near the east entrance) has maps and brochures on a variety of park-related subjects including camping, trails, safety, and regulations. Separate licences must be obtained for angling in national parks and staff has information on the best spots to fish.

Originally called the Banff-Windermere Highway, the Kootenay Parkway was the first road through the Rocky Mountains. It was the brain-child of Invermere businessman Randolph Bruce, who saw a great commercial advantage in having a route connect the northern Columbia Valley with Alberta. Construction began in 1911, but the highway wasn't completed until 1922 – after the federal government had been given land on either side of the proposed roadway in return for financing. The park was established in 1920.

Unlike Glacier National Park to the northwest, where the steep slopes create a harsh and unsympathetic environment, wildlife viewing is excellent here. Mountain goat, deer, elk, and bighorn sheep are commonly seen – drive with caution.

The Hot Springs

The **Radium Hot Springs Aquacourt** (347-9615) pools are just inside the park. Valued by several Native tribes for their soothing powers, pictographs in the area suggest the pools were an ancient meeting place for Interior and Plains Natives. Hot-spring water is heated deep underground, collecting minerals on its

Western or Pacific Yew
Taxus brevifolia

The yew tree is unusual among conifers because its seeds occur in a red berry-like structure rather than the typical evergreen cone.

Ten species occur worldwide, all in the northern hemisphere, but only two in Canada. The Pacific yew, the only species in BC, is found in the coastal forests and the Columbia forests of the southeastern Interior.

Yew tends to grow singly rather than in stands, in moist areas under the canopy of trees such as western hemlock and Douglas fir. Although at lower elevations a single tree can grow up to 20 metres high, at middle elevations they often form an impenetrable, sprawling undergrowth.

The distinctive thin purple bark can be peeled off revealing yellow sapwood and bright-orange or rose-red heartwood that is valued for decorative woodwork. Fine-grained, strong, hard but elastic, the wood was valued by Native cultures for harpoons, bows, canoe paddles, eating utensils, and splitting wedges.

Too slow-growing to be harvested commercially, some English yew trees have reached ages of 1000 to 2000 years. The flat two-toned leaves are poisonous to horses and cattle.

In 1992, taxol, a compound found in yew bark, was approved as an anti-cancer drug.

The federal government expropriated Radium Hot Springs from developer Roland Stuart in 1922 when Kootenay National Park was created. The original Aquacourt was constructed in 1950, with renovations in 1968.

journey to the surface that dissolve, affecting the colour and odour. (The length of time it takes for the water to reach the surface varies. Estimates have the Banff waters taking three months; Yellowstone waters, 50 years.) Some feel the added minerals may have therapeutic properties.

Although the amount of radium in the water here is about equal to what you'd find in the dial of a luminous wrist watch, early settlers flocked to the pools in the belief that the radium content would heal all their ills. In fact, when developer Roland Stuart was trying to find financing for his hot springs project in the early 1900s, he got backing from Perrier multimillionaire John Harmsworth. Harmsworth was completely paralyzed until he spent several weeks soaking in the pool and was finally able to wiggle his foot. Today, most people come simply to relax in the soothing 27°C to 40°C waters. A resort and campgrounds are close by.

Sinclair Canyon

In the fur-trading days, American- and British-backed companies were vying for control of Oregon Territory and the land north of the Columbia River. In 1841, the Hudson's Bay Company sponsored 120 settlers from

Construction of the Kootenay Parkway through Sinclair Canyon took 13 years between 1911 and 1924. The brightly coloured canyon rock is part of the Redwall Fault.

The Kootenay Valley Viewpoint

The Kootenay Valley Viewpoint, 17 kilometres east of Radium Hot Springs, gives an extraordinary view of the Kootenay River. In the autumn the golden needles of western larch turn the hillsides into a blaze of colour. This species, although cone-bearing, is not an evergreen and drops its needles every fall. Its appearance in the national parks in the Rockies is relatively rare. The headwaters of the Kootenay River is just north of Kootenay Crossing, about 15 kilometres east of the viewpoint.

Mountain goats often visit the mineral lick near Mount Wardle on the highway. An estimated 300 mountain goats live in the park.

From 2.5 kilometres south of Vermilion Crossing farther up the valley, it is possible to get a glimpse of 3618-metre Mt. Assiniboine to the south. The highest mountain in this part of the Rockies, it was named after the Assiniboine, or Stoney people.

Paint Pots

Eighty kilometres east of Radium Hot Springs, the half-hour self-guided walk to the **Paint Pots and Ochre Beds** winds through a mossy damp subalpine forest with scenic views of snow-capped peaks.

The Paint Pots are mineral springs that produce iron-rich, slightly heated water that stains the surrounding earth. The colourful residue was collected by Kutenai Natives, who baked the clay in round cakes and used it as the basis of a ceremonial paint. On their way to hunt across the Rockies, the

Manitoba's Red River Colony in an unsuccessful attempt to maintain control of the disputed land. Led by James Sinclair, they travelled through the Rockies using the pass in the spectacular red-rock canyon that bears his name. Part of Redwall Fault, the red-coloured rock was created millions of years ago when limestone, ground into fragments by the shifting of the tectonic plates, was stained by iron oxide.

Five hiking trails of varying lengths start from the canyon, taking in lakes, wildflowers, and creeks. Altogether the park has 200 kilometres of trails. They penetrate the wilderness from several points along the highway, with some short self-guided tours for those with limited time.

Kutenai would stop here to gather the ochre for barter with the Stoney. In the early 1900s, local businessmen tried to export the clay to a paint-manufacturing company in Calgary, but the attempt failed. Remains of the machinery can still be seen at the site.

Before crossing the suspension bridge over the Vermilion River, look for the insectivorous butterwort plant with its violet-coloured flowers. Minute hairs on the sticky, yellow leaves trap tiny insects for sustenance.

The artificial surface on trails in this and other national parks may seem a little disappointing, but it minimizes the effect of many sightseers in a fragile environment.

Marble Canyon

Over 500 million years of geological history is revealed in the limestone and dolomite rock walls of Marble Canyon, 85 kilometres east of Radium Hot Springs. A one-kilometre interpretive trail along Tokumm Creek criss-crosses a 600-metre-long, 36-metre-deep chasm which took nature 8000 years to carve. A national parks information centre is at the site.

Vermilion Pass

Lightning started a forest fire on these slopes in July 1968, which burned for four days, destroying 2400 hectares of trees. A one-kilometre trail through the area gives visitors an opportunity to view natural reforestation at work.

In old growth forests, mature stands of trees dominate the ecosystem. They shade the ground, leave no room for new plants to grow, and eradicate the food supply of animals. After the fire, lodgepole pine – which needs the heat of the fire to pop open its seed pods – began to grow. Fireweed, young spruce, and fir also took root. Shaded by the lodgepole, the fir and spruce will grow to maturity in another hundred years or so, and the cycle will repeat itself. The **Fireweed Trail** is just south of the eastern entrance to Kootenay National Park, at the Continental Divide.

The **Continental Divide** runs along the border between Kootenay, Banff, and Jasper national parks. All rivers and streams along the west side of this ridge run to the Pacific, all those to the east eventually end up in the Arctic Ocean or Hudson Bay.

Mineral springs that produce iron-rich water stain the earth at the Paint Pots and Ochre Beds. Natives derived a coloured pigment from the clay and used it to make decorative paint.

Central Interior

Once part of a difficult canoe and portage route from the Lower Mainland to the Cariboo, Seton Lake near Lillooet has since been flooded as part of the Bridge River hydro-electric project. During construction, a bowl dating back 12,000 years was found at the site, a Native settlement for centuries.

o man stands beside the Fraser River without sensing the precarious hold of his species upon the earth," Bruce Hutchison writes in his book *The Fraser.* When Alexander Mackenzie began his historic journey part way down the Fraser in May 1792, his Native interpreter "shed tears on the reflection of those dangers which we might encounter in our expedition."

For centuries the Fraser River was both a welcome lifeline and a formidable obstacle to the men and women who travelled its waters, prospected its gravel beds, and built trails, roads, and railways along its banks. Never tamed by hydroelectric dams, the mighty Fraser continues to earn the respect of those who know it.

The Central Interior encompasses approximately 100,000 square kilometres of the Fraser River drainage.

Our circle tour of the region begins at Cache Creek. Highway 97 travels north through the Cariboo-Chilcotin region to Prince George over the Interior Plateau. Throughout this area, travellers can see evidence of the early volcanic eruptions and subsequent glacial activity that has shaped the landscape. Huge boulders seemingly out of place in the middle of rolling grasslands can be spotted from time to time. Called erratics, they were deposited by the melting ice sheets. Lava rock, glacial eskers, and canyons are also among the geological attractions.

The Cariboo-Chilcotin is cowboy country. The sparsely populated area to the west of Highway 97 and the Fraser River is popularly referred to as the Chilcotin. Rolling hills, tumbling tumbleweed, and enormous cattle ranches conjure up romantic visions of the Old West in all but the most determined city slickers.

The Cariboo, the region to the east of the highway, is gold country. In the 1860s, thousands of miners rushed to the goldfields at Williams Creek, Quesnel Lake, and Keithley Creek, establishing boom towns like Barkerville and Horsefly. Parts of Highway 97 follow the old Cariboo Wagon Road, one of the first highways in the province.

If you want to holiday in the Cariboo-Chilcotin, you might be just as well off to get a map, close your eyes, and stick a pin in it – you can hardly go wrong. Guest ranches, rodeos, and fishing attract visitors from around the world.

At Prince George, our route continues east along Highway 16 (the Yellowhead Highway) following the Fraser River almost to its headwaters near Mount Robson in the Rocky Mountains. The tour heads south from the old fur-trading centre of Tête Jaune Cache along Highway 5 (the Yellowhead South) accompanying the North Thompson River to Kamloops.

Less developed than the Cariboo-

Buildings at Hat Creek Ranch date back to the 1860s. It was regarded as one of the better roadhouses on the old Cariboo Wagon Road.

Chilcotin, the area is popular with outdoor recreation enthusiasts who enjoy wilderness experiences. One of the major attractions on the Yellowhead South Highway is Wells Gray Provincial Park.

The main industries in the Central Interior are logging, mining, cattle ranching, tourism, and outdoor recreation. Fishing, hiking, backpacking, canoeing, rafting, cross-country skiing, and horseback riding opportunities are plentiful.

Hat Creek Ranch

11 kilometres north of Cache Creek, Box 878, Cache Creek, V0K 1H0. 457-9722

When thousands of prospectors descended on the Cariboo in the 1860s, Governor James Douglas quickly started construction of a road to the goldfields. Construction crews completed the Cariboo Wagon Road in 1865, providing faster and cheaper access to the Interior from the coast. One of the many roadhouses along the route where stagecoach travellers and horses could rest was **Hat**

Creek Ranch, 500 metres off Highway 97 on Highway 12.

Donald McLean, a former Hudson's Bay Company factor, began operating the roadhouse at Hat Creek in 1862. McLean was killed in the Chilcotin War in 1864, but not before he fathered three sons, the infamous McLean Gang, considered by historian T.W. Paterson "the most notorious outlaws in provincial history."

The youngest was 15 when they were hung in 1881 for killing a police constable.

Subsequent owners enlarged and developed the Hat Creek facilities. Stephen Tingley, a legendary stagecoach whip, took over the ranch from McLean. The owner of Barnard's Express (the BX Line) between 1864 and 1897, Tingley claimed he once made the trip between Yale and Soda Creek in 30 hours. He drove a six-horse stagecoach for 28 years without a single accident.

Now preserved and managed by the BC Heritage Trust, the original Hat Creek Ranch buildings have been restored – but only structur-ally. The roadhouse still has the original floorboards and wallpaper. In the summer months, wagon rides and a variety of interpretive services are available, including a first-hand look at a working period ranch.

Stewart Douglas
Blacksmith at Hat Creek Ranch

I'm one of these people who feels like they were born at the wrong time. I always wanted to have a simpler life and do things that felt good and looked good. I want to be independent and not rely on the system to keep me going.

I used to be a carpenter, but I got tired of building places I wouldn't want to live in. I felt sorry for the people who would have to deal with the mortgages.

I moved to Lillooet two years ago because I wanted to find a good dryland place to live. I grew up in a little town big enough to have all the services, but not big enough to have a Macdonalds. I like that. After a couple of years you get to know everyone. For me, Lillooet is the best of all worlds: you can live in the bush and be close to town. I work two days a week at Hat Creek Ranch and work on my place the rest of the time.

Blacksmithing appeals to me because it's a good counterpoint to wood. It's very exacting. Everytime you hit the iron, you make a mark, leave an impression. Originally all the old tools were made by blacksmiths. Toolmaking is a long way off for me, my skills aren't up to it yet. But I'm learning.

Side Trip: Highway 12

Although the main Cariboo Wagon Road from Yale was through Lytton and Cache Creek, Mile 0 is measured from Lillooet where one of the earliest trails to the Cariboo was established via Harrison Lake in 1858. Highway 12 north of Cache Creek off Highway 97 provides an interesting sidetrip to this historic area.

Upper Hat Creek, 22 kilometres west of Highway 97, was an area of controversy in the 1980s when BC Hydro proposed hydroelectric development for the region. As part of the process, archeologists examined the Upper Hat Creek area in the late 1970s and estimate as many as 1350 Native sites exist in the area. At the junction with Hat Creek Road, a steep one-kilometre trail on the north side of Highway 12 leads to Native pictographs.

Marble Canyon Provincial Park is 30 kilometres west of Highway 97. Limestone cliffs and dramatic rock formations tower almost a kilometre above two turquoise lakes. Pictographs, a waterfall, and good swimming and fishing make the park a popular destination. In winter, ice climbers tackle the frozen falls.

At **Pavilion**, Highway 12 heads south to Lillooet along the eroded rocks of the Fraser Canyon. To the north, the Kelly Lake road provides fair-weather access to Clinton. The community of Pavilion has one of the oldest buildings in BC still on its original site, the still-operating **Pavilion Store**.

Lillooet

65 km (40 m) north of Lytton on Highway 12. Population: 1825. Infocentre: 790 Main Street, Box 441, V0K 1V0. 256-4308; Fax: 256-4288

Lillooet recorded one of the highest temperatures in Canadian history when the thermomenter hit 44.4°C on July 16, 1941. As "gateway to the Cariboo," Lillooet was a hotspot of a different kind in 1860, with 13 saloons and an itinerant population of 16,000. The town faded in importance when the main Cariboo Wagon Road bypassed it at Lytton.

One of the most colourful characters of gold rush days was Judge Matthew Begbie. **Hangman's Tree Park** (turn off Main Street at the United Church and head up the hill), is reputed to be one of the places that he meted out his frontier justice. A close reading of history reveals Begbie's label as the "hanging judge" is misleading: he was regarded as strict, but fair.

Once the easy pickings were gone, most of the early gold miners looked elsewhere, but Chinese prospectors often stayed behind, carefully working the spent claims. Near Hangman's Park the **Chinese Rock Pilings** are a testament to the patience of these early settlers.

The **Lillooet Museum** (790 Main Street, 256-4308) housed in a former church, features Native and gold rush history, plus memorabilia and a separate floor featuring legendary newspaperwoman Ma Murray. **Miyazaki Heritage House** (463 Russell Street), built in the 1890s, now honours Dr. Miyazaki, who received the Order of Canada for his medical

work with Japanese-Canadians interned in Lillooet during World War II.

The **Bridge of 23 Camels** south of Lillooet commemorates the beasts of burden that three entrepreneurs imported into the area during the Cariboo Gold Rush. Although the camels required less food and water than traditional pack animals, their tender feet, bad tempers, and foul odor quickly put an end to the scheme. Some of the camels were released into the desert area between Cache Creek and Kamloops. The last one died in 1905.

Rockhounds come to the Lillooet area looking for a variety of semi-precious stones, particularly jade and agate. The largest jade boulder found here weighed more than 16 tonnes.

Golfers will find something a little different in farmer Dave Jones' Sheep Pasture Golf Course located eight kilometres south of Lillooet on Highway 12. Not surprisingly, the natural obstacles include sheep.

In the fall, Native people pursue their ancient technique of fish drying on the banks of the Fraser. Other special events include **Only in Lillooet Days** in June and the **Fall Fair** in September.

West of town, Anderson and Seton lakes were part of one of the earliest routes to the Interior, the Harrison-Lillooet Trail. Completed in 1957, **Seton Lake Dam** provides hydroelectric power to the Lower Mainland. It is part of the Bridge River hydroelectric development, which includes two other dams, four powerhouses, and three reservoirs. BC Hydro's **Seton Lake Recreation Area** has a beach, boat launching area, and interpretive

Left: In the earth beneath Lillooet's "hanging tree" lie the remains of at least two, perhaps eight, criminals sentenced by Judge Matthew Begbie.

Right: Begbie is credited with maintaining law and order during the gold rush years, which stood in sharp contrast to the lawlessness of the American "Wild West." He was knighted by Queen Victoria in 1875.

trail. The steep hillsides around Seton Lake are home to mountain goat, and salmon spawn near Seton Creek and Bridge River.

Farther west, **Bralorne** and **Gold Bridge** developed in 1930s, turned out to be one of the richest gold-producing areas in the province. The **Bralorne Mine** produced over $145 million worth of gold before closing in 1970.

Highway 12 south of Lillooet to Lytton passes through a less travelled section of the Fraser Canyon, but has some of the most spectacular scenery in the province. A self-guided Forests in Action tour brochure, available at Infocentres in Lytton and Lillooet, highlights points of interest along the way. South of Lillooet, the Duffey Lake Road connects the central Interior with Vancouver.

Ma Murray

"Sometimes you have to be a little raw to get the point across," Ma Murray, BC's legendary newspaperwoman, once said.

Although she only had a grade three education, Murray's flamboyant style, down-to-earth language and outspoken opinions put her in the national spotlight.

In 1959 while editing the *Alaska Highway News* in Fort St. John, she wrote about wasteful water consumption. "We sure as hell need to use less if we are going to have this modern convenience," she wrote. "To head off this catastrophe, only flush for Number 2, curtail bathing to the Saturday night tub, go back to the old washrag which could always move a lot of BO if applied often enough." Water consumption dropped 65,000 gallons a day, *Time* magazine ran an article about her, and she became a media celebrity.

Born in Windy Ridge, Kansas in 1888, Murray came to BC in 1912, marrying George Murray in 1913. They moved to Lillooet in 1933, starting the *Bridge River Lillooet News* in 1934. In 1943 they started the *Alaska Highway News* in Fort St. John.

Murray briefly toyed with politics, running provincially in 1945, but gave it up. "I didn't know what the hell they were talking about," she said.

She credited George as her mentor and teacher. "I feel very much like the man who invented the atomic bomb," he once said. "It was a great idea at the time, but now what to do with it."

In 1970, Ma Murray was awarded an honourary doctor of laws degree from Simon Fraser University and in 1971, the Order of Canada. She died in 1982 at the age of 95.

Clinton

40 km (25 mi) north of Cache Creek.
Population: 690. Infocentre: 1400 Cariboo
Highway, PO Box 256, V0K 1K0.
459-2640; Fax: 459-7079

Back on Highway 97, 20 Mile House
marks the road to **Loon Lake,** one of
many fishing resorts in the Cariboo.

Clinton, 15 kilometres farther on
Highway 97 was once an important
town, sitting at the junction of the old
Fraser Canyon and Lillooet gold trails.
The main street retains some of this
Wild West flavour. Among its restored
buildings, the **Clinton Museum** (459-
2442), constructed as a schoolhouse
in 1892 from handmade locally fired
brick, served as courthouse for the
famous Judge Matthew Begbie. Displays feature Chinese and Native artifacts. **Robertson's Store,** built in
1861, was run by the Robertson family until 1978 and is still operating.

Although the original Clinton Hotel
burned to the ground in 1958, an impressive log lodge has replaced it and
displays interesting archival photographs in the lobby.

The **Clinton Ball** was a highly formal affair when it was first held in
1868 at the old Clinton Hotel. Visitors
to Clinton in May are welcome to
attend the party, believed to be the
longest-running event in the province. Other special events include the
Game Dinner (which serves exotic
wild meat like cougar and snake) and
Winter Carnival in January, the **May
Rodeo,** and the **United Native Na-
tions Rodeo** in August. In the winter,
Big Bar forestry trails are used for
cross-country skiing.

At **Lime Mountain,** conditions
for hang gliding are reputed to be
among best in western North
America. Although locals are some-

Miyazaki House is
one of Lillooet's
oldest structures,
built in the 1890s by
early resident
Caspair Phair. Dr.
Masajiro Miyazaki
and his family lived
in the house during
the internment of
Japanese-Canadians
in Lillooet during
World War II.

The Clinton Museum was built as a schoolhouse in 1892 from locally fired brick.

Sidetrip: Empire Valley

Northwest of Clinton, the 45-kilometre drive to **Big Bar Lake Provincial Park** passes through the marshlands and spruce forest of the Chilcotin's Empire Valley, past several guest ranches. Eskers, long gravel ridges formed under retreating glaciers, and drumlins, tear-shaped hills created as ice walls receded, are two geological features highlighted in the park. Ducks Unlimited has a marsh enhancement project here also, with a trail winding along the lake among lava rock, wildflowers, and glacial deposits.

Forty-six kilometres further along this road is 400,000-hectare **Gang Ranch,** at one time the largest cattle ranch in the world. Jerome and Thadeus Harper drove a herd of cattle up from Oregon to Barkerville in the 1860s and bought and leased several tracts of land near Churn Creek, eventually controlling 1.6 million hectares. The ranch got its name from the unique double-furrowed "gang" plough developed to work the fields.

Just a few kilometres from the Gang Ranch on the old Fraser River Trail, **Dog Creek** was once an ancient Indian settlement. A huge cavern below **Dog Creek Dome** was part of Native rituals and contains rock paintings.

It is rumored that Count Versepeuch, a French nobleman and early settler, traded his satin coat and tri-cornered hat to Chief Alexis of the Chilcotin Band for some good horses in the early days. The Count then went on to build BC's first flour mill and a sawmill at Dog Creek in 1866.

what skeptical, aficionados claim that on a good day, gliders can soar all the way to the Okanagan. The annual **Western Canadian Hang-gliding Championships** are held here in May, with a second event in August. Four-wheel drive vehicles can travel to the top of the mountain over a forestry road to a lookout and a view of the surrounding area.

Painted Chasm Provincial Park

Fifteen kilometres north of town on Highway 97, **Painted Chasm Provincial Park** is an impressive sight. Located in a formerly active volcanic area, the spectacular bedrock box canyon is 1.5 kilometres long and 120 metres deep. The chasm was created by glacial meltwater about 10,000 years ago. Layers of bright-orange rock record several volcanic eruptions. The day-use-only park is four kilometres off Highway 97.

The BC Rail line running close to the road here provides passenger service to Prince George.

Twenty-seven kilometres north of the ranch, **Alkali Lake** is popular with dedicated bird-watchers, who come to view rare white pelicans during spring and fall migrations.

Side Trip: Interlakes

Back on Highway 97, 70 Mile House was one of the first stopping places established on the Cariboo Wagon Road, and marks the turnoff to **Green Lake Recreation Area.** Fifteen-kilometre-long Green Lake was on the Fur Brigade Trail between Fort Kamloops and Fort Alexandria. Now the lake is a popular recrea-

Jake Conkin
Cowboy Poet

A cowboy poetry roundup is a group of people who are sharing lies and stories and poetry, telling about the lifestyles of the real cowboy – the cowboy that works on the ranch with the cows and rides horses for most of his life, not the rodeo cowboy or the urban cowboy. Elko, Nevada "the grandaddy" of them all, hosted 10,000 people at its gathering in 1991.

The poetry talks about mother nature in its glory, the bunch grass, the critters, the huge sky, and the life of the cowboy out on the range. It involves certain values that people seem to want to hang on to today, centering on honesty, integrity, good friendships in the old fashioned way. A lot of people seem to be missing that in their lives and I think that's what attracts them to gatherings like this.

A lot of people out there involved in the ranching business fear for their lifestyle to some extent and I guess that's part of what the poetry is about. This lifestyle, of course, has been going on since the 1800s, and cowboys really would be considered some of the first environmentalists. They live off the land, so they really look after the land and everything else.

I've been interested in the lifestyle all my life. I've had horses. My dream has always been of going to ranches and doing the real cowboy things: getting up at three o'clock in the morning and going out and herding cows, this type of thing. I had the opportunity to do that at Douglas Lake, which is one of Canada's largest cattle ranches, at spring turnouts, cattle drives, cow camps, and so on. I had experiences that I felt I would like to share with people and decided to write some of these thoughts down on paper.

Jake Conkin's collection of cowboy poetry, *Silk and Silver and Other Things Too,* is self-published, distributed through Sand Hill Marketing of Kelowna and available at western shops throughout BC and Alberta. He organized BC's first cowboy poetry roundup at O'Keefe Ranch near Vernon in 1991.

Green Lake, now a popular resort area, was on the Fur Brigade Trail linking Fort Alexandria and Fort Kamloops between the 1820s and the 1850s.

tion area. Surrounded by pine, spruce, aspen, and grassy undergrowth harbouring lupin, wild rose and Indian paintbrush, Green Lake is a beautiful spot, but buggy. Anglers fish for kokanee and trout, and birdwatchers can look for osprey and loon. In the winter months, the area is popular with snowmobilers.

Highway 24, just south of 100 Mile House, follows the Fur Brigade Trail as it passes through Bridge Lake to Little Fort. Known as the **Interlakes** area, this is another ancient dwelling place of Native people. Some developments on the lakes have been built above ground so as not to disturb Native artifacts. Canoeing is excellent on the more than 50 lakes in the area, and locals claim the best trout fishing in the world. Guest ranches are plentiful.

Lone Butte, named for obvious reasons, was a busy centre for the ranchers that settled in the area from the early 1900s to the 1950s. The community's lone water tower, one of

the last existing structures of its kind in the province, used to service the steam engines that took the cattle to market.

At **Bridge Lake,** ask for directions to the ice caves, crevasse-like openings in the side of a cliff containing huge ice stalactites, once popular with local ice-cream makers.

Special events in the area are the **Bush-a-thon** in Bridge Lake in July, the **Bridge Lake Rodeo** in July, and the **Bridge Lake Fall Fair** in September.

100 Mile House

80 km (50 mi) north of Clinton. Population: 1630. Infocentre: 422 Cariboo Highway, Box 2312, V0K 2E0. 395-5353; Fax: 395-4085

A station on the Fur Brigade Trail from Kamloops to Fort Alexandria, **100 Mile House** became an important stage coach stop on the Cariboo Wagon Road in the 1860s. At the north end of the village, one of the original

Barnard Express (BX) stage coaches is on display. The town's first road-house, built in 1862, has since burned down, but 100 Mile House remains an important service centre.

In town, to the west of the high-way, an eight-hectare wetland marsh provides easy wildlife viewing. The Infocentre is next door.

Logging is important to the eco-nomy of the area, and tours of woods and mills can be arranged at the Infocentre. An important new indus-try is log-home building. The houses are constructed locally, then disas-sembled and shipped to the United States and Japan.

The **Cariboo Cross-country Ski Marathon** (791-6212), held the first weekend in February, attracts a thou-sand participants annually. Perhaps one of them will be able to use the 12-metre-long racing skis, claimed to be the world's biggest, on display next to the Infocentre. Over 200 kilometres of groomed cross-country ski trails are found at 99 Mile, 108 Mile

House, and Red Coach Inn. Snow-mobiling, ice-fishing, and mushing – dog sledding over frozen lakes and streams – are also popular winter-time activities.

Other annual events include the **Old Time Fiddler's Contest** and **Fron-tier Days Rodeo** in May, **Loggers Sports** in July, the **IRA Rodeo** and the **Great Cariboo Rid**e in August, the **South Cariboo Fall Fair** in Septem-ber and the **Triathlon** in December.

Moose Valley, west of 100 Mile House off Exeter Road (on the way to Dog Lake), is the site of a two-day canoe route through a chain of 12 wilderness lakes. The lakes were cre-ated at the end of the last ice age when the glaciers retreated and the path of the Fraser River was being re-cut. In June and July, paddlers may spot moose calves and sandhill cranes. Locals claim there are very few bothersome bugs. The Info-centre at 100 Mile House has a map.

Sharp-eyed travellers will occasionally be treated to examples of whimsical folk art throughout the Interior.

The historic community of 100 Mile House today boasts the world's biggest cross-country skis and hosts an annual ski marathon that attracts hundreds of participants.

Sidetrip: Canim Lake

35 km (22 mi) east of Highway 97

Archeologists suggest that when prairie buffalo herds diminished, Plains people came to the area around Canim Lake to fish and perhaps search for caribou. There are pictographs and remains of *kekuli,* the native pit houses, in the region.

Canim Lake is popular with 20th-century residents as well, who come here for fishing, hiking, and wildlife viewing.

The end of the road is Mahood Lake in Wells Gray Park (see page 216) and canoe heaven. **Mahood Falls,** a 55-kilometre drive east of the community of Canim Lake, is a magnificent cascade between Canim and Mahood lakes. **Mahood Lake Campground** in Wells Gray Provincial Park was once an important Native settlement and is a good place to search for pictographs.

Some say the Canim River has the best fly-fishing in the Cariboo, but you'll have to get there by trail. Ask locally for directions, and how to get to **Deception Falls**, the **Volcano**

Cones, and other local attractions and good fishing spots. Cross-country skiing is popular in the winter.

The **Canim Lake Rodeo** takes place in July and the **International Native Arts and Crafts Show** is in August and September.

108 Mile House

Just north of 100 Mile House on Highway 97, **108 Mile Heritage Site** (791-5288) has a collection of seven historical buildings on three hectares of lakeside property belonging to a large resort. Visible from the highway, the old Clydesdale barn, built in 1908 and since restored, is one of the largest log barns in Canada. Area resorts offer horse-backriding, fishing, hiking, and cross-country skiing.

Lac La Hache

25 km (16 mi) north of 100 Mile House. Population: 700.
Infocentre: Box 252, V0K 1T0.
396-7620; Fax: 396-7720. Seasonal

Lac La Hache calls itself the "Longest Town in the Cariboo" due to its location on the body of water of the same name. The lake apparently got its name when a French Canadian fur trader dropped his axe through a hole in the ice – *hache* is French for axe.

Resorts, campgrounds, and guest ranches are nearby. The community hosts the **Polar Bear Swim** in January, the **Winter Carnival** in February, the **Cariboo Square Dance Jamboree** in June, the **Cariboo Regatta** in July, and the three-day **Country Music Festival** the second week in August every year.

Gold Country

At **150 Mile House,** fifteen kilometres east of Williams Lake on Highway 97, travellers can follow early gold rush routes to Horsefly, Likely, Quesnel Lake, and dozens of smaller lakes. The Horsefly River winds through a beautiful valley of cottonwood and wild rose. Birdwatchers can view herons, eagles, and sandpipers.

Large spawning runs of kokanee and sockeye occur every fall just south of the community of **Horsefly** (Board of Trade: 620-3440) where the first Cariboo gold was discovered in 1859. Originally called Harper's Camp, after Thadeus Harper of the Gang Ranch, the town's present name is, unfortunately, descriptive and accurate. The **Jack Lynn Museum** (on Campbell Avenue, 620-3304, seasonal) displays artifacts from the early days.

Likely

85 km (53mi) northeast of 150 Mile House. Population: 375. Infocentre: PO Box 10, V0L 1N0. 790-2422. Seasonal

Originally called Quesnel Dam, the town was not renamed by an optimistic prospector, but after successful miner "Plato" John Likely, who searched for gold and spouted philosophy in the 1860s. Appreciative followers gave Likely good tips which he followed to his advantage. Nicknamed "the nugget patch," this is one of the richest areas in the Cariboo goldfields. In 1922, one mine yielded 700 ounces in one week.

The ghost town of **Quesnel Forks,** once a bustling community of 5000, is eight kilometres past Likely. Designated as a heritage site, the town's glory days lasted for five years.

The **Bullion Pit,** an open-pit gold mine from 1892 to 1942, is five kilometres west of Likely. In order to have enough water to feed the mine's hydraulic system, 64 kilometres of canals were built to utilize the resources of nearby lakes and creeks. The pit is 90 metres deep and 3 kilometres long. Between 1892 and 1898 $1.25 million worth of gold was removed. As recently as 1988 a prospector found a nugget worth $10,000.

Quesnel Lake, 100 kilometres long, is the largest in the region. Much of the early search for gold centred in this area, and early gold rush trails to the productive fields around Barkerville were via the lake. Paddling, wildlife viewing, hiking, and fishing are popular, and there are several resorts. Anglers pull out rainbow, kokanee, lake trout, and Dolly Varden. The **Quesnel River Salmon Hatchery,** two kilometres south of Likely, produces 2.3 million chinook fry annually. Self-guided tours are available.

Special events include the annual **Loggers Sports Day** at Likely in July.

Williams Lake

92 km (55 mi) north of 100 Mile House. Population: 10,015. Infocentre: junction of Highways 97 and 20, 1148 Broadway South, V2G 1A2. 392-5025; Fax: 392-4212

Perhaps most famous for its annual stampede, Williams Lake has been a focal point for ranching communities in the Cariboo since the turn

Boy calf-riders at the Williams Lake Stampede in 1924. The annual event attracts thousands of visitors every July 1st weekend.

of the century. The town missed its chance to cash in on the gold-rush boom of the 1860s because a local landowner refused to loan money to the road builders. Annoyed, they routed the highway through the present site of 150 Mile House instead. Although the building of the Pacific Great Eastern Railway (now BC Rail) in 1920 gave Williams Lake the economic edge it needed, the big boom came a full century after the gold rush. Then the population exploded as logging and mining (copper, molybdenum, gold, and silver) became part of the economy. Tours of plywood mills, sawmills, logging sites, and the open-pit **Gilbraltar Copper Mine** can be arranged at the Infocentre. Williams Lake also has the most active cattle stockyard in the province.

The **Williams Lake Historical Museum**, (113 North 4th Avenue, 392-

7404) includes displays about Native artifacts, the Cariboo Road, and early mining, ranching, and logging.

The four-day **Williams Lake Stampede** is held every July 1st weekend. Begun in 1926 as horse races on a local farm, activities now include a parade, pancake breakfasts, and barn dancing. Canadian Professional Rodeo Association events include chuck wagon races, barrel racing, calf roping, and steer wrestling. Make sure to book motel rooms well in advance – the Infocentre estimates as many as 5000 people crowd into town during the stampede. Other special events include the **William Lake Children's Festival** in June, **Loggers Sports Festival** in July, the **Cariboo Fall Fair and Rodeo** in September, and the **Cariboo Medieval Market** in November.

Scout Island Nature Centre (southeast of the intersection of

Highways 97 and 20) on Williams Lake overlooks a major staging area for migrating waterfowl. Hikers might try following the Williams Lake River through a scenic 12-kilometre valley to the Fraser River.

Good fishing for kokanee, rainbow, and char is found in many lakes, such as McKinley, Hen Ingram, Quesnel, Horsefly, Tyee, and Dewar.

Side Trip: Chilcotin Highway

The 458-kilometre Chilcotin Highway (Highway 20) is difficult to class as a "side trip." The route travels east from Williams Lake over the Chilcotin Plateau, the traditional home of the Chilcotin people, through Tweedsmuir Provincial Park (BC's largest), to the ancient Native village of Bella Coola on the Pacific Ocean. The only road out is back over Highway 20. Nearly 300

kilometres of the highway is paved, with gravel sections west of Puntzi and through Tweedsmuir Park. And there isn't one traffic light between Williams Lake and Bella Coola. The highway is well-used by logging trucks, so travel with headlights on.

Alexander Mackenzie trekked through the area in 1793. A Hudson's Bay Company fur-trading post was established in 1828 at the confluence of the Chilko and Chilcotin rivers. The first cattle ranches were established in the 1860s to supply the gold miners. Forestry, ranching, tourism, and outdoor recreation are now the economic lifelines. But the area has not developed like the Cariboo. Known for its rugged individuals, sparse population, and vast uninhabited areas, the Chilcotin is a land where freedom is highly valued and horses outnumber cars.

The rolling grasslands of the Interior Plateau are ideally suited to cattle ranching. This rancher is surveying a portion of the Gang Ranch south of Williams Lake.

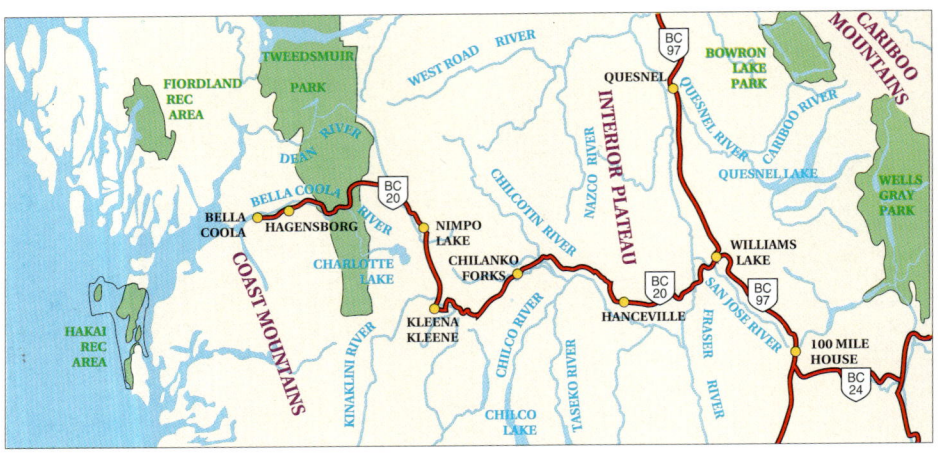

CHILCOTIN HIGHWAY HIGHLIGHTS

For those who can't travel the entire Chilcotin Highway, the short drive along Highway 20 to **Sheep Creek Bridge,** about 23 kilometres west of Williams Lake, gives an excellent view of the Fraser River. During the gold rush, Chinese farmers grew market gardens here.

Across the Fraser River and atop the dry grasslands of 1200-metre high **Chilcotin Plateau,** the Coast Mountains appear. The transmitter at the **Canadian Loran C Station** (north of the highway 13 kilometres west of the bridge) may seem oddly placed, but the facility is part of a marine navigation network that guides ships in the Pacific Ocean. (Open most days from 9 to 4. Phone for a tour: 659-6511.)

Another 26 kilometres west to **Riske Creek** and then 15 kilometres south, the **Bighorn Sheep Reserve** is home to 500 California bighorn sheep, one-fifth of the world's population. And it is worth going another five kilometres to **Farwell Canyon** on the Chilcotin River to view the hoodoo rock formations. Native rock paintings are on the overhang south of the bridge. The Chilcotin River is rated among the best in North America for kayaking, canoeing, and whitewater rafting. Check locally for road information.

Lee's Corner, 42 kilometres west of Riske Creek on Highway 20, is named after Norman Lee, who made an ill-fated attempt to drive 500 head of cattle 2400 kilometres through the wilderness to Dawson City during the Klondike Gold Rush. The lookout here gives a spectacular view of the Chilko Ranch; the church spire belongs to one of the many Native villages along the route.

North of Alexis Creek on Stum Lake, **White Pelican Provincial Park** is a breeding sanctuary for this endangered species. There's no road access.

Bull Canyon Provincial Park (398-4414), located in an aspen grove on the Chilcotin River 10 kilometres west of **Alexis Creek,** is near a historic battleground and cattle round-up point. Temperatures at **Redstone,** a Native settlement 20 kilometres to the west, can fall to -50°C in the winter.

Chilanko Marsh, about 59 kilometres west of Alexis Creek and on the Pacific Flyway, is great for bird-watching. To the north is **Puntzi Lake,** another resting place for white pelicans. Puntzi was once a US Air Force Base.

Tatla Lake, 44 kilometres west of Chilanko Forks (information: 476-1113), offers access to Tatlayoko Lake, Homathko Icefield, and Mount Waddington, at 4016 metres the highest peak in the Coast Range. Guides are available locally for exploration of the Ice Caves in the Potato Range.

An attempt by Alfred Waddington to build a road through this area to the Interior from Bute Inlet was met with fierce resistance by the Chilcotin people in 1864. Nineteen road builders were killed and eventually five Native men were hung for their part in the battle. The ill-conceived road was never completed.

The stampede at **Anahim Lake** promises a real down-to-earth celebration every July. Lessard Lake Road north of here gives access to famous **Dean River** steelhead fishing, abandoned Carrier villages, and the **Alexander Mackenzie Heritage Trail**. (See p. 207.) Richard Hobson and Pan Philips homesteaded nearby in the early 1900s. The deserted Home Ranch remains, as do Hobson's books describing the undertaking, *The Rancher Takes a Wife* and *Grass Beyond the Mountains.*

The **Rainbow Range** of the Coast Mountains displays the purples, reds, and oranges of its 2500 metre peaks several places in this area. There are

several places for hikers and horseback riders to get close-up views. One route is the **Trail to the Rainbows**. (Follow the turnoff at Heckman Pass to the trailhead.)

The portion of the highway that travels through 981,000-hectare **Tweedsmuir Provincial Park** and the Coast Range is dubbed the **"Freedom Road."** Locals, wanting a connection between coastal and Interior communities, built it themselves in 1953 when the government deemed it economically unfeasible. Within park

White Pelican Provincial Park provides pelicans on Stum Lake with a breeding sanctuary. There is no road access to the park.

Chilcotin Special Events

Special events in the Chilcotin include the **Annual Cross Country Ski Race** in Tatla Lake in January; the **Nuxalk Sports Day** in Bella Coola and the **Dean River Canoe Race** at Anahim Lake in May; the **Big Creek Rodeo**, the **Riske Creek Rodeo**, and the **Puntzi Lake Fishing Derby** in June; the **Anahim Lake Stampede** and the Bella Coola **Salmon Queen Festival Rodeo and Dance** in July; the **Alexis Creek Pioneer Days and Fall Fair** in August; the **CRA Rodeo Finals** in Riske Creek and the **Fall Fair and Loggers Sports** in Bella Coola in September.

boundaries, the **Atnarko Valley** is where turn-of-the-century settler Ralph Edwards lived and wrote about Lonesome Lake's trumpeter swans. Leland Stowe's best seller, *Crusoe of Lonesome Lake*, describes the Edwards family's homesteading triumphs. The **Turner Lakes** chain offers wilderness camping, good trout fishing, and sandy beaches to canoers willing to hike or fly in. Backpackers can view spectacular 259-metre **Hunlen Falls** at the top of Turner Lake.

Hagensborg, east of Bella Coola, was settled by Norwegians from Minnesota in 1894.

Bella Coola (population: 850, Infocentre: 799-5919), is at the highway's end on Labouchere Channel. The rock where Alexander Mackenzie noted the termination of his famous journey in 1793 is in Dean Channel to the northwest. The **Bella Coola Museum** (982-2328) has displays on the building of the Freedom Road and early history as well as information on local attractions.

Soda Creek

Soda Creek, 33 kilometres north of Williams Lake on Highway 97, was an important transportation centre during the gold rush days. Having come this far by wagon road, bypassing the unnavigable parts of the Fraser River, travellers took paddlewheelers upriver to Quesnel. Then they followed the Cariboo road to the gold fields of Barkerville.

The **Marguerite Ferry,** 63 kilometres north of Williams Lake, is one of the few reaction ferries left on the Fraser. The free two-vehicle vessel takes travellers across the river between April and September when the river isn't frozen. Just north of the ferry landing, basalt columns jut out of a field on the east side of Highway 97, evidence of ancient volcanic activity. Much volcanic rock is basalt; as the molten rock cools it shrinks and splits into these striking vertical columns.

About halfway between Soda Creek and Quesnel, 67 kilometres north of Williams Lake, a cairn marks the site of the old Hudson's Bay Company post, **Fort Alexandria,** named after early explorer Alexander Mackenzie. This was the northern terminus of the Pacific Fur Brigade Trail and one of the last posts to be built on the Fraser. Supplies were shipped from Fort Astoria at the mouth of the Columbia, through the Okanagan to Fort Kamloops and finally here for distribution throughout New Caledonia. The importance of the fort faded once gold dominated the economy.

Quesnel

120 km (74 mi) north of Williams Lake. Population: 8069. Infocentre: opposite BC Rail Station, Highway 97. 992-8716

During the 1860s many thought Quesnel was destined to become the capital of the province. It reached prominence during the Cariboo gold rush era, and has maintained its economic importance through lumber and pulp production.

Beginning on the Fraser River across the footbridge at Front Street, the **Riverfront Park and Trail** travels past historic points of interest including a restored Hudson's Bay Com-

pany post, manicured residential areas, the Quesnel River, and the rail yards.

Boat trips take visitors either up the Quesnel or along the Fraser rivers; gold panning is offered along with the ride. Recreational gold panners can try their luck at the junction of the Quesnel and Fraser rivers, but serious gold panners should check at the Gold Commissioner's Office (102-350 Barlow Street, V2J 2C1, 992-4301) for rules and regulations.

The **Quesnel Museum** (on Carson Avenue next to the Infocentre, 992-9580) houses one of the strongest collections in the Interior, with displays on mining and ranching, Natives, and Chinese settlers.

About three kilometres north of town on Highway 97, a unique observation tower offers a bird's-eye view of a **forestry industrial complex.** The four lumber mills, two pulp mills, planer mill, and related activities have a production capacity of one billion board feet of lumber and 1700 tonnes of pulp per year.

The four-day **Billy Barker Days** celebration is held the third week of July each year. The Fall Fair is in August, an event started in 1912.

Pinnacles Provincial Park, seven kilometres from downtown Quesnel, features hoodoo rock formations and a panoramic view.

Mackenzie Grease Trail

The **Blackwater River** area west of Quesnel includes excellent fishing, canoeing, kayaking, and wildlife viewing. Natives established the "Mackenzie-Grease" Trail beside the Blackwater River centuries ago, as interior and coastal tribes traded for the oily oolichan fish. They later used

At the confluence of the Fraser and Quesnel rivers, Quesnel was an important point on the transportation route during the Cariboo Gold Rush in the 1860s. Today its main industries are forestry related.

Cottonwood House had a reputation as one of the finest roadhouses on the Cariboo Wagon Road. John and Janet Boyd bought it in 1874, and the Boyd family operated it until 1951.

the same trail to guide Alexander Mackenzie to the Pacific Ocean in 1793. Today experienced backpackers who trek the entire length of the 18-to-24-day **Alexander Mackenzie Heritage Trail** travel 420 kilometres from the mouth of the Blackwater north of Quesnel to **Sir Alexander Mackenzie Provincial Park** in Dean Channel. Information is available at the Williams Lake and Quesnel Infocentres. Or write the Alexander Mackenzie Trail Association (Box 425, Station A, Kelowna BC V1Y 7P1). Access is across the Moffatt Bridge in Quesnel on Nazko Road.

Sidetrip: Highway 26 to Barkerville and Bowron Lake

Two of the Interior's biggest attractions lie east on Highway 26, the last leg of the old Cariboo Wagon Road, the Gold Rush Trail. Markers along the route evoke the past with names like Mexican Hill, Lover's Leap, Robber's Roost, Devil's Canyon, and Jaw Bone Creek.

Very few of the thousands who travelled these roads found what they were looking for. Billy Barker, a typical boom-bust miner, had a town named after him, and a claim valued at $600,000, but he died in Victoria in 1894, alone and broke. However, many are still searching. All along Highway 26 evidence of modern mines and claims abound.

Like early seekers, modern travellers can stop at **Cottonwood House Provincial Historic Park** (994-3332), 24 kilometres east of Quesnel. The old Gold Rush Trail passes right by the front door of the roadhouse, built in 1864.

Besides displays of archival photos and period artifacts in the outbuildings, the interpretive staff offer baked goods fresh from Cottonwood House's wood stove with their descriptions of early days.

Wells

80 km (48 mi) east of Quesnel.
Population: 246.
Infocentre: Box 123, V0K 1R0.
994-3237; Fax: 994-3405. Seasonal

Wells is a relatively new town, created when Fred Marshall Wells discovered gold nearby in 1932, but by 1940, 3000 people lived here. The period-style false front buildings create a charming mining-town atmosphere. **Wells Museum** (Pooley Street, 994-3422) features local history. The town used to be right on Jack of Clubs Lake, but the tailings of a mining operation that closed in 1967 have adjusted the landscape. The lake offers trout fishing and the company of loons.

Special events in Wells: **Home-coming Weekend** in July, the **Island Mountain Arts Festival** in July and August, the **Gold Rush and Casino Night** in August, and the **Heritage Festival** in September.

Barkerville Historic Park and Gold Rush Town

82 km east of Quesnel.
BC Parks: 398-4414.
Interpretive centre (seasonal): 994-3332
A well-known tourist attraction, Barkerville is an exciting "living" museum operated as a heritage site by the provincial government.

One of three "overnight" mining communities on Williams Creek, Barkerville was the hub of the Cariboo gold rush. Cornish prospector Billy Barker had dug down 12 metres and

was about to give up his claim when he struck pay dirt in 1862. Some esti-mate over $40 million worth of gold was taken out of the area. With a population of 10,000 to 20,000 in the

Top: Barkerville, one of the most famous of the Interior's gold rush towns, has been restored by the provincial government. In the summer months, costumed interpretive staff recreate the early days.

Left: Billy Barker, a typical boom-bust miner, had a town named after him and a claim valued at $600,000, but he died penniless in Victoria in 1894.

Sandy Lake in Bowron Lake Provincial Park is one of 10 lakes in a 116-kilometre chain that attracts paddlers from around the world.

round, but the full interpretive program operates only in summer.

Hikers can trek to the old cemetery, "The Last Mile" of the Cariboo Wagon Road into Barkerville, and the ghost town of Richfield. Cross-country skiing is popular in winter.

Special events in Barkerville include the **Dominion Day Celebration** on July 1st weekend, the **Old Fashioned Picnic** also in July, the **St. Saviour's Church Institute Concerts** in August, the **Invitational Hose Carriage Races** on Labour Day Weekend in September, and the **Victorian Christmas** celebrations the weekend before Christmas.

Since there is no overnight accommodation, visitors must stay in Wells, Quesnel, or several area campgrounds.

Bowron Lake

Canoers from around the world come to **Bowron Lake Provincial Park** (398-4414), 29 kilometres east of Wells. The park's ten-lake chain takes seven to ten days and covers a 116-kilometre water and portage circuit through undeveloped wilderness. The best time to make the trip is between June and October. Fishing is unpredictable but kokanee, rainbow trout, Dolly Varden, and whitefish are present. The 121,600-hectare wilderness area is also a wildlife sanctuary. In winter, the circuit can be made by snowshoe or cross-country ski. Local outfitters rent canoes and supplies.

Access to the lakes is on a "first-come, first-serve" basis. Groups of 7 to 14 must make reservations. There ia a fee. Contact the parks office.

The park's namesake was John Bowron, an "Overlander" who came

mid-1860s, Barkerville was a rip-roaring place, the largest town north of San Francisco and west of Chicago.

In October 1868, 116 buildings in the new town burned to the ground in one hour and fifteen minutes, at a loss of close to $700,000. However, gold seekers are a determined lot; the townspeople began rebuilding the next day.

A functioning town until the 1930s, restoration began on Barkerville in 1958. Work is ongoing, and at present there are 75 preserved buildings and displays, including several restaurants, and a theatre offering live performances.

In the summer months, costumed interpretive staff greet visitors as though they had just clambered off the BX stagecoach. Playing the parts of characters from Barkerville's history, the staff offer mining demonstrations, stagecoach rides, school lessons, and guided tours. The park is open year

to the Cariboo in 1862. Besides being Camerontown's first librarian, Bowron was active in Barkerville's Cariboo Amateur Dramatic Association and became the gold commissioner in 1883.

Prince George
120 km (74 mi) north of Quesnel. Population: 65,145. Infocentre: 1198 Victoria Street, V2L 2L2. 562-3700; Fax: 563-3584

Carrier Sekani Natives were the earliest residents of this region, trading with coastal people for centuries before the European explorers and fur traders arrived. Alexander Mackenzie and Simon Fraser paddled past the site on their historic journeys down the Fraser River. Fraser established Fort George here in 1807.

Located at the confluence of the Fraser and Nechako rivers, Prince George continues to be a transporta-

tion hub, today sitting at the junction of two major highways, Highway 16 running east-west and Highway 97 running north-south. It is an important stop on VIA and BC Rail lines.

Logging became viable with the development of the railways; the first sawmills were established in 1906, supplying ties and materials for the Grand Trunk Pacific Railway. Hundreds of small mills flourished until the 1950s and 1960s when they were bought out by larger corporations. Beginning in 1964, three pulp mills opened in Prince George, triggering a population boom that has made it the second largest city in the Interior.

Contact the Infocentre about tours of Northwood Pulp and Timber, one of the largest pulp mills on the planet, and North Central Plywoods.

At the 106-hectare **Forest for the World Park** visitors can learn about

Prince George, one of the Interior's largest cities, is the site of BC's newest university, due to open in 1994.

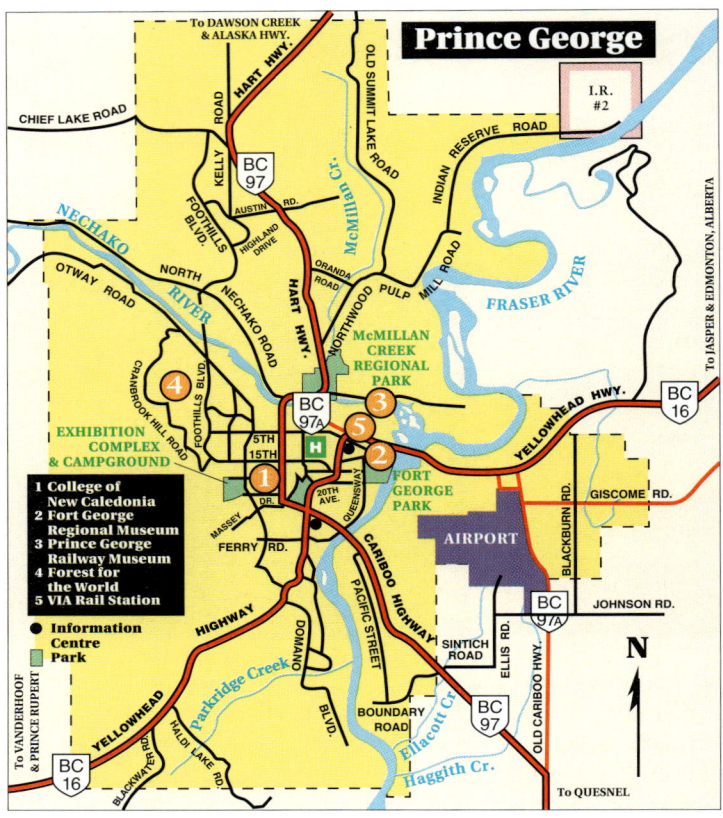

reforestation. The park has eight kilometres of trails.

The **Fraser-Fort George Regional Museum** (in Fort George Park at the end of 20th Avenue, 562-1612), overlooks the site of Fort George. The museum contains local history, natural history, and travelling exhibits. **The Prince George Railway Museum** at Cottonwood Island Nature Park (River Road, two kilometres northeast of downtown) features a variety of railway artifacts and exhibits of early logging, agriculture, and firefighting.

The **Prince George Art Gallery** (2820-15th Avenue, 563-6447) and **Studio 2880** (next door, 562-4526) and the **Native Art Gallery** (144 George Street, 562-7385) display the work of local and international artists and craftspeople.

Annual events include the **Dog Sled Races** at Tabor Lake in January; **Mardi Gras** in February; the **Canadian Northern Children's Festival** and the biennial **Regional Forest Exhibition** in May; the **Prince George Rodeo** in June; **Simon Fraser Days, Sandblast** (skiing on gravel), and the **Prince George Exhibition** in August; and **Oktoberfest** in October.

The **Heritage River Trail** is an 11-kilometre crushed-gravel circuit that includes **Cottonwood Island Nature Park**, a fish hatchery, the railway museum, and **Fort George Park.**

Teapot Mountain Hiking Trail, 50 kilometres north on Highway 97, offers a short but strenuous hike with spectacular scenery and a chance to examine a large basalt flow that helped shape the land in the days before the glaciers. A little less strenuous, **Fort George Canyon Trail,** 30 kilometres southwest, is noted for its wildflowers and plant life.

Over 250 lakes are within an 130-kilometre radius of Prince George. Rainbow, brook, and lake trout, Dolly Varden, char, whitefish, and grayling are among the species.

Highway 16: Yellowhead Highway East

The second part of our circle tour of the Central Interior heads east on the Yellowhead Highway (Highway 16) to Tête Jaune Cache, 266 kilometres east of Prince George.

The Yellowhead gets its name from an Iroquois trapper and guide whose hair had a light tinge to it. *(tête* in French is "head"; *jaune* means yellow.) Accounts differ as to the man's identity but most agree it was Pierre Bostonais, a former North West Company employee. In the early 1800s, Bostonais stashed his furs at a cache to the west of Mt. Robson in the Rocky Mountains, thus Tête Jaune Cache.

The highway was dedicated as the northern Trans-Canada route in 1990 and travels from the Pacific Ocean to Winnipeg, providing the gentlest grades of any route through the

Rockies. The elevation of Yellowhead Pass is 1066 metres, compared with 1327 metres at Rogers Pass, and 1643 metres at Kicking Horse Pass. It was the route through the Rockies favoured by early CPR surveyor Walter Moberly in the 1870s.

Tabor Mountain

Thirty kilometres east of Prince George at Tabor Mountain, **Grove Forest** pull-out is an opportunity to see nature's regenerative powers at work. Over 26,000 hectares of forest were destroyed in a fire here in 1961. In a mature stand, established timber blocks-out the competing vegetation,

Found in mountain areas west of the Rockies, the western anemone is one of 2000 species in the buttercup family. One of the first alpine plants to bloom, the creamy flowers are soon replaced by these large fluffy seed heads. It is also known as western pasque flower, towhead baby, and windflower.

Fireweed is one of the first plants to grow after a forest fire. Although such fires can seem disastrous, they allow re-introduction of a variety of plant and animal life that gets blocked-out by mature timber stands.

discouraging life forms all the way down the food chain. At Grove Forest, deciduous alder and willow are among the new vegetation that has slowly been established. A variety of wildlife exists here now that could not have found sustenance before the fire.

In winter, Prince George skiers are 40 minutes from **Purden Ski Village's** (565-9038) ten runs. **Tabor Mountain** (563-7669), is 15 minutes from Prince George, with 10 alpine runs and nordic trails.

McBride

220 km (136 mi) east of Prince George. Population: 570. Infocentre: 569-3366

The only service area between Prince George and Tête Jaune Cache, McBride came into being with the Grand Trunk Pacific Railway before World War I. The town was named after BC's youngest premier, Sir Richard McBride, who assumed office at age 33 and served from 1903 to 1915.

Surrounded by pristine mountains, waterfalls, meadows and streams, McBride is popular with backpackers, skiers, paddlers, anglers, and bikers.

Special events include the **Yellowhead Loppett Ski Race** in January, **Elks Pioneer Days** in June; the **Great Rocky Mountain Bike Race** in July; and the **Robson Valley Fall Fair** in August.

Tête Jaune Cache

A small town with population estimates ranging from 46 to 300, Tête Jaune Cache was a major construction centre for the Grand Trunk Pacific Railway and the head of navigation for Fraser River sternwheelers in the early part of the 20th century. In its heyday, 5000 people lived here.

Rearguard Falls Provincial Park

Five kilometres east of Tête Jaune Cache, Rearguard Falls Provincial Park marks the farthest point that spawning salmon travel up the Fraser River. The fish begin their journey at Vancouver on the Pacific Ocean some 1200 kilometres away in July

and arrive here in August and September. The lookout provides a place to observe the salmon attempting to leap up the 10-metre-high falls. Eventually they spawn on gravel beds downstream.

A viewpoint just beyond the park reveals 2650-metre-high **Mt. Terry Fox,** honoring the BC athlete who died in 1981. The one-legged runner inspired millions of people around the world with his Marathon of Hope in 1980.

Mt. Robson Provincial Park

Spectacular Mt. Robson, at 3954 metres, is the highest peak in the Canadian Rockies. The 217,200-hectare park contains the headwaters of the Fraser River, at this point only a tiny trickle. Abundant wildlife, 170 species of birds, subalpine forest vegetation, and glaciers make this a backpacker's paradise. The park office (566-4325) at the west gate has information on trails and attractions. Fit hikers enjoy the two-day hike through the Valley of a Thousand Falls to Tumbling Glacier and the beauty of Berg Lake. Moose Lake and Moose River are popular with wildlife viewers. The eastern border of the park is on the Continental Divide.

Yellowhead South

South of Tête Jaune Cache, Highway 5 (the Yellowhead South Highway) follows the North Thompson River to Kamloops. The paved two-lane highway provides access to fishing, wildlife viewing, hiking, and river rafting .

Mt. Robson, the highest peak in the Rockies, is often shrouded in clouds. In 1862, the Overlanders' Native guide claimed he had only seen the peak once in his first 29 visits.

Valemount

20 km (12 mi) south of Tête Jaune Cache. Population: 1055. Infocentre: 566-4846. Seasonal

Valemount's location on the North Thompson River and artificial Kinbasket Lake, (created when the Columbia River was dammed north of Revelstoke), has made it a four sea-

The Overlanders

In August of 1862, the Overlanders, a group of 132 people on their way to the Cariboo goldfields, stood at Tête Jaune Cache wondering how to proceed. They had been sold "the speediest, safest and most economical route to the gold diggings" by the British Columbia Overland Transit Company back east. The original brochure had promised stagecoaches, but by the time the travellers passed over the Great Divide they were using Native *travois* and mules.

The party split up at Tête Jaune Cache, most deciding to travel via the Fraser Rive. A small group of about twenty choose the North Thompson. After several weeks of perilous rafting and portaging with little food, the first of the North Thompson group arrived at Fort Kamloops on October 11. Two days later, another raft arrived, carrying the expedition's only woman, Catherine Schubert. A day after that, Mrs. Schubert gave birth to a daughter, Rose, one of the first European babies born in the Interior.

sons recreational headquarters. River rafting, heli-skiing, and wildlife observation are among the choices.

Trails along the North Thompson River provide viewpoints for salmon spawning. **Cranberry Marsh,** three kilometres south of town, is a wildlife haven.

Clearwater

190 km (114 mi) south of Valemount. Population: 3500. Infocentre: 674-2646

Clearwater is headquarters for Wells Gray Provincial Park and offers a number of services for vacationers. The **Yellowhead Museum** (674-3660) displays pioneer and Native artifacts and photographs as well as natural history displays. The North Thompson River from Clearwater to Kamloops is a favourite with paddlers. Special events include the **Wells Gray Loppet** in February.

Wells Gray Provincial Park

Abandoned homesteads, mineral springs, glaciers, high mountain peaks, extinct volcanoes, waterfalls, spawning salmon, and lava beds are among the many attractions in **Wells Gray Provincial Park** (597-6150), the third largest in BC. **Helmcken Falls,** at 137 metres, is one of the highest waterfalls in North America. Wildlife viewing includes moose, grizzly bear, and 218 species of birds. The park's interpretive services are available only in the summer. Certified guides are available year round.

The park is mostly wilderness, but some vehicular camping is allowed along Clearwater River. One attraction is wilderness camping and ca-

Dawson Falls, one of many in Wells Gray Provincial Park, is part of the 91-metre-wide Murtle River. Located in the Cariboo Mountains, the park was created in 1939.

noeing on the Clearwater-Azure lakes chain and on Murtle Lake, accessible from Blue River. From Hobson Lake in the north end of the park, a 6.5 kilometre portage connects with Quesnel Lake in the Cariboo. Mahood Lake in the south connects with the Cariboo via a gravel road at the west end.

North Thompson Area

South of Clearwater, Highway 5 continues through **Little Fort**, the site of an early Hudson's Bay Company post on the old Fur Brigade Trail. Highway 24 west of here connects with the Cariboo's Interlakes region and excellent fishing. Continuing south, the region around **Barriere** also is a favourite with anglers. South of Barriere, Highway 5 continues to Kam-

loops on the Trans-Canada Highway. Special events include the **North Thompson Fall Fair** in Barriere in September.

Driving on Northern Highways
Alaska Highway and Cassiar Highway

- Be prepared. There are long stretches that go through wilderness, without many services. Carry back-up equipment such as tires and fan belts, and food and water and survival supplies.
- Highways are always at the mercy of the elements: watch for pot holes, frost heaves, and washouts.
- Construction and repair is ongoing: watch for graders and road crews. Be prepared for some delays.
- Travel at an appropriate speed. Visibility will be limited by dust, curves, and hills. Always watch for wildlife.
- Check locally for current road information at the RCMP and Infocentres and on the local radio stations.
- Drive with headlights on low beam and buckle up.

Northern Interior

Aurora borealis or Northern Lights are common in the northern latitudes of the Interior, reaching their maximum displays in March and September. These spectacular light shows result from electrical discharges generated by the solar wind interacting with the Earth's magnetic field.

When Alexander Mackenzie crossed the Rockies and paddled along the Peace and Fraser river systems in 1793, it was the earliest European exploration of the land west of the Rockies. By contrast, modern development of this part of the province occurred relatively late. The Alaska Highway was only built in 1942; the John Hart Highway in 1952, and the Cassiar Highway in 1972.

Although the average tourist does not visit the relatively unpopulated region north of Prince George, it comprises roughly one-half of the province's land area. The terrain varies from muskeg lowlands to rugged mountains and offers a wide range of outdoor recreation activities. (Bugs can be a problem in the summer months: bring mosquito repellent or wear blue and eat lots of garlic.)

The first leg of our route travels northeast from Prince George over the John Hart Highway, cutting through the Rocky Mountains to the agricultural Peace River Country, the only part of the province that lies east of the Rocky Mountains. This triangle of prairie is Cana-

da's northernmost agricultural area of commercial significance. North of Dawson Creek our route follows the scenic Alaska Highway to the Yukon border at Watson Lake. Then the route returns south, travelling the Cassiar Highway through equally spectacular wilderness to meet up with the Yellowhead Route near Hazelton and then east to Prince George.

For tips on driving in the North see page 217.

John Hart Highway

Highway 97 north of Prince George (the John Hart Highway) first winds through rolling hills dotted with lakes and farms, then climbs through Pine Pass in the Murray Range of the Rocky Mountains to the grasslands, aspen forests, and marshes of the boreal plains. The route is a paved two-lane highway stretching 415 kilometres from Prince George to Dawson Creek.

Meandering **Crooked River**, 85 kilometres north of Prince George, was once a fur-trade route. Today it is a wildlife viewing corridor popular with paddlers. The wetland is the most northern wintering site in the Interior for the rare and beautiful trumpeter swans.

Simon Fraser built Fort McLeod at **McLeod Lake** (55 kilometres north of Prince George) in 1805, naming this new and untamed land New Caledonia. The first fur-trading fort west of the Rockies, the site is presently unrestored and on private land. **Carp Lake Provincial Park,** west of McLeod Lake has interesting glacial eskers and historic fur-trading trails.

By the turn of the century, many areas of the southern Interior had been linked by railways. In the 1920s bush pilots began flying into remote areas of the north. Today many small airlines offer charter services for recreational, business, and service activities.

Sidetrip: Mackenzie

190 km (118 mi) north of Prince George on Highway 39. Population: 5615. Infocentre: junction Highways 97 and 39. Box 880, V0J 2C0.
997-5459; Fax: 997-6117. Seasonal Mackenzie was wilderness until the construction of the massive Peace River hydroelectric project in 1965. On display is a legacy of the venture, the world's largest tree crusher. Williston Lake, the largest reservoir in Canada, has 1200 kilometres of shoreline and exceptional fishing and boating.

Today, forestry is the main industry in Mackenzie. Members of the public are welcome to explore the demonstration forest; two of the eight trails are wheelchair accessible.

Special events include the **Winter Carnival** in March, **Kinsmen Indoor Rodeo** in May, and the **Fall Fair and Trade Show** in August.

Pine Pass Area

Back on the John Hart Highway travelling east toward Chetwynd, **Bijoux Falls Park** near Pine Pass has a picnic area and spectacular waterfalls. Keep alert for bears: this area has the highest grizzly-to-people population in the province. (See p. 77.) **Powder King Ski Area** (561-1776) is nearby, offering fine powder skiing, 23 runs, and a vertical drop of 640 metres.

About 10 kilometres east of the summit, the time zone changes. (See Reference section.)

Chetwynd

310 km (192 mi) north of Prince George. Population: 2730. Infocentre: 5217 North Access Road, V0C 1J0. 788-3655. Fax: 788-7843
Formerly known as Little Prairie, this town was renamed in honor of Ralph Chetwynd, a former minister

of highways. The **Caboose Museum** (next to the Infocentre, 788-3345) has an interesting combination of displays which range from dinosaurs to the railway. The **Little Prairie Heritage Museum** is two kilometres west of town in the original post office (788-3358).

Special events include **Chinook Daze** in February, the **Bluegrass Country Music Festival** in June, **West Moberly Days** in July, **Pemmican Days** in August, and the **NRA Rodeo Finals** in September.

Two interesting side trips are possible via Highway 29 which intersects with the John Hart Highway here.

Sidetrip: Tumbler Ridge

105 km (65 mi) south of Chetwynd on Highway 29. Population: 4800. Infocentre: Southgate Road, Box 606, V0C 2W0. 242-4702; Fax: 242-5159

Tumbler Ridge is one of Canada's newest towns. It was created in the early 1980s and has one of the world's largest computerized open-pit coal mines. (Tours of **Quintette Mine** are available, 242-2702.) Nearby is **Monkman Provincial Park** with spectacular **Kinuseo Falls**, at 70 metres, higher than Niagara. The falls are accessible by jetboat (ask at the Infocentre), horseback, or a seasonal gravel road. Annual celebrations include the **Winter Carnival** in March and **Tumbler Ridge Days Fair and Rodeo** in August.

Sidetrip: Hudson's Hope

64 km (40 mi) north of Chetwynd. Population: 1050. Infocentre: 10507 - 105 Avenue, Box 330, V0C 1V0. 783-9154; Fax: 783-5794. Seasonal

Fur traders travelled to this area as early as 1778, establishing a trading post at Rocky Mountain Portage in 1805. Overlooking the Peace River, the town was on the sternwheeler route in the early 1900s.

The **Hudson's Hope Museum** (783-5735), housing everything from "dinosaurs to dynamos," has trapping and coal-mining displays and an extensive fossil collection, including a rare baby icthyosaur specimen. Besides enjoying a great view, at **Alwin Holland Park**, three kilometres from town, visitors can bird-watch and fish.

WAC Bennett Dam (24 kilometres west on Dam Access Road), on the eastern tip of Williston Lake, was built in the 1960s and supplies more than one-third of BC's power. Tours are available daily during the summer (783-5211). **Peace Canyon Dam** (east side of Highway 29, seven kilometres beyond Hudson's Hope), part of the same project, has a self-guided tour that outlines the region's history (783-9943). During the dam building, workers discovered prehistoric tools and artifacts dating back thousands of years, and an 11,600-year-old mammoth tusk.

The varied landscape surrounding Dunlevy Creek north of the WAC Bennett Dam is a wildlife-viewing area.

Special events include the **Ice Carnival** in March, the **NRA Rodeo** and the **Dam Run** in June, and **Dinosaur Daze** and the **Raft Race** in August.

Dawson Creek, a service centre for the Peace River region, is also Mile 0 on the Alaska Highway.

Dawson Creek

102 km (63 mi) north of Chetwynd.
Infocentre: 900 Alaska Avenue, V1G 4T6.
782-9595; Fax: 782-9538

Dawson Creek may be famous as Mile 0 of the Alaska Highway, but only 16 kilometres from the Alberta border, it is also a centre for the Peace River's rich farmlands. Compared with other areas of the province, non-Native settlement was late. Although on the edge of the Klondike Gold Rush Trail in 1898, the first homesteaders didn't arrive until 1907. The Northern Alberta Railway built its terminus here in 1931, but the town only had 500 residents in 1941. In 1942 the construction of the Alaska Highway began, and Dawson Creek was changed forever as thousands of workers poured into the area.

The award-winning **Northern Alberta Railway (NAR) Park** is downtown. Features include the **Dawson Creek Station Museum** (782-9595), displaying human, geological, and archeological history; and the **Dawson Creek Art Gallery** (782-2601), in a restored grain elevator. Other attractions include the **Mile 0 Post of the Alaska Highway** at the east end of the NAR parking lot, the **Alaska Highway Cairn** in the heart of downtown at 10th Street and 102nd Avene, and the **Pioneer Village** (782-9595) at the junction of the John Hart and Alaska highways.

Special events include **Mile Zero Days** in June, the **Pouce Coupe Barbecue** in July, the **Fall Fair and Rodeo** in August, and the **Rotary Carol Fest** in December.

Alaska Highway

Highway 97 north of Dawson Creek is known as the Alaska Highway (formerly the Alcan Highway), with Dawson Creek designated as Mile 0. Built in nine months by 11,000 American troops under a joint Canada-US agreement as a supply route during World War II, the highway opened to the public in 1947. The route, mostly paved now with some gravel sections, is constantly being improved and shortened. Current distance from Dawson Creek to Fairbanks, Alaska is 2451 km (1523 miles). Road conditions change due to weather and construction, with June through September the best times to travel. (See page 217.)

Mainly a two-lane highway, the road narrows to a single lane in places, and flying gravel can be a problem. It is possible to go 160 kilometres without services, but on average, food, gas, and accommodation are found every 30 to 80 kilometres. Over 200,000 vehicles travel this road every year.

Building the Alaska Highway

An amazingly audacious task at the time, the men charged with creating this route through the wilderness were often raw recruits in the US Army or civilians with little knowledge of road-building. Construction started in March, 1942 and the first truck pushed through to Whitehorse in September that same year. However, during the following spring 150 bridges washed out and 240 kilometres of road disappeared in mud and muskeg. Conversion of the road to an all-weather route began the same year. At the height of activity in September 1943, 17,000 workers, 54 separate contractors, and over 11,000 pieces of equipment valued at $27 million were on the job. Total cost of the project in 1991 dollars is estimated at about $1.4 billion.

The southern part of the highway travels through a wide plateau of grasslands, forests, wetlands, and muskeg. The highway turns back toward the Rocky Mountains west of Fort Nelson, entering the Liard Basin just south of the Yukon border. As one might expect in such vast wilderness, wildlife viewing, wilderness recreation, and fishing are excellent. Paddling and river rafting are also popular. Contact the Infocentre.

Fort St. John
75 km (47 mi) north of Dawson Creek. Population: 12,743. Infocentre: 9323 - 100th Street, V1J 4N4. 785-6037; Fax: 785-7181

Dubbing itself "the energy capital of BC" because of its expanding gas, coal, and oil fields, Fort St. John also relies on forestry and agriculture. Ranchers herd buffalo and reindeer as well as cattle.

The region was inhabited by Beaver and Sekani Natives when fur traders first arrived. Some experts theorize that during the last glaciation, the area was part of an ice-free corridor used by people who crossed from Asia and migrated south. At nearby **Charlie Lake**, archeologists have unearthed 10,500-year-old artifacts and animal bones. Simon Fraser University is holding most of these pieces for study, but the **North Peace Pioneer and Petroleum Museum** (787-0430) displays a replica of the oldest artifact found in BC, a bead from Charlie Lake estimated to be 10,500 years old. **Rocky Mountain House** is 10 kilometres upstream, built by the North West Company in 1797.

The museum displays feature pioneer history, Alaska Highway construction, and early oil and gas exploration. Other attractions include tours of **Bickford's Buffalo Ranch** (781-3507); **Canadian Forest Products** (785-8906); and **The Honey Place** (785-4808), containing the world's largest glass beehive.

Special events in Fort St. John include the **Ice Carnival** in March, the **Kinsmen Summerfest** in June, and the **Fort St. John Rodeo** in July.

The **Peace River Lookout** (south of 100th Street, 2.3 kilometres past the traffic lights on the Alaska Highway) has a breathtaking view of the river and its surrounding fields and hills.

Pink Mountain
Access road is 160 km (100 mi) north of Fort St. John

Pink Mountain (elevation:1784 m) has the only wild buffalo habitat in BC, as well as the Arctic butterfly and other wildlife, including caribou, moose, grizzly, and black bear.

The access road is difficult and not for the faint of heart. Check at Pink Mountain service station for current conditions.

A time-zone boundary is about 12 kilometres north of Pink Mountain. Check locally. (See Reference section.)

Fort Nelson
383 km (237 mi) north of Fort St. John. Population: 3690. Infocentre: Mile 300.5 Alaska Highway, Bag Service 399, V0C 1R0. 774-2541; Fax: 774-6794

Like many northern communities, Fort Nelson was first established in

1805 as a fur-trading post, although it has been rebuilt several times. At the confluence of the Nelson, Prophet, and Muskwa rivers, the town is the northernmost point on BC Rail's freight line. The local economy is supported by forestry and natural gas processing. An unusual special event is the **Canadian Open Sled Dog Races**, held here every December. The **Fort Nelson Rodeo** and the **Fall Fair** are in August.

Fort Nelson claims the easiest access to **Kwadacha Wilderness Provincial Park.** The 158,457-hectare recreation area has no road access, but users can fly, horseback ride, or hike in. Contact the Info-centre for guides. Attractions include alpine meadows, hoodoos, and wildlife: grizzly bears are common. (See p. 77.)

Stone Mountain Provincial Park and Wokkpash Recreation Area

Located on the Alaska Highway amid the alpine tundra, spruce forest, and glaciers of the northern Rockies, motorists can view fantastic landscapes and a wide variety of wildlife, including stone mountain sheep, mountain caribou, and moose. A trail for experienced hikers leads to a five-kilometre line of "hoodoo" erosion pillars in Wokkpash Valley. Some are 100 metres tall. A less vigorous view of hoodoos is via the short walk at Summit Pass. At Summit Lake, **Flower Springs Trail** takes hikers on a five-kilometre walk, among wildflowers and waterfalls.

Muncho Lake Provincial Park

Muncho Lake Provincial Park's natural mineral licks attract wildlife that include deer and stone sheep (up to 200 in the summer). Migrating birds such as grebes, loons, hummingbirds, nuthatches, and flycatchers are also common. The town of Mucho Lake is in the park, 261 kilometres (162 miles) north of Fort Nelson. Gas, food, and accommodations are available. Ask about the **Bush Pilot Film Festival**.

Liard River Hotsprings Provincial Park

It seems impossible that a "tropical" oasis could exist north of the 56th parallel. At Liard River Hotsprings Provincial Park, water in the natural pool is 43°C, raising the air temperature to create frost-free, unfrozen soils. Of the 250 species of boreal forest plants growing here, 14 occur only because of the springs. Flora include such exotic species as monkey flower, ostrich fern, lobelia, violets, 14 species of orchids, and several carnivorous plants such as sundew, butterwort, and aquatic bladderwort.

The hot springs are also one of the best places in the province to view moose. Of particular interest are the "hanging gardens" of tufa, formed when spring water reacts with air, creating surreal mineral deposits.

The 668-hectare park is located in the Liard Plateau, north of the Rocky Mountains. The hot springs are mentioned in Hudson's Bay Company factor Robert Campbell's diary in 1835, and likely they were used by the

Glacier-fed Atlin Lake is BC's largest natural lake. It includes over 795 square kilometres of bays, arms, and channels.

Teslin Natives long before that. US troops working on the Alaska Highway constructed a boardwalk and pool facilities at the hot springs in 1942.

The Yukon Border

Watson Lake, Yukon, 532 kilometres north of Fort Nelson, is famous for its international sign-forest. At the border (60° North) Highway 97 becomes Highway 1. Twenty-one kilometres west on Highway 1 just past Upper Liard, is the junction with Highway 37, the Cassiar Highway.

Sidetrip: Atlin

467 km (290 mi) northwest of Watson Lake. Population: 500. Infocentre: Box 111, V0W 1A0. 651-7522

Searchers for Shangri-La might wish to push on to Atlin, in BC's northwest corner. Located on the shores of Atlin Lake, BC's largest natural lake and headwaters of the Yukon River, the picturesque town is far off the beaten track.

Known for its placer gold claims, the town had 5000 residents during its gold rush days at the turn of the century. The **Atlin Historical Museum** (651-7522) contains gold rush, Tinglit Native, and early transportation displays. The 29°C pools of **Atlin Mineral Springs** are 24 kilometres south of town, close to the lake.

Atlin is also a base for exploring the spectacular glaciers of the Juneau Ice Cap in **Atlin Provincial Park** (847-7320). Gold panners can try their luck at the provincial government placer lease on Spruce Creek, eight kilometres from town. Houseboat rentals are available on the lake and trout fishing is good.

Cassiar Highway

Completed in 1972, Highway 37 travels 746 kilometres south from its junction with the Alaska Highway near Upper Liard, Yukon Territory, to the junction with Highway 16 near Hazelton. Many believe the scenery is among the most magnificent in the country. Most of the route is through wilderness, with occasional towns and ghost towns along the way.

The road is a combination of gravel, pavement, and seal-coated surfaces. As with the Alaska Highway, conditions depend on the weather, the season, and ongoing construction projects. (See Reference section.) Check locally for current information. Repair services are limited. The longest stretch without gas pumps is the 160 kilometres between Tatogga Lake and Bell II.

The mineral-rich Cassiar, Stikine, Skeena, and Coast mountains dominate the landscape. The province's newest ghost town, **Cassiar,** 120 kilometres south of the junction, shut down when the asbestos mine closed in 1992. The area is also a source of jade, with **Jade City** and **Dease Lake** (117 kilometres to the south) luring rockhounds from around the world.

Side Trip: Telegraph Creek

A rough but scenic road travels from Dease Lake to Telegraph Creek, a centuries-old Tahltan Indian settlement that has seen its share of gold rushes. Trailers have to stay behind in Dease Lake, but the two-hour, 120-kilometre trip is very scenic, passing Native settlements, caribou meadows, lava beds, and ranchland.

Left: Watson Lake's "sign forest" was begun by military personnel working on the Alaska Highway in 1942.

Right: The two hot pools and warm-water swamps at Liard Hot Springs have created an exotic ecosystem in the northern Interior.

Telegraph Creek became an important stopover during the Klondike Gold Rush of 1898. The CPR originally planned to operate 20 paddlewheelers from the town as part of an all-Canadian route to the Yukon, but cancelled the ships when a proposed railway was not approved.

Telegraph Creek was the terminus of the Telegraph Trail, built in the 1860s when the Collins Overland Telegraph Company was attempting to establish the first cable line to Europe. From 1861 when Telegraph Creek enjoyed a minor gold rush, the town was the head of navigation for Stikine River sternwheelers from Wrangell, Alaska, 260 kilometres downstream. The river served as a transportation route for the next 100 years.

Stikine River

Highway 37 crosses 644-kilometre-long Stikine River about 60 kilometres south of Dease Lake. In the 100-kilometre-long Grand Canyon of the Stikine River, the water surges between rock walls 300 metres high. The recently created **Stikine River Recreation Area** is very popular with canoers and kayakers, but the canyon itself is considered unnavigable. Environmentalists have opposed a proposal for hydro development on the Stikine River for many years.

Two Wilderness Parks

Mt. Edziza and **Spatsizi Plateau Wilderness provincial parks** are two of the route's other major features. Mt. Edziza is one of Canada's most significant volcanic areas with 2787-metre Ice Mountain dominating the scenery, and 2500-metre Eve Cone and the colourful **Spectrum Range** adding to the attraction. Many outfitters and guides based in **Iskut** (84 kilometres south of Dease Lake) and the surrounding area offer hiking, rafting, float plane, or horseback trips into both parks.

Spatsizi, at 656,785 hectares, is BC's second largest park. Wildlife includes caribou, Stone sheep, mountain goats, moose, grizzly bear, and 140 species of birds. Adventurers should remember these are wilderness areas and come prepared. (See p. 77.)

Sidetrip: Stewart

The lure of **Bear** and **Salmon glaciers** may convince motorists to make the 67-kilometre side trip to Stewart. (Drive west via Highway 37A at

Meziadin Junction. The Stewart Infocentre is between 6th and 7th on Columbia; 636-2568.). The astonishing Bear Glacier cascades down the mountain just across the lake from the highway, and the ice glows at night, just so you can't miss it.

Stewart, Canada's most northern ice-free port, is also the movie capital of the north *(Bear Island, Iceman, The Thing)*. At the end of the road a few minutes away is **Hyder, Alaska** (population 80). During its hey-day, miners signed dollar bills and tacked them to the wall of the bar to ensure that when they returned, they wouldn't be broke. The tradition still exists, and travellers are welcome to add more to the collection. Grizzly and black bears feed on spawning salmon at local rivers near both communities in the fall. During the summer months the Alaska State ferry system connects with Stewart.

Sidetrip: Tseax

The last volcanic eruption in BC occurred at Tseax about 230 years ago. Take the Nass Road south at Cranberry Junction (83 kilometres south of Meziadin Junction) to 17,783-hectare **Nisga'a Memorial Lava Bed Provincial Park**. Created in 1992, the park is administered jointly by BC Parks and the Nisga'a Band.

Totem Pole Country

The southern end of Highway 37 is totem pole country, providing an opportunity to learn about northwest Native culture. At **Kitwancool** (849-5703), 20 poles stand outside the band office, including the oldest standing totem pole in the world, "Hole in the

Ice." At **Kitwanga** (849-5591), **Battle Hill** is the first National Historic Site in Western Canada to commemorate Native culture. A self-guided trail and nearby totem poles tell the story. (The Kitwanga Infocentre is in the video store: 849-5760.)

At the junction with Highway 16, the route travels west to Terrace and Prince Rupert. That's another book, but Prince Rupert is a major fishing port and the terminus for both Alaska and BC ferry routes. Canada's first grizzly preserve, the Khutzeymateen, is just north of Prince Rupert. Among Terrace's attractions is the opportunity to view the unusual Kermode

Secluded Spatzizi Plateau Wilderness Provincial Park is described as the "Serengeti of North America" because of the minimal human impact on indigenous wildlife. Spatzizi means "red goat" and describes the coats of mountain goats that roll in the iron-oxide-rich soil near Gladys Lake in the park.

Totem poles carved from cedar served as signboards, genealogical records, and memorials in Northwest Native cultures. K'san village at Hazelton is a major attraction.

bear. Our circle tour goes in the opposite direction, however, following the Yellowhead route east to Prince George.

Yellowhead East

The final portion of the Northern Interior Circle Tour travels east through the Bulkley and Nechako valleys. Generally, the region is dry Interior forest of the Interior Plateau with some grasslands along the valley floor. The Skeena and Omineca mountains lie to the north. The highway is paved, but adverse weather can make it perilous. Check locally for current conditions.

The Carrier tribes of the Athapaskan language family were the earliest residents of the Bulkley Valley. The Nass and Skeena valleys were inhabited by the Tsimshians, who, along with the Haida on the Queen

Charlotte Islands are noted for their totem carving.

Noted for its outdoor recreation, the area is popular for fishing, paddling, wildlife viewing, and skiing.

Hazelton

Population: 1275. Infocentre: Box 340, New Hazelton, V0J 2J0. 842-6571; Fax: 842-6077

At the confluence of the Bulkley and Skeena rivers, the towns of New Hazelton and Old Hazelton are dominated by the Roche Deboule Mountains. One of the major attractions is **K'san Village,** site of native settlements for 7000 years. Reconstructed longhouses, guided tours, totem poles, a carving school, the **Northwestern National Exhibition Centre** (842-5723), and performances by the internationally recognized K'san dancers are among the attractions.

A self-guided "Hands of History" tour of the area, the ancestral home of the Gitksan and Wet'suwe'ten people, includes totem poles at Kispiox (Band Council: 842-5248), Kitwancool (849-5703), and Kitwanga (849-5591). West of Hazelton near Moricetown, the Carrier village, **Kyah Wiget,** is the oldest settlement in the Bulkley Valley.

The Gitskan and Wet-suwe-ten are leaders in the struggle by Native people to have their land claims recognized in British Columbia.

With European settlement in the area, notably the rush to the Omineca goldfields in the 1870s, Hazelton became the sternwheeler terminus on the Skeena River, celebrated in the "old town" pioneer village.

Special events include the **Kispiox Rodeo** in June and **Hazelton Pioneer Days** in August.

Smithers
68 km (42 mi) east of Hazelton.
Population: 4850. Infocentre:
1425 Main Street, Box 2379, V0J 2N0.
847-9854; Fax: 847-3337

With the Babine Mountains as a backdrop, this "Bavarian" town is a popular destination for outdoor adventurers and a service centre for logging, agriculture, and mining. A number of outfitters make their headquarters here, and shops sell the work of local artisans.

The **Central Park Building** (1425 Main, behind the Infocentre) is a heritage structure built in 1925. It houses the **Art Gallery** (847-3898) and the **Bulkley Valley Museum** (847-5322). One of the largest agricultural exhibitions in the province,

the annual **Bulkley Valley Exhibition** occurs in the last weekend in August, with the BC Championship Heavy Horse Pull, logging sports, and art exhibitions. Other attractions include an old time fiddler's contest, a midway, art exhibitions, a canoe race, and a petting zoo.

Other special events include the **Bulkley Valley Cross-country Ski Marathon** in January, the **Smithers Winter Festival** in February, and the **Smithers Rodeo** and **Midsummer Festival** in June.

The Collins Overland Telegraph

In 1865, under Col. C.S. Bulkley, the Collins Overland Telegraph Company began construction of a line connecting the US to Europe via BC, the Yukon, Alaska, and Siberia. The race was lost in 1866 when an Atlantic cable was laid, but not before the Collins line had been pushed from New Westminster to 25 kilometres north of Hazelton.

When the company left the area, some of the discarded cable was used by the Natives to build a bridge across the Hagwilget Canyon on the Bulkley River near Hazelton.

The ski season stretches from mid-November through April at **Ski Smithers** on 2575-metre **Hudson Bay Mountain** (847-5327; 1-800-665-4299). Powder skiing is excellent. Nordic trails are also an attraction with ice fishing, skating, snowmobiling among the other winter activities.

The **Babine Mountains Provincial Recreation Area** is also accessible from Smithers. Its many hiking trails make it popular in any season. The **Babine River,** noted for its steelhead fishing, is also an internationally known whitewater route for rafters and kayakers.

Sidetrip: Telkwa High Road

The Telkwa High Road starts 22 kilometres west of Smithers at Moricetown or 12 kilometres east of Smithers at Telkwa. The route passes through rolling farmland to Driftwood Creek Road and access to **Driftwood Canyon Provincial Park** (847-7320), or follow the signs just west of Smithers on Highway 16. Waterfalls, glacial deposits, and 40- to 70-million year old fossil beds are among the park's attractions. An interpretive display describes the specimens from the Tertiary periods found here. Fossil collectors should check with the BC Parks office in Smithers for information.

Simon Gun-an-Noot

In the early hours of June 19, 1906, two men were found dead outside the remote village of Hazelton. When police investigated, they discovered that one of the men, Alex MacIntosh, had earlier argued violently with Simon Gun-an-Noot, a Git'ksan trapper and merchant.

Without a trial or representation for the accused, two days later a coroner's jury convicted Gun-an-Noot and his cousin, Peter Himadam, of the murders. The two men disappeared into the wilderness.

An expert trapper and packer, Gun-an-Noot eluded capture for thirteen years, during which time public perception of him changed from being "a murdering Indian" to a national folk hero.

While on the run, Gun-an-Noot and Himadam were accompanied by Gun-an-Noot's wife Sarah, their three children, his mother and father, and Himadam's wife. Sarah Gun-an-Noot gave birth to two more children during their exile.

Supported by sympathizers who included prominent criminal lawyer Stuart Henderson of Victoria, Gun-an-Noot turned himself in in 1919. He was acquitted of all charges. The murderer was never found.

Telkwa

What better reason to stop at the small community of Telkwa (10 kilometres west of Smithers; information: 846-5212), than fishing from the main street? At the convergence of the Bulkley and Telkwa rivers, Telkwa was created when the Collins Overland Telegraph Line was built in the 1860s. Heritage buildings include turn-of-the-century **St. Stephen's Anglican Church** on Highway 16. The **Telkwa Barbecue** is held every August. The Telkwa River has novice and intermediate runs for paddlers.

Houston

50 km (31 mi) east of Telkwa.
Population: 3510. Infocentre:
3289 Highway 16, Box 396, V0J 1Z0.
845-7640; 845-3682

At the confluence of the Morice and Bulkley rivers, Houston calls itself "the world steelhead capital" and claims the world's largest fly-fishing rod (18.3 metres long).

Created during the Grand Trunk Pacific Railway construction, today Houston's economy is based on forestry and ranching. The community offers forestry awareness tours and nature trails with wheelchair access.

The Bulkley Valley is noted for its paddling opportunities, and one of the best routes is the 80-kilometre day-trip from Houston to Smithers on the Bulkley River. This is the same route that the Bulkley Valley Fall Fair Canoe Race uses. The Morice River is also popular.

Industrial tours include the Equity Silver Mine and two high-tech sawmills. (Contact the Infocentre.) Special events include **Pleasant Valley Days** in May.

Fossil hunters at Driftwood Canyon Provincial Park should NOT search the cliff for specimens – it is too unstable. Check with BC Parks in Smithers for regulations.

Burns Lake

80 km (50 mi) east of Houston.
Population: 1635. Infocentre: Box 339,
VOJ 1E0. 692-3773; Fax: 692-3493
Like Houston, Burns Lake began as
a railway construction camp in
1911, supplying hand-hewn ties to

Carrier Natives

The Carrier are a branch of the western Dene people who
have inhabited this part of the Interior Plateau for
centuries. It was the custom for widowed women of the
tribe to carry the ashes of their deceased husbands on
their backs until a potlatch was held, thus the name
"carriers."

Like coastal tribes, the Carrier relied heavily on
salmon for survival, spearing and trapping the fish as
they came upriver to spawn. The diet of dried salmon was
supplemented by hunting and by gathering of wild plants
and berries. Trapper "Six Mile Mary," above, was 106
years old when this photo was taken in the early 1900s.

the Grank Trunk Pacific. Today the
town is the centre of the "Lakes District," an area stretching from Ootsa
to the south and Babine to the north
– 17 fishing lakes within a 100-kilo-
metre radius. At Babine Lake, BC's
longest natural lake, anglers catch
rainbow trout up to 3.5 kilograms
and lake trout up to 18 kilograms.
The lake is also one of the largest
freshwater habitats for sockeye
salmon in the province.

The **Lakes Disrict Museum** (692-
7450) is in the 1925 Heritage Centre
and features logging exhibits. Gift
shops in town feature beadwork and
painting by Carrier Natives.

Rockhounds should investigate
Eagle Creek, 6.5 kilometres west of
Burns Lake, for agates and opals.
Special events include the annual
**Bluegrass and Country Music Fes-
tival** in July.

Burns Lake is the northern gate-
way to **Tweedsmuir Provincial
Park,** BC's largest (see page 205).
Access here is by boat only. By con-
trast, **Deadman's Island Provincial
Park,** a short boat ride away, is BC's
smallest provincial park. Highway
35 south of town gives access to
Ootsa Lake, part of the Nechako
Reservoir, created in 1952 for the
Alcan smelter in Kitimat.

Vanderhoof

135 km(83 mi) east of Burns Lake.
Population: 3130. Infocentre: Box 126,
VOJ 3A0. 567-2124; Fax: 567-3316
The first agricultural settlement in
BC and still largely a farming com-
munity, Vanderhoof is the geographi-
cal centre of British Columbia.
William Vanderhoof had dreams of

making the town into a writers' colony when he settled here in the early 1900s, but it was not to be.

Located on the Nechako River, in the spring and fall the **Vanderhoof Bird Sanctuary** offers a resting place to over 50,000 migrating Canada Geese. Check locally for up-to-date information on the popular three-to-five-day canoe trip to the confluence of the Stuart and Nechako rivers. Other attractions include the **Family Farm** (567-9192) and the **Pioneer Village** (567-2991) with its restored OK Cafe (567-2594), both on Highway 16. The **International Airshow** is in July and the annual **Fall Fair and Rodeo** is in August.

Sidetrip: Fort St. James

60 km (37 mi) north of Vanderhoof. Population:1925. Infocentre: 115 Douglas Avenue, Box 1164, V0J 1P0. 996-7023; Fax: 996-7047

Simon Fraser first crossed the Rocky Mountains in 1805, establishing a post on McLeod Lake. In July of 1806, he built a fort near a Carrier village on Sturgeon (later Stuart) Lake. The post, Fort St. James, became the administrative centre for the large trading area of New Caledonia. As the fur trade waned in the 1880s, so did the fortunes of the fort, but it remained part of the Hudson's Bay Company empire until the 1930s, when it was abandoned in favour of a modern retail store.

In 1971 historians, archeologists, carpenters, and a host of other experts began work on a multimillion

dollar program to create **Fort St. James National Historic Park** (996-7191). Open from mid-May to October, the fort has been restored to its 1896 appearance. The town claims to be the longest continuously inhabited white settlement west of the Rockies.

Other attractions include **Lady of Good Hope Church,** one of the oldest in BC, and the **Russ Baker Memorial.** Baker was founder of one of BC's early airlines. **Murray Ridge Ski Hill** (996-2200), 20 minutes away, has the longest T-Bar in North America and 16 kilometres of groomed nordic trails .

A popular canoe trip follows Simon Fraser's route from Stuart Lake down the Stuart River to the Nechako River and on to Prince George. Moose, mule deer, and many birds are among the wildlife along the way. The Nation Lakes chain and Takla Lake also offer remote, but enjoyable, paddling.

Fort St. James was one of the first fur-trading posts west of the Rockies. Established by Simon Fraser in 1806, it is now a national historic site.

Reference

Access

AIR
From outside BC
Vancouver International Airport, located in the suburb of Richmond, a half-hour bus ride from downtown, serves as a destination to 26 scheduled airlines. Banking, money exchange, restaurant, car rental, accommodation reservations, and shopping services are available at the airport. Several hotels are close at hand.

Calgary and Edmonton in Alberta also have international airports. Victoria International Airport at Sidney on Vancouver Island has commuter service to and from Seattle, Washington.

To the Interior
From Vancouver, connector flights are available to all major centres in the Interior via Air BC and TimeAir. Smaller commuter and charter airlines also provide services that make most destinations in the province easily accessible. Vacationers seeking remote fishing or other outdoor recreation experiences often use these smaller airlines. Some airlines offering service in the Interior:
• Air BC: 688-5515; 1-800-663-3721 (BC); 1-800-663-8868 (US). Scheduled flights to Castlegar, Cranbrook, Dawson Creek, Fort St. John, Kamloops, Kelowna, Penticton, Prince George, Prince Rupert, Quesnel, Smithers, Terrace, Vernon, and Williams Lake.
• Pacific Coastal Airlines (Richmond): 273-8666. Interior service includes Vernon and Bella Bella.

• Shuswap Air (Salmon Arm): 832-8830; 1-800-363-4074 (BC). Interior service to Kelowna and Salmon Arm.
• TimeAir: 279-6611; 1-800-663-3502 (BC). Scheduled service to Castlegar, Cranbrook, Fort Nelson, Fort St. John, Kamloops, Kelowna, Penticton, and Smithers.
• Trans Provincial Airlines (Prince Rupert): 279-9082. Interior service includes Prince Rupert and Stewart.
• Wilderness Airline (Hagensborg): 982-2225; 1-800-665-9453. Interior service includes: Anahim Lake, Bella Coola, Dean River, and Shearwater.

FERRIES
From outside BC
• Alaska Marine Highway System, Box 458, Prince Rupert, BC V8J 3R2, 627-1744; 1-800-642-0066 (US). Prince Rupert, Skagway, Ketchikan, Wrangell, Petersburg, Sitka, Stewart, Juneau, and Haines.
• Black Ball Transport, 430 Belleville Street, Victoria, BC V8V 1W9, 386-2202; 206-457-4491 (Port Angeles). Victoria and Port Angeles on the Olympic Peninsula.
• Clipper Navigation, 1000-A Wharf Street, Victoria BC V8W 1T4, 1-800-888-2535. Seattle to Victoria.
• Washington State Ferries, 2499 Ocean Avenue, Sidney, BC V8L 1T3, 656-1531; 381-1551 (Victoria); 206-464-6400 (Seattle).

In BC
The government-operated BC Ferry Corporation provides regular and frequent service between Vancouver Island, the Gulf Islands and the mainland. During the summer months traffic is heavy. Reservations are required for the "Inside Passage" trip between Port Hardy and Prince Rupert.
• BC Ferry Corporation, 1112 Fort Street, Victoria BC V8V 4V2, 386-3431. Regular and frequent service. Some waits during summer months. Bus service, which includes ferry transportation, from Victoria and Nanaimo to Vancouver is also available. Call 662-8074 (Vancouver) for further information.

BUS
Regular bus services connect BC with the rest of Canada and the United States. Greyhound Bus Lines (Vancouver, 662-3222) has scheduled service to many communities in BC's Interior.

Several companies offer bus tours of popular destinations in BC's Interior. Travel agents will have information.

RAIL
• BC Rail, owned by the provincial government, offers regularly scheduled service to the Interior from North Vancouver to Prince George (North Vancouver, 984-5246).
• Rocky Mountaineer Railtours has a seasonal rail service between Vancouver and Banff or Jasper with a stopover in Kamloops. Scheduled so all travel is during daylight hours, the service only operates from April to October (1-800-665-RAIL).

• VIA Rail, Canada's only remaining national passenger railway, accesses the province from the east through Edmonton and Jasper. From Jasper, service is offered to Prince Rupert via Prince George, or to Vancouver via Kamloops. Plan to book at least six months in advance for travel between April and October (1-800-561-8630).

PRIVATE MOTOR VEHICLE
There are 17official points of entry along the southern border between the United States and British Columbia. Those at Boundary Bay, the Blaine crossings of Douglas and Pacific Highway, Huntingdon, Osoyoos, Kingsgate, and Roosville are open 24 hours.

Major highways entering BC
• From the south: Interstate 5, Highway 97, and Highway 395 from Washington state, Highway 95 from Idaho, and Highway 93 from Montana.
• From Alberta: Highway 3 (the Crowsnest route), Highway 1 (the Trans-Canada) from Banff and Calgary, Highway 16 from Edmonton and Jasper, and Highways 2, 34, and 43 from Edmonton to Dawson Creek.
• From the north: the Alaska Highway from Fairbanks, Alaska and Whitehorse, Yukon Territory.

Major highways in BC
• Highway 1 (the Trans-Canada Highway). Vancouver to the Alberta border via Hope, the Fraser Canyon, Kamloops, Revelstoke, and Golden.
• Highway 3 (the Crowsnest Highway). Hope to the Alberta border via Osoyoos, Castlegar, and Cranbrook.
• Highway 5 (the Coquihalla Highway). Controlled-access toll route from Hope north to Kamloops.
• Highway 5 (the Yellowhead Highway South). Kamloops to Tête Jaune Cache.
• Highway 16 (the Yellowhead Highway). Prince Rupert to the Alberta border via Prince George.
• Highway 97. From the US border near Osoyoos to the Yukon border. The only highway to cover the entire length of the province.

Entering Canada

Customs and Excise officials of **Revenue Canada** can supply border-crossing information. (Public Relations Branch, Ottawa ON K1Z 0L5, 613-993-6220, or, 1101 West Pender, Vancouver BC V6E 2M8, 666-0545.) US citizens do not require passports, but should carry appropriate identification. Visitors from other countries should carry passports or other recognized travel documents. Check with the nearest Canadian Consulate or Embassy for current regulations.

Driving a Car in BC

• International and US drivers' licences are valid in BC. Motor vehicle registration forms must be carried. If the driver is not the registered owner, she or he must have a letter of authorization from the registered owner. If the vehicle is a rental, a copy of the rental contract should be with the vehicle.
• Drinking and driving in Canada is a serious offence. If asked by a police officer, a driver must provide a breath or blood sample for testing. Operating a motor vehicle while under the influence of drugs is also a criminal offence.
• Seat belts must be worn by all passengers in motor vehicles. Motorcycle riders must wear safety helmets. Car seats must be provided for infants up to nine kilograms.
• In winter, carry tire chains and emergency supplies.

• Motorists involved in motor vehicle accidents should contact the nearest Insurance Corporation of British Columbia office.
• Canada is on the metric system. Speed limits and distances are posted in kilometres. In most cities the speed limit is 50 km/h, which is about 30 mph. An average speed limit on rural two-lane highways is 80 or 90 km/h (about 50 to 55 mph). On most controlled access highways, 100 or 110 km/h (65 or 70 mph) is the limit.

Highway Information
Ministry of Transport and Highways
Infoline: 1-800-663-4997
BC Road Fax Report:
    1-800-567-MOTH
Vancouver: 525-4997
Kelowna: 860-4997
Kamloops: 371-4997
Penticton: 490-4997

Tourist Information

INFOCENTRES

Most Interior communities, in cooperation with the provincial government, sponsor Infocentres, which have up-to-date information on sightseeing, recreation, accommodation, and special events. Usually located on or near the highway with identifiable red, white, and blue signs, Infocentre staff supply information on a wide variety of subjects. Locations are indicated on the maps.

TOURIST REGIONS

The provincial government has divided the province into nine tourist regions. Each one has a central office with information about its attractions and services. The regions are marked on the BC government road map (available free at Infocentres and many government offices). Eight of these regions are in the Interior.

Legal Holidays in BC

New Year's Day: January 1
Good Friday: Friday before
   Easter Sunday
Easter Monday: First Monday
   after Easter
Victoria Day: Third Monday in May
Canada Day: July 1
BC Day: First Monday in August
Labour Day: First Monday in
   September
Thanksgiving Day: Second Monday
   in October
Remembrance Day: November 11
Christmas Day: December 25
Boxing Day: December 26

• Tourism Association of Southwestern BC, 304 - 828 West 8th Avenue, Vancouver BC V5Z 1E2. 876-3088; Fax: 876-8916. Vancouver and the Lower Mainland make up most of the region, but the zone also includes the Interior community of Hope, a portion of the Fraser Canyon, a portion of the Coquihalla Highway, and Manning Park.

• Okanagan-Similkameen Tourism Association, #104-515 Highway 97S, Kelowna BC V1Z 3J2. 769-5959; Fax: 861-7493. Includes Princeton and area, the Similkameen and Okanagan valleys, and the Kettle River Valley.

• Kootenay Country Tourist Association, 610 Railway Street, Nelson BC V1L 1H4. 352-6033; Fax: 352-1656. Includes those communities along the Crowsnest Highway between Rock Creek and Creston as well as the southern Monashee Mountains, the Arrow Lakes and Kootenay Lake. The West Kootenay area in this book, including Nelson and the Slocan Valley, is part of this region.

• BC Rocky Mountain Visitor Association, 495 Wallinger Avenue, Box 10, Kimberley BC V1A 2Y5. 427-4838; Fax: 427-3344. Includes the southern Rocky Mountains, the Rocky Mountain Trench, and the Purcell Mountains and stretches from Kinbasket Lake near Golden south along the Columbia Valley to the US border.

• High Country Tourism Association, Box 962, Kamloops BC V2C 5N4. 372-7770; Fax: 828-4656. Extends from Merritt and the Nicola Valley through Kamloops to include Wells Gray Provincial Park, all the southern Yellowhead Highway, and Mt. Robson Provincial Park near Jasper, as well as Glacier National Park and Revelstoke on the Trans-Canada Highway.

• Cariboo Tourist Association, 190 Yorston Avenue, Box 4900, Williams Lake BC V2G 2V8, 392-2226; 1-800-663-5885; Fax: 392-2838. Includes the areas to the west of the Fraser River (the Chilcotin), to the east of the Fraser River (the Cariboo), and Highway 97 from Cache Creek north to Prince George.

• North by Northwest Tourism Association of BC, 3840 Alfred Avenue, Box 1030, Smithers BC V0J 2N0. 847-5227; Fax: 847-7585. Includes Prince George, most of the Yellowhead Highway to Prince Rupert and the wilderness area traversed by the Cassiar Highway.

• Peace River Alaska Highway Tourist Association, 10631-100th Street, Box 6850, Fort St. John BC V1J 4J8. 785-2544; Fax: 785-4224. Includes the John Hart Highway to Dawson Creek and the Alaska Highway north to the Yukon border.

• The ninth tourist region, not included in this book, is Vancouver Island. (Tourism Association of Vancouver Island, 302-45 Bastion Square, Victoria, BC V8W 1J1. 382-3551; Fax: 382-3523)

TOURISM BC

Ministry of Tourism
Parliament Buildings
Victoria BC V8V 1X4
387-1642
1-800-663-6000

For Further Information ...

FREE PUBLICATIONS

The provincial government has a number of free publications that can be very useful to travellers. They are available at Infocentres and other tourist outlets. Titles include:
• *British Columbia Accommodation Guide*
• *British Columbia Outdoor and Adventure Guide*
• *Super Camping*
• *British Columbia Skiing*
• *British Columbia Freshwater Fishing Regulations Synopsis*
• Road maps, camping maps, forestry maps, maps of major provincial parks.

ACCOMMODATION

Canadian Hostelling Association
1515 Discovery Street
Vancouver BC V6R 4K5
224-7111

British Columbia Automobile
Associaton
999 West Broadway
Vancouver BC V5Z 1K5
732-3911

BC and Yukon Hotels
Association
1st Floor, Hotel Vancouver
900 West Georgia Street
Vancouver BC V6C 2W6
681-7164; 1-800-663-3153

BC Bed and Breakfast
Association
810 West Broadway
Box 593
Vancouver BC V5Z 4E2

BC Motels, Campgrounds,
Resorts Association
980-555 West Hastings Street
Box 12105
Vancouver, BC V6B 4N6
682-8883; Fax: 682-8839

BC Fishing Resorts and Outfitters
Association
Box 3301
Kamloops BC V2C 6B9
828-1553; Fax: 828-1586

CANADA CUSTOMS

Public Relations Branch
1001 West Pender Street
Vancouver BC V6E 2M8
665-0545

FISH AND WILDLIFE

Ministry of Environment, Lands
and Parks,
7870 Blanchard Street,
Victoria BC V8V 1X5
Infoline: 387-9737

Tourism BC Toll Free Fishing
Information: 1-800-663-6000

Regional offices
• Cariboo
540 Borland Street
Williams Lake BC V2G 1R8
•East Kootenay
106 - 5th Avenue S
Cranbrook BC V1C 2G2
•Northern Interior
1011 Fourth Avenue
Prince George BC V2L 3H9
•Okanagan
3457 Skaha Lake Road
Penticton BC V2Z 7K2
• Peace-Liard
10142-101 Avenue
Fort St John BC V1J 2B3
• Skeena
3726 Alfred Avenue Bag 5000
Smithers BC V0J 2N0
•Southern Interior
1259 Dalhousie Drive
Kamloops BC V2C 5Z5
•West Kootenay
617 Vernon Street
Nelson BC V1L 4V9

GUIDES, NATURALISTS, AND TOUR OPERATORS

Association of Mountain Guides
Box 1537
Banff AB T0L 0C0
403-762-3761.

BC Fishing Resorts and Outfitters'
Association
Box 3301
Kamloops BC V2C 6B9
828-1553

Federation of BC Naturalists
Room 321, 1361 W Broadway
Vancouver BC V6H 4A9
737-3057; Fax: 738-7175

Guide Outfitters'
Association of BC
Box 759
100 Mile House BC V0K 2E0
396-2438; Fax: 395-4085

SPECIAL TRAILS ASSOCIATIONS

Alexander Mackenzie Heritage
Trail Association
Box 425, Station A
Kelowna, BC V1Y 7P1

Centennial Trails Trust
203-1646 West 7th Avenue
Vancouver BC V6J 1S5
731-9195
    This is an umbrella organization co-ordinating efforts to create uniform standards on 1400 kilometres of trail from Victoria to Banff through the southern Interior. It is currently possible to make this trek, although some sections are poorly maintained.

Rails to Trails
c/o Sue Thompson
Box 2437
Grand Forks BC V0H 1H0
442-81831; Fax: 442-8111.
    This group is co-ordinating the reclamation of abandoned railway lines for recreational use.

RECREATION ASSOCIATIONS
Outdoor Recreation Council of
British Columbia
334 - 1367 W Broadway
Vancouver, BC V6H 4A9
737-3059
Member organizations:
• BC Bicycle Association
  (737-7433)
• Cross Country BC (737-3058)
• Federation of Mountain Clubs
  of BC (737-3053)
• Recreation Canoeing
  Association of BC (737-3058)
• River Rafters Association of BC
  (737-3058)
• Whitewater Canoeing
  Association of BC (737-3058)

BC Fishing Resorts and Outfitters
Association
Box 3301
Kamloops BC V2C 6B9
828-1553

BC Speleological Federation
Box 733
Gold River BC V0P 1G0
283-2691

Dive BC
5824 Ash Street
Powell River BC V8A 4R4
483-9740

Sierra Club of Western Canada
314-626 View Street
Victoria BC V8W 1J4
467-1766 or 368-5255

Western Canada Wilderness
Committee
20 Water Street
Vancouver BC V6B 1A4
683-8220

PARKS, RESERVES, AND RECREATION AREAS
Forest Service Recreation Areas
•Cariboo Forest Region
540 Borland Street
Williams Lake BC V2G lR8
398-4345

•Kamloops Forest Region
515 Columbia Street
Kamloops BC V2C 2I7
828-4131
•Nelson Forest Region
518 Lake Street
Nelson BC V1L 4C6
354-6200
•Prince George Forest Region
1011-4th Avenue
Prince George BC V2L 3H9
656-6100
•Prince Rupert Forest Region
Bag 5000, 3726 Alfred Avenue
Smithers BC V0J 2N0
847-7500

Ministry of Parks
2nd Floor, 800 Johnson Street
Victoria BC V8V IX4
387-5002; Fax: 387-5757

District offices: write to the
Visitor Services Co-ordinator, BC
Parks:
• Cariboo District
540 Borland Street
Williams Lake BC V2G 1R8
398-4414
• East Kootenay District
Box 118
Wasa BC V0B 2K0
422-3212 or 422-3213
• Northern Region
1011-4th Avenue
Prince George BC V2L 3H9
565-6270
• Okanagan District
Box 399
Summerland BC V0H 1Z0
828-4501
• Peace-Liard District
9512-100th Street
Fort St. John BC V1J 3X6
787-3407
• Prince George District
Box 2045
Prince George BC V2N 2J6
565-6340
• Skeena District
Bag 5000
Smithers BC V0J 2N0
847-7320 or 847-7565

• Southern Interior Region
101-1050 West Columbia St
Kamloops BC V2C 1L4
828-4501
• Thompson River District
1265 Dalhousie Drive
Kamloops BC V2C 5Z5
828-4494
• West Kootenay District
RR3 Nelson BC V1L 5P6
825-4421 or 825-4422

Ecological Reserves
Ministry of Parks
4000 Seymour Place
Victoria, BC V8V 1X5
387-5002

National Parks
Visitors Services
Canadian Parks Service
Box 2989, Station M
Calgary, AB T2P 3H8
403-292-4401; Fax: 403-292-4746

Alcohol Consumption in BC
• Legal drinking age is 19.
• It is unlawful to drive with an open bottle of alcohol in a vehicle.
• It is unlawful to consume alcohol in a public place such as a beach or park.
• In BC alcohol is only sold at government liquor stores or specially licensed beer and wine stores. Grocery stores are not normally permitted to sell alcoholic beverages, although some grocery stores in small rural communities may be so licensed.

Tax Refunds for Travellers

Under certain circumstances visitors are eligible for rebates on the 7 percent federal Goods and Services Tax (GST) paid on accommodation and goods purchased. Forms and information are available at Canada Customs, Infocentres, and duty-free shops. For more information call 1-800-66VISIT (668-4748) within Canada or 1-613-991-3346 outside Canada; or write Revenue Canada, Customs and Excise, Visitors Rebate Program, Ottawa ON K1A 1J5 Canada.

Currency and Banking

Canada's money system is based on the decimal system. Paper denominations are $2 (orange), $5 (blue), $10 (purple), $20 (green), $50 (red), $100 (brown), and up. Dollar coins are known as loonies. Other coins are used for amounts less than a dollar.

American money is accepted in most businesses, but you may get the best exchange rate at a bank or currency exchange desk.

Major credit cards are widely used, and travellers will find bank machines in most towns.

Time Zones

BC's Interior has two time zones. The Pacific Time Zone covers most of the province. However, the Mountain Time Zone is in effect in the area around Dawson Creek and Fort St. John, and, in the Columbia River Valley along a corridor west of the Rockies from Mt. Robson Provincial Park to the US border. This corridor includes Golden, Invermere, Kimberley, Moyie, Cranbrook, Fernie, and Sparwood. The zone is marked by a yellow line on the provincial government road map.

Travellers going from west to east move their clocks ahead one hour when they enter the Mountain Time Zone. When coming from the east, they move their clocks back an hour when entering the Pacific Time Zone.

In both time zones, Daylight Savings Time is in effect between April and October. "Spring ahead, fall back" is the saying that helps people remember how to adjust their clocks. On the first Sunday of April, time pieces are turned ahead one hour. On the last Sunday in October, they are turned back an hour.

But not in Creston or the Dawson Creek area. When Daylight Savings Time comes into effect in the spring, Creston stays on Pacific Standard Time and Dawson Creek stays on Mountain Standard Time.

To be sure, check locally.

Metric Conversion Tables

British Columbia, along with the rest of Canada, uses the metric system for measurement. Distance is measured by kilometres, speed signs are in kilometres per hour (km/h), gas is sold by the litre (L), and temperature is measured on the Celsius scale (°C).

1 centimetre (cm)	0.39 inches
1 metre (m)	3.28 feet
1 kilometre (km)	0.62 miles
1 hectare (ha)	2.47 acres
1 square kilometre	0.36 sq mi
1 kilogram (kg)	2.2 pounds
1 tonne (t)	1.10 US tons
	0.98 UK tons
1 litre (L)	0.26 US gallons
	0.22 Imp. gallons
1° Celsius (C)	1.8° Farenheit (F)

Speed (approximate)

10 mph	15 km/h
20 mph	30 km/h
30 mph	50 km/h
40 mph	65 km/h
50 mph	80 km/h
60 mph	95 km/h
70 mph	110 km/h

Temperature

100°C	Boiling point	212°F
30°C	Hot summer day	86°F
20°C	Comfortable room	68°F
0°C	Freezing	32°F
-18°C	Cold winter day	0°F

Popular Hiking Places

TRANS-CANADA HIGHWAY
• **Glacier National Park** East of Revelstoke. Several trails
• **Mt. Revelstoke National Park** Summit accessible by vehicle. Over 64 km of improved trails
• **Stein Valley** Near Lillooet. Several trails through old growth forest and sacred Native land
• **Yoho National Park** East of Golden. Several trails

CROWSNEST HIGHWAY
• **Cathedral Provincial Park** Southwest of Keremeos. Several trails in wilderness area
• **Dewdney Trail** Historic trail from Hope to Fort Steele. Access points include Manning Park, Christina Lake, Rossland. (442-5411)
• **Kettle Valley Railway** Several sections of abandoned rail line used for hiking and biking. Check at Infocentres in Hope, Princeton, Osoyoos, Rock Creek, Kelowna, Penticton

---

Maps
For topographic maps write:

Canada Map Office
615 Booth Street
Ottawa ON K1A 0E9

Map and Publication Sales
Geological Survey of Canada
100 West Pender Street
Vancouver BC V6B 1R8
666-0271

Surveys and Mapping Branch
Parliament Buildings
Victoria BC V8V 1X5
387-1441

• **Manning Provincial Park** East of Hope. Heritage trails, Pacific Crest Trail, and others

OKANAGAN
• **Antlers Beach Provincial Park** On Okanagan Lake near Peachland. Easy route beside Deep Creek to waterfall
• **Kettle Valley Railway** (See above)
• **Okanagan Mountain Provincial Park** Wilderness area. Secluded beaches. Wild Horse Canyon and historic park trails

WEST KOOTENAY
• **Cody Caves Provincial Park** Near Ainsworth. Underground caves
• **Kokanee Glacier Provincial Park** Near Nelson. Several trails
• **Valhalla Provincial Park** Access from Slocan Valley. Wilderness area. Several trails

EAST KOOTENAY
• **Bugaboo Glacier Provincial Park and Alpine Recreation Area** Access from Brisco. Several trails. Wilderness area
• **Elk Lakes Provincial Park** Access from Sparwood. Several routes around Elk Lake. Wilderness
• **Elkford Interpretive Trail System** North of Sparwood. 40 km of trails for beginner to advanced hiker
• **Kootenay National Park** Borders both Banff and Yoho national parks. Many trails
• **Mt. Assiniboine Provincial Park** In the Rocky Mountains. 12 trails. Wilderness area

• **Purcell Wilderness Conservancy** West of Invermere. Earl Grey Trail to Kootenay Lake
• **Top of the World Provincial Park** Access from Canal Flats. Wilderness

CENTRAL INTERIOR
• **Alexander Mackenzie Heritage Trail** Historic route begins near Quesnel through Tweedsmuir Provincial Park to Bella Coola area. For experienced hikers. (See p. 239.)
• **Mt. Robson Provincial Park** In Rocky Mountains adjacent to Jasper National Park. Several trails from easy to taxing. Wilderness area
• **Tweedsmuir Provincial Park (North and South)** Several trails. Hunlen Falls, Turner Lake, Rainbow Range are among attractions. Wilderness area
• **Wells Gray Provincial Park** Over 20 trails in wilderness area

NORTHERN INTERIOR
• **Mt. Edziza Provincial Park** Volcanic landscape. Unmarked trails. Only for experienced hikers
• **Muncho Lake Provincial Park** No signed trails. Open terrain to alpine valleys
• **Murray Ridge** Near Pine Pass. Four hour hike from highway
• **Stone Mountain Provincial Park** Near Fort Nelson. Summit Peak Trail for experienced hikers; Flower Springs Trail and Lake Trail for easier hiking

Hot Springs

TRANS-CANADA HIGHWAY
• **Canyon Hot Springs**
A privately owned, fully
developed resort about 37 km
east of Revelstoke on the Trans-
Canada Highway. Box 2400,
Revelstoke BC V0E 2S0, 837-2420
(page 69)

WEST KOOTENAY
• **Halcyon Hot Springs**
Once a resort, now an undevel-
oped hot springs on privately
owned land, 33 km north of
Nakusp (page 166)
• **St. Leon Hot Springs**
Also once a resort. 22 km north
of Nakusp (page166)
• **Nakusp Hot Springs**
Developed facility in a provincial
park. Turn-off is 1.5 km north of
the town, 14 km to the pool.
Box 280, Nakusp BC V0G 1R0.
352-4033 (page 166)
• **Ainsworth Hot Springs**
A privately owned resort beside
Kootenay Lake. 46 km north of
Nelson. Box 1268, Ainsworth Hot
Springs BC V0G 1A0. 229-4212
(page 160)

Gold Panning

Barkerville 208
East Kootenays 178
Emory Creek 47
Fraser Canyon 52
Lytton 51
Moyie River 107
Princeton area 86
Quesnel 207
Revelstoke 68
Rock Creek 93

EAST KOOTENAY
• **Dewar Creek Hot Springs**
Undeveloped hot springs west
of Kimberley. Take the logging
road north at Dewar Creek to its
end, and hike 13 miles.
• **Lussier Hot Springs**
Undeveloped site with log pool
and bathhouse. Take White
Swan Lake road 6.5 km south of
Canal Flats (page 178)
• **Fairmont Hot Springs**
A major resort in the Columbia
Valley. 35 km south of Radium
and 32 km north of Canal Flats.
Day-users are welcomed. Box 10,
Fairmont Hot Springs BC
V0B 1L0. 345-6311 (page 179)
• **Radium Hot Springs**
Developed pools at the
Aquacourt in Kootenay National
Park. Box 220, Radium Hot
Springs BC V0A 1M0. 347-9485
(page 184)

CENTRAL INTERIOR
• **Canoe River Hot Springs**
Undeveloped hot springs 15
km southeast of Valemont on
Highway 5A north of
Kamloops.

NORTHERN INTERIOR
• **Liard Hot Springs**
In a provincial park close to
Yukon border. Some develop-
ment (page 225)

For a detailed description, refer
to *Hotsprings of Western
Canada: A Complete Guide* by
Jim McDonald (Vancouver:
Waterwheel Press, 1991).

River Rafting

*Following is an alphabetical list
of companies licensed under the
provincial Commercial River
Rafting Safety Act.*

• Alpine Rafting, Box 1409,
Golden BC V0A 1H0. Phone
collect: 344-5016; 344-5129;
US toll free: 1-800-663-7080; Fax:
344-7102. One-half to three-day
trips on Kicking Horse River
• Canadian River Expeditions,
1 - 3524 West 16th Avenue,
Vancouver BC V6R 3C1.
738-4449; Fax: 736-5526. Eleven-
day trips on Chilko, Chilcotin,
Fraser, Skeena, Alesk, and
Tatshenshini rivers
• Clearwater Expeditions,
613 Bissette Road, Kamloops BC
V2B 6L3. 579-8360; 674-3354
(Clearwater, summer only); Fax:
554-1357. One-half to six-day
trips on Clearwater, Thompson
and Chilko-Chilcotin rivers
• Far North Rafting Company,
9103 - 91st Avenue, Fort St.
John BC V1J 1C7. 787-3049.
Two- to three-hour trips on the
Prophet River
• Fort Sasquatch, Box 133,
Groundbirch BC V0C 1T0 (near
Chetwynd). 788-9671;
Fax: 785-4424
• Fraser River Raft Expeditions,
Box 10, Yale BC V0K 2S0.
863-2336; Fax: c/o 869-7690.
One-half day to 10-day trips on
Nahatlatch, Coquihalla, Fraser,
Chilliwack, Thompson and
Chilko/Chilcotin rivers
• Great Expeditions, 5915 West
Boulevard, Vancouver BC
V6M 3X1. 263-1476;
Fax: 263-8422. Six-day trips on
Chilko, Chilcotin, Fraser, Babine,
and Skeena rivers
• Hyak Wilderness Adventures,
1975 Maple Street, Vancouver BC
V6J 3S9. 734-8622;

Fax: 734-5718. One- to six-day trips on the Thompson, Chilliwack, Chilko, Chilcotin, and Fraser rivers.

• Interior Whitewater Expeditions, Box 129, Celista BC V0E 1L0. 955-2447; Fax: 955-2534. Two-hour to 10-day trips on Adams, Clearwater, Babine, Skeena, and Tatshenshini rivers.

• Kootenay River Runners, Box 81, Edgewater BC V0A 1E0. 347-9210. One-half to two-day trips on Kootenay, White and the Kicking Horse rivers.

• Kumsheen Raft Adventures, 281 Main Street, Box 30, Lytton BC V0K 1Z0, 455-2296; BC toll free: 1-800-663-6667; Fax: 455-2297. One-to three-day trips on Fraser and Thompson rivers.

• North South Expedition Services, 100-1159 West Broadway, Vancouver BC V6H 1G1. 736-7447; Fax: 736-6513. One- to 15-day trips from Vancouver, Smithers, and Whitehorse operating on Chilko, Chilcotin, Thompson, Fraser, Babine, and Tatshenshini rivers.

• Off the Wall Adventures, Panorama Resort, Panorama, BC V0A 1T0. 342-6941 ext. 328. Two-hour trips on Toby Creek, departing from Panorama Resort.

• Reo Rafting Adventures, Suite 390, 1199 West Pender Street, Vancouver BC V6E 2R1. 684-4438; 879-2010 winter; Fax: 684-4438. Trips ranging from four to six hours or four to six days operating from Chilliwack, Boston Bar, and Lytton on Nahatlatch, Thompson, and Taseko rivers.

• River Rogues Adventures, Box 115, Spences Bridge BC V0K 2L0. 458-2252. Daily three-hour trips on Thompson River.

• Ryan's Rapid Rafting, Box 600, 1755 Robson Street, Vancouver BC V6G 3B7. 875-9745. Trips from two hours to three days, departing from Spences Bridge, operating on the Thompson, Nicola, and Nahatlatch rivers.

• Suskwa Adventure Outfitters, Box 3262, Smithers BC V0J 2N0. 847-2885; Fax: c/o 847-7585. One- to 12-day trips on Bulkley, Babine, Skeena, and Tatshenshini rivers.

• Whistler River Adventures, Box 202, Whistler BC V0N 1B0. 932-3532; Fax: 932-3559. Two-hour to five-day trips on Green, Birkenhead, Squamish, Thompson, and Chilcotin rivers.

• Whitewater Voyageurs Rafting, Box 1983, Golden BC V0A 1H0. 344-7335; Fax: 344-6688. One-half day to two-day trips on Kicking Horse and Blaeberry rivers.

For more information:

• Registrar of River Rafting Ministry of Environment, Lands and Parks 800 Johnson Street, 2nd floor Victoria BC V8V 1X4 (604)387-5002

• River Outfitters Association of BC 1367 West Broadway Vancouver BC V6H 4A9 737-3058

For more information read:
Betty Pratt-Johnson's *Whitewater Trips for Kayakers, Canoeists and Rafters in British Columbia* (Vancouver: Adventure Publishing, 1986).

Ghost Towns

TRANS-CANADA HIGHWAY
• **Donald** In the East Kootenay on the bank of the Columbia River near Golden. A construction centre and divisional point for the CPR. It was the chief town of the Kootenays in 1889. During its heyday, gold dust was accepted as payment for groceries.

• **Three Valley Gap** 19 km west of Revelstoke. Consists of more than 20 buildings restored and furnished with antiques.

• **Walhachin** South side of Thompson River, 18 km east of Cache Creek. English settlers came in 1907 to create an elegant society in the sagebrush desert. Ruins of flumes, buildings, and a few skeletons of apple trees remain.

CROWSNEST HIGHWAY
• **Ashnola** On the west side of Similkameen River, 13 km south of Princeton. The doorpost of the Ashnola Hotel (built in 1902 but destroyed by fire in 1945) carried the inscription: "James MacLaren invested $50,000 in venture and bang went sixpence."

• **Granite City** In the Tulameen region northwest of Princeton, at one time it was considered the third largest settlement in BC. By 1900 all the streams and creeks were completely mined and the town had been swept by fire twice.

• **Waldo** In 1905 this was a lumbering town with two mills and 700 people, located 46 km southwest of Fernie. The town was flooded by Lake Koocanusa after the Libby dam was built in 1972.

OKANAGAN
• **Fairview** West of Oliver on the hillside on Fairview Road, this was one of the most famous gold mines in the province. A marker is all that is visible today.

WEST KOOTENAY
• **Ainsworth** North of Nelson on Kootenay Lake, one of many West Kootenay mining towns that boomed during the 1890s, but embattled with fires and bad luck. Now the site of a hot springs resort; a few original buildings remain.
• **Phoenix** Near Greenwood off Highway 3. A major centre in the boom years of the 1890s, today a strip mine covers the townsite.
• **Poplar** In the Lardeau Valley 144 km north of Nelson. It was a gold prospecting town with a population of 3000 at the turn of the century, reduced to four by 1947.
• **Sandon** Between New Denver and Kaslo, the heart of the Silvery Slocan mining boom of the 1890s. At the outbreak of the World War II the town housed 1000 Japanese-Canadians.

EAST KOOTENAY
• **Baynes Lake** 42 km south of Fernie, an operating general store is all that's left of this mill town that once contained two schools and a hospital. Its heyday was from 1902 to 1925.
• **Bull River** A few false-front buildings remain of this placer gold town 20 km south of Fort Steele. It appeared in the late 1860s but disappeared when the gold ran out around 1900.

• **Fisherville** 11 km from Fort Steele, northeast of Cranbrook. It was the major gold rush town in the 1860s. Scattered remains of a town and a graveyard still exist.
• **Fort Steele** A major tourist attraction 16 km northeast of Cranbrook on Highway 93/95. The first North West Mounted Police post in BC from 1877 to 1888; the town was empty by 1910. In 1961 it became a provincial historical park.

CENTRAL INTERIOR
• **Barkerville** At the end of the old Cariboo Wagon Road east of Quesnel, the town was known as the "Gold Capital of the Word" in the 1860s. Restoration began in 1958 and continues today.
• **Cedar Creek** Near Likely. A ghost town known for a big gold strike in 1922; it is also referred to as the Nugget Patch.
• **Quesnelle Forks** At the junction of Quesnel and Cariboo rivers, near the town of Likely. Dating back to 1859, this was the first permanent mining community in BC. It once housed the largest Chinese community north of San Francisco.

For a more complete listing, refer to N.L. Barlee's *Gold Creeks and Ghost Towns* (Surrey, BC: Hancock House, 1984).

Guest Ranches

The following are 1992 Members of the BC Guest Ranches Association (Box 4501, Williams Lake BC V2G 2V8).

TRANS-CANADA HIGHWAY
• Sundance Guest Ranch, Box 489, Ashcroft BC V0K 1A0. 453-2422. In Fraser Canyon. Ranch dates back to 1864. Cookout rides, tennis, pool

OKANAGAN
• Apex Mountain Guest Ranch, Box 426, Green Mountain Road,Penticton BC V2A 6K6. 492-2454. In the Okanagan, near Alpine Apex Ski area. Elevation 914 m (3000 ft). Trail rides, horse pack trips, children's summer riding camp, and other activities

EAST KOOTENAY
• Three Bars Cattle and Guest Ranch, SS 1, Site 19-62, Cranbrook BC V1C 4H4. 426-5230; Fax: 426-8240. Authentic working ranch. pool, tennis court, riding program, hay rides, fishing, packtrips, winter skiing
• Top of the World Guest Ranch. Box 29, Fort Steele BC V0B 1N0. 426-6306. In Rocky Mountains. 1600-hectare working ranch. Riding, canoeing, fishing, swimming, hiking, wildlife viewing

CENTRAL INTERIOR
• Big Bar Guest Ranch, Box 27, Jesmond BC V0K 1K0. 459-2333; radio phone: 395-7101. Empire Valley of the Chilcotin near Fraser Canyon and Marble Mountains
• Cariboo Rose Guest Ranch, Box 160, Clinton BC V0K 1K0. 459-2255. Adult-oriented ranch (maxiumum 10 guests). Wilderness riding, indoor riding clinics

• Circle H Mountain Lodge, Box 7, Jesmond, Clinton BC V0K 1K0. Phone or fax: 459-2565. In the Chilcotin, Marble Mountains west of Clinton. Guided trail rides, swimming, fishing, hiking
• Elkin Creek Guest Ranch, Nemaiah Valley BC V0L 1X0. Phone: H497533. Mail: 4462 Marion Road, North Vancouver BC V7K 2V2. 984-4666; Fax: 984-4686. In the Chilcotin. Horseback riding, fishing, swimming, sailing, windsurfing, canoeing
• The Hills Health and Guest Ranch, C-26, 108 Ranch, 100 Mile House BC V0K 2E0. 791-5225; Fax: 791-6384. In the Cariboo. Family oriented. Horseback riding, hay rides, guided hikes, fishing, aerobics, swimming pool
• The McLeans River Ridge Resort, Box 2560, Williams Lake BC V2G 4P2. 398-7755; Fax: 398-7487. In the Chilcotin at the north end of Chilko Lake. Riding, fishing, canoeing, hiking, photo hunts
• Teepee Heart Ranch, Box 6, RR 1, Big Creek BC V0L 1K0. 392-5015. In the Chilcotin,135 km southwest of Williams Lake. Wilderness pack trips, fishing, spring wild horse round up, May horse drive, horse packing clinics, trail rides
• Tyax Mountain Lake Resort, Tyaughton Lake Road, Gold Bridge BC V0K 1P0. 238-2221; Fax: 238-2528. In the Chilcotin Mountains. Fishing, boating, goldpanning, tennis, volleyball, hiking, horseback riding

Ski Resorts

Many communities in BC have ski facilities.They range from modest family-oriented hills to deluxe fully developed resorts. Here are some of the most popular alpine and nordic destinations, in alpahabetical order.

ALPINE (DOWNHILL) AND NORDIC (CROSS-COUNTRY)

• **Apex Alpine** Near Penticton. Vertical drop of 610 metres (2000 feet). 36 runs. Night skiing, nordic trails, on-mountain accommodation. Box 1060, Penticton BC V2A 7N7. 292-8222; toll free (BC, Alberta and Washington): 1-800-663-1900
• **Big White** Near Kelowna. Vertical drop of 625 metres (2050 feet) with 47 runs. Night skiing, nordic trails, on-mountain accommodation. Box 2039, Station R, Kelowna BC V1X 4K5. 765-8888; toll free (Western Canada and US): 1-800-663-2772
• **Fairmont Hot Springs Resort** Near Invermere. Vertical drop of 300 metres (1000 feet) with 12 runs. Night skiing, nordic trails, and on-mountain accommodation. Box 10, Fairmont Hot Springs, BC V0B 1L0. 345-6311; toll free: 1-800-663-4979
• **Fernie Snow Valley Resort** Vertical drop of 730 metres (2400 feet) with 40 runs. Nordic trails and on-mountain accommodation. Ski Area Road, Fernie, BC V0B 1M1. 423-4655
• **Harper Mountain** Near Kamloops. Vertical drop of 425 metres (1400 feet) with 13 runs. Night skiing and nordic trails. 2042 Valleyview Drive, Kamloops BC V2C 4C5. 372-2119

• **Kimberley Ski and Summer Resort** Vertical drop of 701 metres (2300 feet) with 34 runs. Night skiing, nordic trails, on-mountain accommodation. Box 40, Kimberley, BC V1A 2Y5. 427-4881; toll free: 1-800-667-0808.
• **Manning Park Resort.** In the northern Cascade Mountains near Hope. Vertical drop of 431 metres (1417 feet). Over 20 runs. Nordic trails. On-mountain accommodation. Manning Park BC V0X 1R0. 840-8822
• **Mt. Mackenzie Ski Area** Near Revelstoke. Vertical drop of 610 metres (2000 feet) with 20 runs. Night skiing and nordic trails. Box 1000, Revelstoke BC V0E 2S0. 837-5268
• **Mt. Timothy** Near Lac La Hache and north of 100 Mile House. Vertical drop of 260 metres (850 feet) with 27 runs. Nordic trails. Box 33, 100 Mile House BC V0K 2E0. 396-4244
• **Murray Ridge** Near Fort St. James. Vertical drop of 522 metres (1740 feet) with 19 runs. Night skiing and nordic trails. Box 866, Fort St. James BC V0J 1P0. 996-8513
• **Panorama Resort** Near Invermere. Vertical drop of 1156 metres (3800 feet) with 32 runs. Nordic trails and on-mountain accommodation. Panorama BC V0A 1T0. 342-6941; toll free (Western Canada): 1-800-663-2929
• **Powder King Ski Village** Near Mackenzie. Vertical drop of 640 metres (2100 feet) with 19 runs. Nordic trails. On-mountain accommodation. Box 2405, Mackenzie BC V0J 2C0. 561-1776
• **Purden Ski Village** Near Prince George. Vertical drop of 332 metres (1090 feet) with 10 runs. Box 1239, Prince George BC V2L 4V3. 565-9038

• **Red Mountain Resorts** Near Rossland. Vertical drop of 850 metres (2800 feet). Thirty runs. On-mountain accommodation. Box 670, Rossland BC V0G 1Y0. 362-7384; Toll Free (BC, Alberta, and Washington): 1-800-663-0105

• **Silver Star Mountain Resort** Near Vernon. Vertical drop of 760 metres (2500 feet), 59 runs. Night skiing, nordic trails, and accommodation on the mountain. Box 2, Silver Star Mountain BC V0E 1G0. 542-1224; toll free (Canada and Northwest US): 1-800-663-4431

• **Ski Smithers** Vertical drop of 530 metres (1750 feet) with 18 runs. Nordic trails. Box 492, Smithers, BC V0J 2N0. 847-2058

• **Tod Mountain** Near Kamloops. Vertical drop of 945 metres (3100 feet) with 47 runs. Nordic trails and on-mountain accommodation. Box 869, Kamloops BC V2C 5M8. 578-7222

• **Whitetooth Ski Area** Near Golden. Vertical drop of 522 metres (1740 feet) with eight runs. Box 1925, Golden BC V0A 1H0. 344-6114

• **Whitewater Ski Resort** Near Nelson. Vertical drop of 395 metres (1300 feet) with 21 runs. Box 60, Nelson, BC V1L 5P7. 354-4944

NORDIC ONLY

The following all offer instruction, rentals, day lodge, and accommodation. Other amenities vary.

• **Apex Mountain Guest Ranch** Forty-eight kilometres of groomed trails, nine kilometres of ski-skating lanes. Box 426, Penticton BC V2A 6K6. 492-2454

• **Emerald Lake Lodge** In Yoho National Park in the Rocky Mountains. 25 km of groomed trails. Box 10, Field BC V0A 1G0. 1-800-343-6321; Fax: 343-6321

• **Helmcken Falls Lodge** 100 km of groomed trails. Wells Gray Provincial Park, Box 239, Clearwater BC V0E 1N0. 674-3657; Fax 674-3657. Snow report: 674-2464

• **Kimberley Nordic Centre** 26 km of groomed trails, 26 km of ski-skating lanes. Night-lit trails. Box 464, Kimberley BC V1A 2Y5. 427-4881; Fax: 427-3927

• **Lac Le Jeune Resort and Conference Centre** 100 km of groomed trails, 80 km of ski-skating lanes. Alpine facilities. Box 3215, Kamloops BC V2C 6B8. 372-2722; Fax 372-8755.

• **Lemon Creek Lodge** In the West Kootenay. 10 km of groomed trails. (No rentals.) Box 68, Slocan, BC V0G 2C0. 355-2403.

• **Logan Lake Hotel** In the Nicola Valley. 36 km of groomed trails, 36 kilometres of ski-skating lanes. Night-lit trails. Box 1190, Logan Lake BC V0K 1W0. 523-6211. Snow report 523-6322. (Also contact the Highland Valley Outdoor Association, Box 145, Logan Lake BC V0K 1W0. 523-6791; Fax 523-6678.)

• **Manning Park Resort** 30 km of groomed trails, 26 km of ski-skating lanes. Alpine skiing (See above.)

• **Mt. Assiniboine Lodge** In the Rocky Mountains. 60 km of groomed trails. Box 1527, Canmore AB T0L 0M0. 403-678-2883; Fax 403-678-4877

• **108 Resort** 100 km of groomed trails. Night-lit trails. C2, RR 1, 108 Ranch, 100 Mile House BC, V0K 2E0. 791-5211.; 1-800-452-5233 (BC); Fax 791-6537

• **Red Coach Inn** 100 km of groomed trails, 35 km of ski-skating lanes. Night-lit trails. c/o Red Coach Inn, Box 760, Highway 97, 100 Mile House BC V0K 2E0. 395-2266; 1-800-663-8422; Fax 395-2446.

• **The Hills Health and Guest Ranch** 100 km of groomed trails, 20 km of ski-skating lanes. Night- lit trails. C 26, 108 Ranch, 100 Mile House, BC V0K 2E0. 791-5225; Fax: 791-6384

• **Tyax Mountain Lake Resort** Near Lillooet. 30 kmof groomed trails. Tyaughton Lake Road, Gold Bridge BC V0K 1P0. 238-2221; Fax: 238-2528

• **Wells-Barkerville** In the Cariboo. 70 km of groomed trails. Wells and District Chamber of Commerce, Box 123, Wells BC V0K 2R0. 994-3265; Fax: 994-3405. Snow report 994-3412

• **Whitewater Inn** In the West Kootenay. 30 km of groomed trails, 15 km of ski-skating lanes. Box 532, Nelson BC V1L 5R3. 352-9150

• **Woody Life Village Resort** 100 km of groomed trails, 80 km of ski-skating lanes. Box 3100, Kamloops BC V2C 6B8. 374-3833; Fax: 374-3800

Rockhounding

Burns Lake	234
Cache Creek	55
Cassiar Highway	227
Cranbrook	109
Fernie	112
Fraser Canyon	47
Keremeos	90
Lillooet	193
Okanagan Falls	128
Penticton	131
Princeton	86
Shuswap Lake	61
Skookumchuck Creek	178
Smithers	232
Vernon	144

Emergencies

Frostbite

If your body gets too cold, it reacts by closing down the blood supply to areas it deems less important – toes, fingers, nose, ears – in order to preserve precious energy for the vital organs. The affected parts will become numb, pale, and waxy looking.

If the frostbite is severe, hospital treatment is necessary to avoid further damage to the victim. If it's superficial, the best way to regain circulation is to warm the affected areas with body heat – either your own or somebody elses. Put affected fingers in your armpits, for example, or between your thighs. Don't rub the skin; that can cause damage and infection.

Hypothermia

Beware of hypothermia in boating or hiking or winter activities, especially if you are feeling fatigued and you are in wet or windy conditions. Hypothermia occurs when the core body temperature lowers beyond normal (37.4°C, 98.6°F). Symptoms include shivering, slurred or incoherent speech, and unco-ordinated body movements. Beware: the victim may deny anything is wrong.

If you find your self shivering (an early warning sign), stop, rest, put on warm, dry clothing, and eat a high-energy snack or drink a sweetened, hot, nonalcoholic beverage. The best thing to do in a severe case, is to bundle the victim into a sleeping bag with another person.

To protect against hypothermia stay dry, keep your head warm and eat high-energy snacks. Boaters should always wear life jackets. Even in the summer, survival time in BC's colder waters will be less than two to three hours.

Hyperthermia

This is the opposite of hypothermia, and occurs when the body becomes overheated and dehydrated. Symptoms include headache, dizziness, an inability to sweat, muscle cramps, and high body temperature. Get in the shade. Cool the body with ice or water. Drink a cold, slightly salted beverage. Avoid hyperthermia by drinking lots of fluids, especially before you begin a journey.

Avalanches

Specialists employed by the Canadian National Parks Service, ski resorts, and other agencies carefully monitor snow conditions throughout the winter and update avalanche forecasts frequently. Check with park officials or other local authorities before heading into mountainous terrain.

The downhill ski resorts have avalanche control programs where slopes are tested and occasionally slides are deliberately triggered to prevent a dangerous buildup of snow.

Groomed cross-country trails have been laid out to generally stay clear of common avalanche paths.

Some avalanche terrain is easy to spot since the slides leave a swath through forested areas.

Watch for other signs of avalanche activity, such as slopes where layers of snow have broken loose and form a jumbled mass at the bottom.

Take special care when travelling in the backcountry after a heavy snowfall and avoid steep terrain, especially if the slope is topped by a cornice, an overhanging lip of windblown snow. If you are travelling in a group and must cross a suspect slope, do it one at a time.

Skieres who venture ionto the backcountry should carry electronic avalanche beacons that aid in locating victims if they are caught in a slide. Lightweight snow shovels should also be carried by those who travel in potentially dangerous areas since time is crucial in rescuing someone trapped in a slide.

The chance of survival is slim for anyone buried for more than half an hour.

Anyone trapped in a slide should try a swimming motion to stay near the surface of the moving snow. If you are beneath the surface as the slide comes to a halt, try to make a bit of breathing room before the snowpack solidifies.

Snowblindness and Sunburn

Spring skiers can bask in bright sunshine and work on an early tan, but high-quality sunglasses and sunscreen are needed to guard against bright sunshine that is intensified by high altitude and reflections off the snow. Even on cloudy days the hazard is great.

Golf Courses

TRANS-CANADA HIGHWAY

Golf courses of the Interior are listed by region, then alphabetically by community.

Anglemont
• Anglemont Golf Course. Public; 9 holes. Box 48, Anglemont BC V0E 1A0. 955-2323; Fax: 955-2212

Blind Bay
• Shuswap Lake Estates Golf Course. Public; 9 holes. On Trans- Canada Highway, 25 km west of Salmon Arm. Box 150, Blind Bay BC V0E 1H0. 675-2315; Fax: 675-2526

Cache Creek
• Semlin Valley Golf Club. Public; 9 holes. 1 km east of Cache Creek on Highway 1. Box 421, Cache Creek BC V0K 1H0. 457-6666

Chase
• Sunshore Golf Club. Public; 9 holes. On Little Shuswap Lake. Box 260, Chase BC V0E 1H0. 679-3021

Golden
• GoldenGolf and Country Club Public; 18 holes. Box 1615, Golden BC V0A 1H0. 344-2700

Kamloops
• DBA Aberdeen Hills Golf Course. Semi-private; 18 holes. Box 3066, Kamloops BC V2C 6B8. 828-1143
• Eagle Point Golf & Country Club. Public; 18 holes. 20 km east of Kamloops. 8888 Barnhartuale Road, Site 5, Comp 12, RR#2, Kamloops BC V2C 2S3. 573-2453 pro shop; Fax: 573-4810
• Kamloops Golf and Country Club. Semi-private; 18 holes. #16 - 2960 Tranquille Highway, Kamloops BC V2B 8B6. 376-3231
• Mt. Paul Golf Course and Driving Range. Public; 9 holes. 615 Mt. Paul Way, Kamloops BC V2H 1A9. 374-4653
• Pineridge Golf Course. Public; 18 holes. East of Kamloops on Highway l. 4725 East Trans-Canada Highway, Kamloops BC V2C 5X4. 573-4333; Fax: 573-5275

• Rivershore Golf Club. Semi-private; 18 holes. 19 km east of downtown on north side of Trans-Canada Highway. Turn right after Wildlife Park sign. RR#2, Kamloops BC V2C 2J3. 573-4622; Fax: 573-3996

Revelstoke
• Revelstoke Golf Club. Public; 18 holes. At Columbia Park. Box 1860, Revelstoke BC V0E 2S0. 837-4276

Salmon Arm
• Salmon Arm Golf Course. Public; 18 holes. On Highway 97B, 5 km south of Salmon Arm. Box 1525, Salmon Arm BC V1E 4P6. 832-4727
• Shannon's Recreation Park. Public; 18 holes. 7 km east of Salmon Arm at Canoe turnoff. 832-7345

Sicamous
• Birchdale Par 3 Golf. Public; 9 holes. Highway 97A, 10 km south of Mara Lake. 838-7740
• Eagle River Golf & Country Club. Public; 9 holes. Box 16, Sicamous, BC V0E 2V0. 836-4454

CROWSNEST HIGHWAY

Castlegar
• Castlegar Golf Course. Public; 18 holes. East of the airport. Follow the signs off Highway 3 or 3B east. Box 3430, Castlegar BC V1N 3N8. 365-5006; Fax: 365-7788

Christina Lake
• Cascade Par 3 Golf Course. Public; 9 holes. On 2nd Avenue in Christina Lake, Box 253, Christina Lake BC V0H 1E0. 447-9705
• Christina Lake Golf and Country Club. Semi-private; 18 holes. Box 1106, Grand Forks BC V0H 1H0. 447-9313

Creston
• Creston Golf Club. Public; 18 holes. 5 km south of Creston off Highway 21S. Box 2013, Creston BC V0B 1G0. 428-5515; Fax: 428-3320

Elkford
Mountain Meadows Golf Club. Semi-private; 9 holes. Box 4, Elkford BC V0B 1H0. 865-7413

Fernie
Fernie Golf and Country Club. Public; 18 holes. At east end of 2nd Avenue. Box 1507, Fernie BC V0B 1M0. 423-7773; Fax: 423-6575

Fruitvale
• Champion Lakes Golf and Country Club. Box 158, Fruitvale BC V0G 1L0

Osoyoos
• Osoyoos Golf and Country Club. Public; 18 holes. Located at West Bench, 2.4 km southwest of Osoyoos. Box 798, Osoyoos BC V0H 1V0. 495-7003; Fax: 495-3511

Princeton
• Princeton Golf Club. Public; 9 holes. On Darcy Mountain Road, Highway 3 East, 3 km south of Princeton. Box 1346, Princeton BC V0X 1W0. 295-6123

Rock Creek
Kettle Valley Golf Club. Public; 9 holes. 8 km east of junction of Highways 3 and 33. 446-2826

Rossland/Trail
Birchbank Golf Course. Public; 18 holes. Located 10 km north of Trail, on Highway 22. Box 221, Trail BC V1R 4L5. 693-2255; Fax: 693-2366
• Rossland-Trail Golf and Country Club. Public; 18 holes. 5 km west of Trail on the Trail-Rossland Highway 3B. Box 221, Trail BC V1R 4L5. 362-5045; Fax: 693-2366

Salmo
• Salmo and District Golf Club. Public; 9 holes. On Airport Road. Box 308, Salmo BC V0G 1Z0. 357-2068; Fax: 357-2280

Sparwood
•Sparwood Golf Club. Public; 9 holes. Box 1525, Sparwood BC V0B 2G0. 425-2612

COQUIHALLA-NICOLA
Logan Lake
• Meadow Creek Golf Club. Public; 9 holes. Box 827, Logan Lake BC V0K 1W0. 523-6666 (Apr.-Oct.)
Merritt
• Merritt Golf and Country Club. Public; 9 holes. Take Highway 8 west to Juniper Drive, turn right at sign. Box 909, Merritt BC V0K 2B0. 378-9414
Nicola Valley
• Nicola Valley Golf Course & R.V. Park. Public; 9 holes. On Highway 5A, beside Nicola Lake. Address: Highway 5A, Quilchena BC V0E 2R0. 378-2923

OKANAGAN
Armstrong
• Birchdale Golf Course. North of Armstrong at junction of Highways 97A and 97B. Grindrod BC V0H 2A0. 838-7740
• Royal York Golf Course. Public; 9 holes. 16 km north of Vernon off Highway 97. Take Rosedale or Harding exits to Okanagan St 546-9700
Kaleden
• Twin Lakes Golf and RV Resort. Public; 18 holes. 23 km southwest of Penticton on Highway 3A. Box 112, Kaleden BC V0H 1K0. 497-5359; Fax: 497-8377
Kelowna
Central Park Golf Club. Public; 9 holes. 1 km east of Orchard Park Mall. 2430 Harvey Avenue, Kelowna BC V1X 4J1. 860-5121
• Fairview Par 3 Golf Course. Two 9-hole courses. 4091 Lakeshore Road, Kelowna BC. 764-4104
• Gallaghers Canyon Golf Resort. Public; 18 holes. 16 km southeast of Kelowna. RR #3, McCulloch Road, Kelowna BC V1Y 7R2. 861-4240; Fax: 861-1852

• Kelowna Golf and Country Club. Semi-private; 18 holes. 1297 Glenmore Drive, Kelowna BC V1Y 4P4. 762-2736; Fax: 868-3360
• Kelowna Springs Golf Club. Semi-private; 18 holes. 480 Penno Road, Kelowna BC V1X 6S3. 765-8511
• Mission Creek Golf and Country Club. Public; 18 holes. 1959 KLO Road, Kelowna BC V1W 2H8. 860-3210
• Shadow Ridge Golf Course. Public; 18 holes. 2 km south of Kelowna airport, east side of Highway 97. Box 1046, Station A, Kelowna BC V1Y 7P7. 765-7777
• Sunset Ranch Golf and Country Club. East of Highway 97 off Old Vernon Road. Semi-private; 18 holes. 4001 Anderson Road, Kelowna BC 765-7700; Fax 765-7733
Oliver
• Cherry Grove Golf Course . Semi-private; 9 holes. On Park Drive. RR 3, Oliver BC V0H 1T0. 498-2880
• Fairview Mountain Golf Club. Public; 18 holes. On Golf Course Road. Box 821, Oliver BC V0H 1T0. 498-3521; Fax: 498-3077
Osoyoos
• Osoyoos Golf and Country Club. Public; 18 holes. At West Bench, 2.4 km SW. Box 798, Osoyoos BC V0H 1V0. 495-7003; Fax: 495-3511
Peachland
Ponderosa Golf and Country Club. Public; 18 holes. On Ponderosa Drive 30 minutes south of Kelowna. Box 336, Peachland BC V0H 1X0. 767-2149; Toll free in BC: 1-800-663-6110
Penticton
• Penticton Golf and Country Club. Semi-private; 18 holes. On West Eckhardt Avenue. Box 158, Penticton BC V2A 6K8. 492-8727

• Pine Hills Golf and Country Club. Public; 9 holes. 1.6 km north of Penticton on Highway 97. Site 39, Comp 2, RR#3, Penticton BC V2A 7K8. 492-5731
• Pleasant Valley Par 3 Golf Course. Public; 9 holes. 2.4 km east of Main Street. #41-1701 Penticton Avenue, Penticton BC V2A 2N6. 492-6988
Summerland
• Sumac Ridge Golf Club. Public; 9 holes. On Highway 97 north of Summerland. RR#1, Site 314, Comp 41, Summerland BC V0H 1Z0. 494-3122
• Summerland Golf and Country Club. Public; 18 holes. 6 km from downtown at 2405 Mountain Avenue. Box 348, Summerland BC V0H 1Z0. 494-9554
Vernon
• Hillview Golf Club. Public; 18 holes. Off Highway 6 to 15th Avenue. Turn right at 14th. 1101-14th Avenue, Vernon BC V1B 2S6. 549-4653
• Predator Ridge Golf Resort. 10 km south of Vernon off Highway 97. Take Bailey Road exit to Commonage. Public; 18 holes. 542-3436; Fax: 542-3835
• Spallumcheen Golf and Tennis Club. Public; 18 holes. 11.2 km north of Vernon, on Highway 97N, opposite the O'Keefe Ranch. Box 218, Vernon BC V1T 6M2. 545-5824 pro shop; Fax: 549-7476
• Vernon Golf & Country Club. Public; 18 holes. On Kalamalka Lake Road. 800-23rd Street, Vernon BC V1T 6V2. 542-9126; Fax: 542-5468
Westbank
• Shannon Lake Golf Course. Public; 18 holes. Between Kelowna and Westbank off Highway 97 at Shannon Lake Road. 768-4577

Winfield
• Aspen Grove Golf Club Public; 9 holes. On Bottom Wood Lake Road, 1/2 block east off Highway 97. Box 195, Winfield BC V0H 2C0.
766-3933

WEST KOOTENAY
Balfour
• Balfour Golf and Country Club. Public; 9 holes. Box 83, Balfour BC V0G 1C0. 229-5655
Crawford Bay
• Kokanee Springs Golf Resort. Public; 18 holes. On east shore Kootenay Lake. 10 km south of Kootenay Bay, 80 km north of Creston on Highway 3A. Box 96, Crawford Bay BC V0B 1E0. 227-9362; Fax: 227-9220
Kaslo
• Kaslo Golf and Country Club. Public; 9 holes. Box 436, Kaslo BC V0G 1H0. 353-2262
Nakusp
• Nakusp Centennial Golf Club. Public; 9 holes. 3 km east of Nakusp on Highway 6. Box 148, Nakusp BC V0G 1R0. 265-4531; Fax: 265-3703
Nelson
• Granite Pointe. Semi-private; 18 holes. On West Richards Street, in the Rosemont district. Box 141, Nelson BC V1L 5P7. 352-2264.
New Denver
• Slocan Lake Golf Club. Semi-private; 9 holes. On Highway 6, north of New Denver. Box 297, New Denver BC V0G 1S0. 358-2408.
Riondel
• Riondel Golf Club. Public; 9 holes. On Kootenay Lake, 94 km north of Creston, 17 km from Kootenay Bay ferry dock. Box 125, Riondel BC V0B 2B0. 225-5384

EAST KOOTENAY
Cranbrook
• Cranbrook Golf Club. Semi-private; 18 holes. At 2nd Street South in Cranbrook. Box 297, Cranbrook BC V1C 4H8. 426-6462
Fairmont Hot Springs
• Fairmont Hot Springs Mountainside Resort. Public; 18 holes. Box 10, Fairmont Hot Springs BC V0B 1L0. 345-6514
• Fairmont Hot Springs Riverside Resort. Public; 18 holes. Box 127, Fairmont Hot Springs BC V0B 1L0. 345-6346; Fax: 345-6595
Invermere
• Windermere Valley Golf Course. Public; 18 holes. Box 2677, Invermere BC V0A 1K0. 342-3004, Fax: 342-0119
Kimberley
• Kimberley Golf and Country Club. Public; 18 holes. On Highway 95. Box 241, Kimberley BC V1A 2Y6. 427-4161 summer; Fax: 427-7416
• Trickle Creek Golf Resort. Public; 18 holes. On North Star Mountain. 340 Spokane Street, Kimberley BC V1A 2E8. 427-4877; Fax: 427-3922
Radium Hot Springs
• Radium Hot Springs Resort Public; 18 holes. On Highway 93/95, 1.6 km south of Radium Hot Springs. Box 310, Radium Hot Springs BC V0A 1M0. 347-9311; 1-800-665-3585; Fax: 347-9588
• The Springs at Radium Golf Course. Public; 18 holes. 2 blocks east of Highway 95. Box 430, Radium Hot Springs BC V0A 1M0. 347-6444; Fax: 347-9707

CENTRAL INTERIOR
Clearwater
• Lacarya Golf Course. Public; 9 holes. Box 3613, RR#2, Clearwater BC V0E 1N0. 587-6100; Fax: 587-6100

108 Mile House
• 108 Mile House Resort Golf Club. Public; 18 holes. 13 km north of 100 Mile House on Highway 97. Comp 2, RR 1, 108 Ranch, 100 Mile House BC V0K 2E0. 791-5211; 791-6537
Prince George
• Aspen Grove Golf Club. Turn right at Leno Road, Mile 9 south. Public; 18 holes. RR #8, Site 6, Comp. 63, Prince George BC V2N 4M6. 963-9650
• Pine Valley Golf Centre. Public; 18 holes. 2.4 km west on Highway 16. Box 1754, Prince George BC V2L 4V7. 562-4811; Fax: 562-4887
• Prince George Golf and Curling Club. Semi-private; 18 holes. Junction of Highways 16 and 97. Box 242, Prince George BC V2L 4S1. 563-0357; Fax: 563-4136
Quesnel
• Quesnel Golf Course. Semi-private; 18 holes. On 6 Mile Road, across Fraser Bridge. 1862 Crystal Street, Quesnel BC V2J 4R8. 249-5550
• Dragon Lake Golf Course. Semi-private; 9 holes. 1692 Flint Street, Quesnel BC V2J 4M1. 747-1358; Fax: 992-7040
Williams Lake
• Williams Lake Golf and Tennis Club. Public; 18 holes. Box 4006, Williams Lake BC V2G 2V2. 392-6026

NORTHERN INTERIOR
Burns Lake
• Carnoustie Golf Course. Public; 9 holes. 16 km west of Burns Lake on Highway 16. RR #1, Burns Lake BC V0J 1E0. 698-7680
Chetwynd
• Moberly Lake Golf Club. Public; 9 holes. At Moberly Lake, 30 km north on Highway 29. Box 1267, Chetwynd BC V0C 1J0. 788-3880

Dawson Creek
• Dawson Creek Golf and Country Club. Public; 18 holes. On Mile 2.5 of Alaska Highway. Box 325, Dawson Creek BC V1G 4G7. 782-7882

Fort Nelson
• Poplar Hills Golf and Country Club. Public; 9 holes. 5 km north off Alaska Highway. Box 1989, Fort Nelson BC V0C 1R0. 774-3862; Fax: 774-6767

Fort St. John
• Lakepoint Golf and Country Club. Semi-private; 18 holes. At Charlie Lake, Mile 54 of Alaska Highway. Box 6208, Fort St. John BC V1J 4H7. 785-5566

Fraser Lake
• Mollyhills Golf Club. Public; 9 holes. In Glenannan tourist area at east end of François Lake. Box 268, Fraser Lake BC V0J 1S0. 699-7761

Houston
• Houston Golf Course. Semi-private; 9 holes. 1.6 km east of Houston on Highway 16. Box 1207, Houston BC V0J 1Z0. 845-2913
• Willow Grove Golf and Country Club. Public; 9 holes. 5 km east on Highway 16. Box 982, Houston BC V0J 1Z0. 845-3770

Mackenzie
• Mackenzie Golf Course. Public; 9 holes. Box 1535, Mackenzie, BC V0J 2C0. 997-4004

Smithers
• Smithers Golf and Country Club. Public; 18 holes. 1 km west on Scotia Road (Highway 16). Box 502, Smithers BC V0J 2N0. 847-3581

Vanderhoof
• Omenica Golf Course. Public; 9 holes. 2 km north of Vanderhoof on Highway 27. Box 1754, Vanderhoof BC V0J 3A0. 567-2920.

Further Reading

• Barlee, N.L., *Gold Creeks and Ghost Towns.* Surrey, BC: Hancock House, 1984.
• Barman, Jean. *The West Beyond the West.* University of Toronto Press, 1991
• Bryan, Liz and Jack Bryan. *Backroads of British Columbia.* Vancouver: Sunflower Books, 1975
• Brough, Sherman B. *Wild Trees of British Columbia.* Vancouver: Pacific Educational Press, 1990
• Gaal, Arlene. *Ogopogo.* Surrey, BC: Hancock House, 1985
• Gould, Stephen Jay. *Wonderful Life: the Burgess Shale and the Nature of History.* Norton, 1989
• Hammond, Herb. *Seeing the Forest Among the Trees.* Winlaw, BC: Polestar, 1991
• Hill, Beth. *Exploring the Kettle Valley Railway.* Winlaw, BC: Polestar, 1989
• Lyons, C.P. *Trees, Shrubs, and Flowers to Know in British Columbia.* Toronto: Dent, 1976
• McDonald, Jim. *Hotsprings of Western Canada: a Complete Guide.* Vancouver: Waterwheel Press: 1991
• Nanton, Isabel and Mary Simpson. *Adventuring in British Columbia.* Douglas & McIntyre, 1991
• Paquet, Maggie. *Parks of British Columbia.* Vancouver: Maia Publishing, 1990
• Pole, Graeme. *Walks and Easy Hikes in the Canadian Rockies.* Banff: Altitude, 1992
• Pratt-Johnson, Betty. *Whitewater Trips for Kayakers, Canoeists and Rafters in British Columbia.* Vancouver: Adventure Publishing, 1986
• Turner, Nancy J. *Plants in British Columbia Indian Technology.* Royal British Columbia Museum, 1992
• Wareham, Bill. *British Columbia Wildlife Viewing Guide.* Edmonton: Lone Pine, 1991
• Woodock, George and Ivan Avakumovic. *The Doukhobors.* McClelland & Stewart, 1977
• Wright, Richard and Rochelle Wright. *Canoe Routes: British Columbia.* Douglas & McIntyre, 1980

Rodeos

100 Mile House 199	Hudson's Hope 221
Anahim Lake 205	Kamloops Pro Rodeo 59
Armstrong 149	Keremeos 90
Ashcroft 55	Kispiox 231
BC High School Rodeo 59	Lytton 52
Bridge Lake 198	Mackenzie 220
Canim Lake 200	Merritt 117
Chetwynd 221	Midway 94
Chilcotin 205	Prince George 212
Clinton 195	Princeton 85
Cranbrook 110	Quilchena 119
Dawson Creek 222	Salmon Arm 62
Falkland 147	Tumbler Ridge 221
Fort Nelson 225	Vanderhoof 235
Fort St. John 224	Vernon 144
	Williams Lake 202

Index

Emergency Numbers

Most communities in the Interior do not have 911 emergency numbers. Local police, fire, and ambulance services are listed in local phone directories or on pay phones.

The Royal Canadian Mounted Police (RCMP) are the police force in many Interior communities.

Forest fires: dial 0, ask for Zenith 5555.

Tourist alert: contact local RCMP for emergency messages.

Earthquake, flood, dangerous goods spills (24 hours): 1-800-663-3456

Helpline for children: dial 0, ask for Zenith 1234.

Photography Credits
Page numbers precede names of photographers or archives.

Contemporary photographs
Photographs by Ron Woodward except as follows:
Front cover Myron Kozak; *back cover* Fred Huser, courtesy of Interior Whitewater Expeditions; *p 8* Larry Doell; *p 19* Jeremy Addington; *p 29* Tania Conley; *p 34* Larry Doell; *p 39* Joe Scanlon; *p 74* Environment Canada, Canadian Parks Service/Wayne Lynch; *p 76* Meredith Bain Woodward; *p 77* Erica Mallam; *p 82* BC Parks; *p 85* Environment Canada, Canadian Parks Service; *p 98* Doug Leighton; *pp 99, 122* Larry Doell; *p 126* Hugo Redivo; *p 131* Greg Young-Ing; *p 132* Richard Wright; *pp 133, 136, 141* Larry Doell; *pp 144, 145* Don Weixl; *p 146* Katie Kidwell; *p 150* BC Parks; *p 151* Don Weixl; *pp 155, 156* Jeremy Addington; *p 160* BC Parks; *p 166* Bryan Anglin; *p 173* Joe Scanlon; *p 176* BC Parks; *p 177* Joe Scanlon; *pp 178, 183* BC Parks; *p 203* Joe Scanlon; *p 205, 210* BC Parks; *p 211* Myron Kozak; *p 213* Ken Ferch; *p 215* Don Harmon; *p 218* Lawrence McGillvray; *p 219* BC Parks; *p 222* Lawrence McGillvray; *p 226* Sheila Kirkwood; *p 227* Paul Dampier (left), Lawrence McGillvray (right); *p 228* Myron Kozak; *p 229* BC Parks; *p 230* Myron Kozak; *p 233* BC Parks; *p. 235* Myron Kozak

Archival photographs
PABC courtesy of Public Archives of British Columbia, Victoria; **VPL** courtesy of Vancouver Public Library; **UBCLA** courtesy of UBC Laboratory of Archaeology; **UBCSC** courtesy of University of British Columbia Library, Special Collections and University Archives Division
Cover inset VPL 16727; *p 20* PABC 759; *p 22* UBCSC BC188/22; *p 23* UBCLA; *p 24* VPL 915; *p 25* VPL 698; *p 48* VPL 390; *p 49* PABC 10230; *p 56* PABC 64053; *p 83* PABC 2526; *p 95* VPL 1771; *p 100* PABC 68579; *p 120* PABC 3275 (left), VPL 1786 (right); *p 130* VPL 510; *p 134* Eric Parmenter, courtesy of Arlene Gaal; *p 137* PABC 98105-1; *p 138* Kelowna Museum; *p 165* PABC 93754; *p 167* VPL 2213; *p 180* UBCSC BC188/25; *p 193* PABC 35310; *p 194* VPL 40325; *p 202* PABC 94157; *p 209* VPL 914; *p 216* PABC 7106; *p 223* PABC 48534; *p 231* VPL 6396; *p 232* PABC 12931; *p 234* UBCSC BC928

Meredith Bain Woodward was born and raised in Vancouver and for 20 years lived in Winlaw in the West Kootenay region. A former travel counsellor for the BC Automobile Association, she has also toured the province many times as a professional actress. She holds a BA and an MFA from UBC and is a past editor of the *Kootenay Business Journal*. She currently lives in Vancouver.

Ron Woodward has been a photographer, designer, print-production manager, and publisher for 20 years. He taught photography, graphic design, and electronic publishing for nine years at Selkirk College in Castlegar and is currently a PhD candidate in the Department of Communication at Simon Fraser University. Born and raised in Cincinnati, Ohio, he has been a Canadian citizen since 1974.